Strategic Trade Policy and the New International Economics

Strategic Trade Policy and the New International Economics

edited by
Paul R. Krugman

The MIT Press
Cambridge, Massachusetts
London, England

57-359

Second printing, 1987

© 1986 by The Massachusetts Institute of Technology

This book was set in Palatino by Achorn Graphic Services, and printed and bound by The Murray Printing Co. in the United States of America.

Library of Congress Cataloging-in-Publication Data

Strategic trade policy and the new international
  economics.

  Includes bibliographies and index.
  1. Commercial policy—Addresses, essays, lectures.
  2. International economic relations—Addresses, essays,
  lectures.   I. Krugman, Paul R.
  HF1411.S82   1986   382'.3   86-2758
  ISBN 0-262-11112-8

Contents

List of Contributors

Michael Borrus
University of California, Berkeley

James A. Brander
University of British Columbia

William H. Branson
Princeton University

Geoffrey Carliner
National Bureau of Economic Research

William R. Cline
Institute for International Economics

Avinash K. Dixit
Princeton University

Jonathan Eaton
University of Virginia and the National Bureau of Economic Research

Gene M. Grossman
Princeton University

Alvin K. Klevorick
Yale University and National Bureau of Economic Research

Paul R. Krugman
Massachusetts Institute of Technology

J. David Richardson
University of Wisconsin

Barbara J. Spencer
Boston College and the National Bureau of Economic Research

Laura D'Andrea Tyson
University of California, Berkeley

Kozo Yamamura
University of Washington

John Zysman
University of California, Berkeley

Preface

In 1984 the Export-Import Bank of the United States celebrated its fiftieth anniversary. To commemorate this occasion, major corporate and trade organizations sponsored an international conference in Washington, D.C., on October 25 and 26, 1984. The papers delivered at the conference are presented in this volume, which is dedicated to the memory of Walter C. Sauer, formerly first vice president and vice chairman of the Bank.

Like many federal agencies whose origins can be traced to the New Deal era, the Export-Import Bank must respond to both an environment that has changed radically and new intellectual currents. The organizers of the conference, Rosemary A. Mazon, director of international affairs of Allied-Signals Inc. and Rita M. Rodriguez, director of the Export-Import Bank of the United States, decided that the conference should reflect this state of flux. Thus they asked me to invite papers from a group of experts disparate in views but united by their willingness to challenge conventional wisdom about international trade. Many of the authors have been contributors to the recent surge of "new wave" trade theory, with its emphasis on imperfect and dynamic competition. The mix is also leavened, however, with representatives of other schools and other disciplines.

All of the authors made a determined effort to present subtle ideas clearly, with a minimum of jargon and formalism. The result is a collection of papers that will, I hope, help stimulate the creative discussion that can best help not only the Export-Import Bank but all our institutions cope with the changing international economy.

Strategic Trade Policy and the New International Economics

1

Introduction: New Thinking about Trade Policy

Paul R. Krugman

The papers in this volume were prepared for an unusual conference, one that brought together two groups of people who rarely communicate with each other directly. On one side are those who are concerned with the real world of trade policy on a daily basis: government officials and representatives of private business. On the other side are academic economists and political scientists—people who *think* about trade policy rather than make it or cope with it. Some of the "real world" participants in this conference have connections with academic research, and some of the academics have put in time in business or government. Basically, however, what the organizers of the conference engineered was a meeting of two quite different worlds.

The purpose of this paper is to help explain why such a meeting of worlds is necessary. Since the volume, like the conference, is primarily aimed at the business and policy communities rather than the academic world, my main purpose is to explain why new thinking about trade policy—thinking that may at times seem abstract and only distantly related to the real problems that arise on a daily basis—is important to practical people. I also want to explain, however, why the gain is mutual, why the academics need to have contact with those who actually make trade policy or live with its consequences.

Theory and Practice in Trade Policy

Practical men and women often have a hard time taking abstract analysis seriously. The equations, diagrams, and jargon that fill most articles in economics seem a long way from reality and of doubtful usefulness. Nor is this prejudice all wrong. It is certainly true that academics often prefer rigor to relevance, mathematical precision to the difficult task of coping with the messy problems of the real world.

Yet it is a mistake for business and government leaders to dismiss theoretical economic analysis as irrelevant or useless. It is a mistake for two reasons. First, like it or not, what economists say matters for policy. It may seem like a hardheaded and realistic view to say that in practice economic policies reflect politics, not analysis, but it would be wrong. In fact theoretical analysis has a way of setting the terms of policy discussion, and often has a more influential role than is widely appreciated.

John Maynard Keynes made this point best in a famous passage with which he closed his book, *The General Theory of Employment, Interest, and Money*:

[T]he ideas of economists and political philosophers, both when they are right and when they are wrong, are more powerful than is commonly understood. Indeed the world is ruled by little else. Practical men, who believe themselves to be quite exempt from any intellectual influences, are usually the slaves of some defunct economist. Madmen in authority, who hear voices in the air, are distilling their frenzy from some academic scribbler of a few years back. I am sure that the power of vested interests is vastly exaggerated compared with the gradual encroachment of ideas . . . soon or late, it is ideas, not vested interests, which are dangerous for good or evil.

The influence of Keynes's work is itself an illustration of his point. Whether he was right or not, Keynes offered a coherent framework for monetary and fiscal policies that others could not match, and Keynesian thinking has shaped these policies throughout the world for forty years. And as Keynes would have expected, the theoretical arguments of his time have become the common sense of ours, so that men and women who think they are only talking realistically are actually using the language and ideas of the Keynesianism of thirty years ago.

More recently, economic policy on a grand scale has been drastically shaped by ideas originating from the academic world. Monetarism and supply-side economics may or may not be good theories, but their application has certainly made a difference to recent real events.

On a more modest level, theoretical arguments play a much more important role in day-to-day policy formation than one might think. Everyone knows that government decisions respond to interest groups and political considerations. It is excessively cynical, however, to imagine that only these considerations matter. The intellectual quality of an argument may not always be decisive, but other things equal it can make a great deal of difference. Anyone who has participated in the decision process in the U.S. government knows that agencies that are able to back their policy proposals with coherent, well-thought-out analyses have an advantage that can offset substantial political odds, and that conversely even a proposal that has clear political support can fail because it is not well argued. During my own brief period in the government, I often saw economic analyses overridden by political considerations—but that was not surprising. What was more surprising was the way that even strong political considerations could sometimes be held at bay when a proposal seemed clearly without a good analytical foundation. I know of one corporation that had a demand widely supported by other businesses and highly placed friends in the government, yet got nowhere for more than a year, largely because the company's arguments were so easily torn apart by government economists. In the end the corporation hired some high-quality economists to help produce a well-argued report, and for that or other reasons finally got some action. The point is that this firm discovered that the quality of analysis really made a difference to its ability to argue its case.

A very senior U.S. trade official once, in reviewing the political pressures on trade policy, remarked, "All that the protectionists need is a theoretical guru—an Art Laffer of protectionism." I am not proposing anyone in this volume for the honor, but this official was again making the point that analysis matters a great deal. No matter how powerful the interests behind a policy may be, they will have substantial difficulty if their policy cannot be backed by a convincing theory.

So far I have argued only that economic analysis needs to be taken seriously because it plays a real role in policy formation. This may be a critical practical reason, but there is another and better reason: often the analysis is right, revealing considerations that would not otherwise be taken into account. We often expect that because a high-level businessman is an expert in the workings of his own business or industry, he will also be an authority on the impacts of policies that affect his industry. If the policies have their main effect directly, this may well be true. But in economic policy often the most important effects work *indirectly*. In these cases it becomes essential that there be an analysis that steps back from the details to take a more comprehensive view. It is here that economists have something to contribute, for it is in the tracking of indirect effects that theoretical analysis and mathematical modeling become most useful. Let me illustrate the point with three examples from trade policy.

The first example concerns agricultural trade. Here the conflict with the EEC over agricultural exports has led the United States on occasion to consider using subsidies or special inducements to get a foreign government to buy from the United States rather than our European competitors. The advocates of such moves typically provide an estimate of the additional exports to be generated by the subsidy, based on the direct effect of capture of the targeted market. Yet these estimates are always far too high because they neglect indirect effects. European grain, for example, diverted from one market will have to go somewhere else. Unless the EEC is willing to cut its exports, the result will be U.S. loss of markets elsewhere, with much less net increase in exports than the initial estimate.

A second example is given by the relationship between budgetary policy and international competitiveness. Many economists now believe that the U.S. budget deficit is largely responsible for the rise in the U.S. trade deficit, because the budget deficit drives up interest rates, high interest rates attract foreign capital inflows, these inflows raise the value of the dollar, and the strength of the dollar reduces U.S. competitiveness. The point here is that the most important single factor currently affecting the international competitiveness of U.S. firms appears to arise from policies that are not directly aimed at the markets that are affected and are liable to be poorly understood even by managers with a broad strategic grasp of their own industries. It takes a willingness to engage in abstract reasoning, to get away from the particulars of industries, to understand this kind of policy impact.

Finally, a third example comes from one of the papers in this volume. Gene Grossman, in his paper (chapter 3), points out that exporting sectors must compete with each other for limited resources such as skilled labor. An export promotion policy that favors some sectors will bid up the cost of these resources and lead to reduced competitiveness of others. This means that any program of selective export promotion must be based on a very clear idea of which exports are more desirable at the margin than others, or it is liable to be counterproductive.

What these examples show is that theoretical economic analysis is necessary to make sensible evaluations of trade policy. However, the fact that an economist offers a theoretical analysis does not and should not automatically command respect. What is needed is some assurance that the analysis is actually relevant. On this score the standard economic analysis of trade policy has begun to look a little wobbly. Although most economists—including at least some of the authors of the papers for this volume—continue to have a strong belief in the desirability of free trade, the economic analysis on which the classical case for free trade was based is beginning to look increasingly unrealistic.

In part this is because the world has changed. For reasons that will be discussed in the next section, the classical case for free trade may have been more in tune with the workings of the economy in 1880 or even 1950 than with the world economy of 1984. In part it is because we have become more sophisticated about the way markets actually work. In either case the point is that although economists may continue to advocate free trade, they will have to update their arguments if they expect to retain their credibility.

The Changing Landscape of Trade Policy

In the first section of this paper I argued that economic analysis of international trade and trade policy is important for businessmen and government officials to understand. The subject of this volume, however, is not simply economic analysis of trade, but "new thinking" about trade policy. Over the last few years the ways in which economists analyze trade have begun to change. This change may in the end change trade policy itself, as we will discuss later. The first step toward understanding the implications of this new thinking, however, must be to look at the reasons for changing ideas.

We can identify three reasons why the economic analysis of trade policy is changing. First, the role of trade in the U.S. economy and the role of the United States in the world economy have changed. Second, the character of international trade itself has been shifting, affecting the United States along with other countries. Third, changing view within the field of economics, especially in the analysis of industrial structure and competition, have affected the views of economists dealing with trade policy as well.

The Changing Position of the United States in the World Economy

The most important change in the U.S. position in the world economy over the past generation has been the steadily increasing importance of trade. In a simple quantitative measure, the shares of imports and exports in U.S. manufacturing value-added both more than doubled from 1960 to 1980. But the change was more than a quantitative one—it amounted to a qualitative change in the importance of international considerations to the U.S. economy. In 1960 the typical U.S. manufacturing firm was basically oriented toward selling to U.S. consumers and competing with U.S. rivals. If it exported, this was usually a secondary activity; if it faced foreign competition, this was usually a minor irritant. By contrast, in the 1980s international considerations have become a key factor. Many, perhaps most, firms either rely heavily on export sales or face important foreign competitors in the U.S. market.

How does this affect our view of trade policy? What it does is to make some issues traditionally viewed as domestic in nature into issues that have a vital trade policy component. In particular, the issues of market power and excessive rates of return, on one hand, and of innovation and technological change, on the other, cannot now be treated without a serious consideration of trade policy as well.

Consider first the issue of market power. A traditional concern of U.S. policy has been to limit the ability of firms in concentrated industries to raise prices and earn excessive profits at the expense of consumers. Now that the United States has become so much a trading nation, however, the aim becomes more complicated. Protection of the consumer from exploitation remains an issue. To the extent that high returns remain, however, there is the additional concern of trying to maintain or enlarge the share of these returns that goes to domestic firms. As we will see in the course of this volume, there are reasons to believe either that in concentrated industries trade policy can usefully take on an active role in promoting the interests of domestic firms against their foreign competitors, or that we should at least be concerned about the possibility that foreign governments will use trade policies to promote their firms in these industries.

Turning to innovation and technological change, the traditional concern of U.S. policy here has been with promoting activities, such as basic research, that yield valuable spillovers to the rest of the economy. What makes this a trade policy issue is the fact that the United States is now only one of a number of countries engaging in activities that can be argued to yield such spillovers. This means that trade policy can be an important factor in determining the pace of technological change. For example, foreign "targeting" of high-technology sectors through subsidies or protection of home markets might cause a shrinkage of U.S. industries which in fact yields valuable spillovers to the rest of the U.S. economy—a possibility that is at the heart of concern over the international repercussion of industrial policy.

The Changing Character of Trade

The rapid growth in the importance of trade has also highlighted another change that is not as recent but whose significance is only now beginning to be fully appreciated. This is a change in the *character* of trade, which is no longer very much like the kind of exchange envisaged in classical theory and still taught in textbooks.

Traditional theories of international trade view trade as essentially a way for countries to benefit from their differences. Because countries differ in climate, culture, skills, resources, and so on, each country will have a comparative advantage in producing goods for which its particular character suits it. Such a theory leads one to expect to see trade dominated by exchanges that reflect the particular strengths of economies—for instance, exports of manufactures by advanced countries and exports of raw materials by underdeveloped countries.

Now it remains true that underlying characteristics of countries shape the pattern of international trade. Countries with highly skilled work forces tend to export goods that require skill-intensive production, countries with abundant land export agricultural products, and so on. Since World War II, however, a large and generally growing part of world trade has come to consist of exchanges that cannot be attributed so easily to underlying advantages of the countries that export particular goods. Instead, trade seems to reflect arbitrary or temporary advantages resulting from economies of scale or shifting leads in close technological races.

To understand the kind of transformation that has occurred, consider how the trade of the United Kingdom has shifted over time. In the nineteenth century, the high point of classical economics, one would have had little difficulty in seeing how national characteristics were shaping U.K. trade. The United Kingdom, with its skilled labor, abundant capital, and experience had a comparative advantage in manufactures, and it basically exported manufactures and imported raw materials. By the 1970s, however, U.K. trade consisted primarily of manufactured goods on the import as well as the export side. Even if one looks more closely at the trade data, it is hard to find much of a pattern in the manufactured goods the U.K. exports and imports; indeed, in many cases very similar goods appear on both sides of the balance.

The reasons for the massive two-way trade in products in which countries have no underlying comparative advantage are not particularly hard to find. They lie in the advantages of large-scale production, which lead to an essentially random divison of labor among countries, in the cumulative advantages ot experience which sometimes perpetuate accidental initial advantages, in the temporary advantages conveyed by innovation. What is important is that the conventional economic analysis of trade policy is based on a theory of trade that does not allow for these kinds of motives for international specialization. As I will argue in the next section, traditional conclusions about trade policy may therefore not be right for the kind of world we live in, where these motives are as important in explaining trade as the better-understood forces of comparative advantage.

We should also note a related change in international trade. Among the forces that seem to be driving international specialization, an increasingly important one seems to be technology. In many industries competitive advantage seems to be determined neither by underlying national characteristics, nor by the static advantages of large-scale production, but rather by the knowledge generated by firms through R&D and experience. As we have already noted, however, technological innovation is an activity that may well generate important spillovers to the rest of the economy. Its growing importance in international trade thus reinforces the need for a rethinking of the analytical basis for trade policy.

New Tools for Analysis

The final strand in the changing nature of trade policy analysis is the application to international economics of new ideas coming from other fields of economics. In particular, the 1970s were marked by major innovations in the field of industrial organization, with new approaches developed for the analysis of industries in which only a small number of firms are competing at any one time—"oligopolies," in the jargon of the economics profession.

Much traditional economic analysis is based on the working assumption that markets are not too far from being "perfectly competitive"—that is, there are many producers, each of whom is too small to attempt to influence prices or the future actions of his competitors. What the changing pattern of trade has done, however, is to make this a clearly unworkable assumption for trade policy. As just noted, a good deal of trade now seems to arise because of the advantages of large-scale production, the advantages of cumulative experience, and transitory advantages resulting from innovation. In industries where these factors are important, we are not going to see the kind of atomistic competition between many small firms that is necessary for "perfect" competition to be a good description of the world. Major U.S. exporters like Boeing or Caterpillar, and many smaller firms as well, are in a different kind of competition from that facing wheat farmers or garment manufacturers. They face a few identifiable rivals, they have some direct ability to affect prices, and they make *strategic* moves designed to affect their rivals' actions.

Firms in this situation are described by economists as being in "imperfectly competitive" markets. This does not mean that competition is not fierce or that the firms are somehow misbehaving. What it means is simply that what can happen in these markets is different from, and more complicated than, what is captured by the simple concepts of supply and demand. The imperfection, in other words, is in the economist's understanding, not in the world.

Although our understanding is imperfect, it is getting better. Important new work has helped reveal, in particular, how the strategic choices of firms are influenced by and in turn help to determine the structure of industries. This new work was originally intended for thinking about domestic issues such as antitrust, regulation, and innovation policy. As we have seen, however, the distinctions between domestic and international issues have been breaking down. Thanks to the new work on imperfectly competitive industries, international economists are in a position to approach the problems raised by the changing environment with an expanded set of tools.

In summary, then, the rethinking of the analytical basis for trade policy is a response to both a real change in the environment and intellectual progress within the field of economics. First, the increased importance of trade has made necessary consideration of the international dimension to issues traditionally viewed as purely domestic. Second, the changing character of trade, away from trade based on simple comparative advantage and toward trade based on a more complex set of factors, has required a reconsideration of traditional arguments about trade policy. Finally, increased sophistication within the economics profession has made practitioners willing to abandon some of their traditional but increasingly untenable simplifying assumptions.

But what difference does this make for the conduct of trade policy? The next item in this paper must be a discussion of the difference that the changed view of trade makes.

New Approaches to Trade Policy

The Traditional Case for Free Trade

When economists call for free trade, this is not a blind prejudice. Rather, it is based on a theoretical framework that is compelling in its logic. Even the new ideas that have begun to change our way of looking at trade amount to a modification rather than a wholesale rejection of this framework.

The case for free trade is of course part of the general case for free markets. This case is familiar, but it does not hurt to restate it briefly. The argument runs as follows. Except for the problem of unemployment—which economists normally regard as a problem of demand that can be handled through monetary policy—the basic economic problem is how to allocate scarce resources: capital, skilled labor, raw materials, and so on. The limitation on resources available forces some choice among activities. What the market system offers is a decentralized way of making this choice. Instead of requiring that anyone explicitly decide what should be produced and how, the market system allows individuals and firms to set priorities implicitly, via the prices they offer.

Now the belief of most economists is that the decentralized process of allocation through the market is a highly effective one. In idealized mathematical models of market economies the market works so well that it in fact cannot be improved on. Although most economists would agree that these models idealize too much, the conventional wisdom is still that markets do a very good job.

How is this relevant to the case for free trade? The essence of the economist's view is that exporting and importing are basically no different from other economic activities. International trade can be viewed as a productive process, whereby goods that are relatively cheap in our country are in effect converted into relatively expensive goods. And like other activities, foreign trade is likely to be most efficiently carried out if it is left up to a decentralized market mechanism.

There is a technical qualification to this argument. Countries that have a large market share in a particular good can benefit themselves by restricting exports to raise world prices. Nobody would suggest that Saudi Arabia would be richer with free trade. Aside from this qualification, however, the basic message of conventional theory is that international markets are not very different from domestic markets, so a general policy of letting markets work should be applied to both.

It is particularly important to stress one not-so-fine point about this argument. The conventional case for free trade does not break down just because other countries do not themselves have free trade. Suppose, for example, that world wheat prices are depressed by export subsidies. The economically rational response for, say, Australia is to produce less wheat and more of other things—and this is what will happen if the Australian government allows events to take their course. No special intervention is called for. There is an old economist's analogy, which runs as follows: To say that our government must depart from free trade because other governments are not free traders is like saying that because other countries have rocky coasts, we must block up our own harbors.

Conventional economic analysis, then, makes a strong case for free trade—even in a world where other countries do not have anything like free trade. But conventional analysis, as we have seen, is under considerable challenge as an appropriate framework for thinking about trade. The next question is, What difference does a modification of that analysis make for economist's views about trade? In effect this whole volume is an answer to that question. Let us, however, begin the discussion with a brief overview.

Implications of New Ideas

The conventional case for the desirability of free trade rests, in part, on idealized theoretical models in which free trade can be shown to be perfectly efficient. Economists have always known that the conclusion that markets are efficient becomes suspect when one abandons some of the idealizations of these theoretical cases. Yet they have tended to regard the idealized models as giving a basically correct view, with the deviations from the ideal adding only minor complications. This traditional faith in the efficacy of markets partly reflected a judgment about reality; equally it reflected a lack of any ability to describe precisely what difference deviations from perfect markets make.

The combination of a changing character of trade and a growing sophistication of theory undercuts this way of justifying free trade. On one side, we are forced to recognize that the industries that account for much of world trade are not at all well described by the supply and demand analysis that lies behind the assertion that markets are best left to themselves. As we have seen, much of trade appears to require an explanation in terms of economies of scale, learning curves, and the dynamics of innovation—all phenomena incompatible with the kind of idealizations under which free trade is always the best policy. Economists refer to such phenomena as "market imperfections," a term that in itself conveys the presumption that these are marginal to a system that approaches ideal performance fairly closely. In reality, however, it may be that imperfections are the rule rather than the exception.

On the other side, the increased sophistication of the analytical toolbox has removed at least part of the reason for clinging to the assumption of perfect markets. Fifteen years ago economists could and did assert that so little was known about the implications of imperfect competition for international trade policy that nothing useful could be said on the matter. There is still considerable uncertainty, but not so much that economists are without useful insights.

What are these insights? The rethinking of the basis of trade policy that is now occurring suggests two ways in which an activist trade policy can benefit a country relative to free trade, perhaps at the expense of its competitors. The first is through the ability of government policies to secure for a nation a larger share of "rent"; the second is through the ability of these policies to get the country more "external economies." The first term means something different to economists than it does to real people; the second is basically meaningless in English. Both need explaining.

"Rent," in economic parlance, means "payment to an input higher than what that input could earn in an alternative use." It could mean a higher rate of profit in an industry than is earned in other industries of equivalent riskiness, or higher wages in an industry than equally skilled workers earn in other sectors. If there are important rents in certain sectors, trade policy can raise national income by securing for a country a larger share of the rent-yielding industries.

Now the conventional view is that who gets the rent is not an important issue because in a competitive economy there will be very little rent. If profits or wages are unusually high in an industry, capital or labor will come in and quickly eliminate the unusual returns.

If, however, the new view of trade is right, important trading sectors are also sectors in which rent may not be so easily competed away. If there are important advantages to large-scale production or a steep learning curve, for example, new entry into an industry may look unprofitable even though existing firms are making exceptionally high profits, paying unusually high wages, or both.

Once we begin to believe that substantial amounts of rent are really out there, it becomes possible at least in principle for trade policy to be used as a way to secure more rent for a country. Suppose, for example, that the nature of the world market for some products is such that it can support two highly profitable producers but addition of a third would eliminate the profits. In this case what we will end up with is two firms earning considerable rent, without any way for that rent to be competed away. Clearly a country would like one of its firms to be one of the lucky pair. Common sense suggests, and mathematical theorizing confirms, that subsidies or protection can in fact be used to increase a country's share of rent in a way that raises national income at other countries' expense.

External economies present a different justification for activist trade policies. By an "external economy" economists mean a benefit from some activity that accrues to other individuals or firms than those engaging in the activity. The most plausible example is the diffusion of knowledge generated in one area to other firms and other sectors. Although external economies are different conceptually from rents, they likewise provide a reason to favor particular sectors. This time the point is not that capital and labor in the sector will themselves earn exceptionally high returns; rather, they will yield high returns to society because in addition to their own earnings they provide benefits to capital and labor employed elsewhere.

The reason why external economies have become more of a trade issue is that, as noted earlier, the reassessment of trade gives technological innovation an enlarged role. Innovation, because it involves the generation of knowledge, is particularly likely also to generate valuable spillovers. So there is now good reason to suspect that trade policy can be used to encourage external-economy-producing activities. Suppose, for example, that we conclude that certain high-technology sectors generate large technological spillovers to the rest of the economy. We could then conclude that promoting these sectors, through protection, export subsidies, and so on, might raise national income. Conversely, foreign promotion of these sectors might be depriving us of valuable spillovers and should be countered, contrary to the conventional argument that free trade is appropriate whatever other countries do.

Central Questions

Traditional trade analysis and the new wave of analysis share certain important features. Both take the view that trade is not a zero-sum game, that it offers an opportunity for mutual gains by all trading nations. Also the new analysis has not lost sight of the crucial point that industries within a country compete with each other for limited supplies of labor and capital, as well as competing with their opposite numbers in other countries for markets. This means that an attempt to promote or protect some particular sector within our country means promoting or protecting that sector at the expense of other sectors. This is true whether foreign competition is fair or unfair, whether it is coming from the underlying comparative advantage of other countries or is a result of government subsidy.

The difference in the new analysis is on the question of whether changes in the allocation of resources matter. For example, if foreign trade policies cause some U.S. sectors to contract and others to expand, can this lower U.S. national income? Alternatively, can the United States raise its national income by actively favoring certain key sectors?

The answer to these questions depends on whether it is possible to identify some sectors that at the margin are more valuable than others. Are there "strategic" activities in the economy, where labor and capital either directly receive a higher return than they could elsewhere or generate special benefits for the rest of the economy? This is the question on which old and new thinking about trade differs.

What the conventional view argues is that there are no "strategic" sectors. Competition, it is argued, eliminates any large deviations between what equivalent qualities of labor or capital can earn in different sectors. Market prices, which guide the allocation of resources, are good indicators of social return, so that basically producers are paid what their output is worth.

The new approaches open up the possibility that there may be "strategic" sectors after all. Because of the important roles now being given to economies of scale, advantages of experience, and innovation as explanations of trading patterns, it seems more likely that rent will not be fully competed away—that is, that labor or capital will sometimes earn significantly higher returns in some industries than in others. Because of the increased role of technological competition, it has become more plausible to argue that certain sectors yield important external economies, so producers are not in fact paid the full social value of their production.

What all this means is that the extreme pro-free-trade position—that markets work so well that they cannot be improved on—has become untenable. In this sense the new approaches to international trade provide a potential rationale for a turn by the United States toward a more activist trade policy.

There is, however, a large gap between showing that free trade is not perfect and arguing for any particular alternative. The papers in this volume, in general, agree on the need for an updating of our framework for thinking about trade policy. They are far less in agreement about how we should make use of the new framework, and it is to the sources of this disagreement that we must now turn.

Policy Questions

The new thinking about trade that was described in earlier sections makes one thing clear: the idealized theoretical model on which the classical case for free trade is based will not serve us anymore. The world is more complex than that, and there is no question that the complexities do open, in principle, the possibility of successful activist trade or industrial policy.

But this does not mean that anything goes. Serious questions remain about the way in which new ideas about trade should affect U.S. trade policy. In this paper I will suggest only the questions; other papers will provide at least the beginning of an attempt at answers.

Can We Identify Strategic Sectors?

As I argued earlier, modern analysis of trade suggests that contrary to what classical theory taught us, there are sectors that at the margin are more valuable to the economy than others. This cannot be read as a recommendation for active effects to protect or promote particular sectors, however, unless we have some reasonably reliable way of identifying which sectors these are.

One criterion I suggested for a strategic sector is a sector where there is substantial "rent," that is, where the return to labor or capital is exceptionally high. Identifying sectors where wages or profits are high may not seem like a difficult task. Several factors may, however, confuse the picture.

First of these is the problem of separating rent from quality differences. If one industry pays higher wages than another, does that represent a true differential for equivalent labor, or the fact that the high-wage industry employs higher-skilled and better-qualified workers? In the latter case there is no special case for promoting the high-wage industry—indeed, an attempt to expand high-skill sectors without increasing the number of highly skilled workers can lead to increased unemployment among the less skilled. One sometimes hears proposals for a national policy of targeting sectors that yield high value-added per worker. Such proposals are misguided when, as is usually the case, they fail to ask whether high value-added simply reflects high input.

A second problem is the possibility that industries that appear to earn high rates of return do so because we are only counting the successes, not the failures. Suppose that only half of those firms that invest in an industry succeed in establishing themselves, while the other half lose their investments. Even if the surviving firms are later observed to achieve twice the average rate of return on their investment, the properly computed rate is only average.

Related to the issue of lucky firms is the problem of lucky industries. If favorable technological developments or shifts in demand lead to rapid growth in an industry, firms and workers already in the industry will typically receive a windfall of temporarily high profits and wages. This windfall gain, however, does not accrue to *new* firms and workers entering the industry—so a policy of promoting the industry will not actually be moving resources to where they can earn high returns.

These objections do not mean that we cannot hope to identify industries where the returns to capital and labor actually are high and where public policy could raise national income by encouraging them to move into the sector. The point is rather that identifying strategic sectors is not a simple matter of looking at profit rates and wage rates over the past five years; it instead requires careful and detailed analysis.

What about our other criterion, external economies? Here the problem is that spillovers from one firm's R&D or experience to other firms are hard to measure. The point is that by definition a spillover is something that does not command a market price—and therefore leaves no "paper trail" by which we can trace it. Few attempts to measure external economies have been made; those that have been made are always historical studies of past relationships. What we need for trade policy of course is forward-looking assessments. For example, how will the pace of innovation in the computer industry be affected by the size of the domestic semiconductor industry? At this point the only way to make such assessments is to combine detailed knowledge of the industries with a heavy reliance on guesswork.

What we have to conclude, then, is that identifying strategic sectors is not something we know how to do with any confidence. One may take one of several policy morals from this conclusion, as we will discuss shortly.

Can We Successfully Pursue a Strategic Policy?

Suppose that we suppress some of the doubts just raised, and imagine that through a program of careful study we can identify a set of industries that are likely candidates for special concern. The next question is whether we can actually devise a policy that will successfully promote these sectors.

From the theoretical and empirical analysis that has been carried out so far on this issue, two points stand out, which raise doubts—though not necessarily critical ones—about the efficacy of policy in this area.

The first problem is that the sectors that one might want to promote are, to an important extent, likely to be competing with each other for such scarce resources as technically trained manpower. Given this competition among industries, government policy could easily end up encouraging the wrong things.

A hypothetical example may make the point. Suppose that the U.S. government were to offer a subsidy for R&D in the software industry. Such a subsidy, unless it were carefully constructed, could easily end up favoring large firms with formal research departments over smaller firms where the line between research and other activities is not a clear-cut one. Skilled programmers would thus be bid away from the smaller firms. If it turns out that it is the small firms, not the larger ones, that generate valuable spillovers, the subsidy could be counterproductive.

The second problem with devising policies to help high-value industries is the problem of predicting effects in a complex strategic environment. The whole point of new thinking about trade is the observation that many industries are not as simple as the supply and demand industries described in economic textbooks. The problem this raises is that the effects of policies on industry behavior are much more difficult to predict in complex industries than in simpler markets. For example, an export subsidy may, by discouraging foreign competition, sharply raise the profits of the subsidized firms. On the other hand, it could provoke a price war that lowers profits. It is very difficult to determine on purely theoretical grounds which outcome will actually occur.

Once more, the point of these questions is not to suggest that nothing can be done but only to indicate that new theoretical arguments do not, at least so far, provide straightforward guidelines for policy.

Can We Trust Ourselves to Use the New Ideas Wisely?

Given the uncertainty about exactly what we might want to promote and how we can promote it, there are some natural doubts about whether the real world of policy can be expected to use new ideas well. The doubt is partly about competence, partly about objectivity.

New thinking about trade does not yet provide simple guidelines for policy. Can the U.S. government usefully act on the basis of concepts that raise more questions than they answer? Policy decisions are ultimately based on three-page memos, not five-hundred-page reports. Can the new concepts be useful given this reality?

A parallel may be instructive. The issues raised by the new trade theory are related to the problems of corporate strategy—but raised to a higher and more diffuse level. We know that during the 1970s strategic planning was looked to for great results by many firms, but that in retrospect it has turned out to be a disappointment. The theoretical concepts turned out to be hard to make operational, while the emphasis on high strategy may have distracted some firms from the basics of their businesses. It is not farfetched to suggest that similar problems could easily arise if the United States tried to have too complex a trade policy.

Moreover, can the U.S. political system actually respond objectively to complex arguments? As several of the papers will emphasize, there is a risk that interest groups that have a stake in trade policy will simply find in new ideas an excuse to advocate policies that are not likely to benefit the nation as a whole. There are already some signs that this is happening—I know that some of the participants in this volume have been surprised and perhaps worried at the places they find themselves cited.

How Will Other Governments Respond?

A final set of questions is raised by uncertainty about the implications of any change in U.S. policy for trade relations with other countries. This is an issue that cuts both ways.

The current international trading system is based on formal, legalistic agreements that limit certain kinds of trade policy. It is clear that these agreements do have some effect in placing bounds on what countries feel free to do. It is also clear that a good deal of nationalistic trade and industrial policy goes on anyway, some of it at the expense of U.S. interests.

What would happen if the U.S. were, on the basis of new theories of international trade, to become more willing to adopt an activist trade on industrial policy? Opinions differ sharply. Some would argue that the main result would be that U.S. bargaining power would be strengthened and that the United States would thus be more effective at persuading other countries to abandon policies that hurt our interests. Others would argue that the result would be to undermine what cooperation there is, and lead us into a world of beggar-my-neighbor trade policies.

Policy Recommendations

It is not the point of this conference to produce any unified recommendations about policy. In this paper I certainly want to avoid prejudging the policy implications of the other conference papers. As an organizing device, however, let me suggest four "generic" policy positions that one might take in response to the new thinking we have been discussing. All four views are represented in this volume.

1. *Immediate activism.* On this view, although there are substantial uncertainties about appropriate trade policies, we should nevertheless act strongly on the basis of the best analysis we can do. Behind this position might be a belief that the stakes are high, and perhaps that other countries are already successfully playing the game at our expense.

2. *Cautious activism.* This position would call for immediate action only where the case seems most clear-cut (perhaps in some high-technology sectors). However, the philosophy of U.S. trade policy would shift from one of free trade except in extremis to one of sophisticated intervention. A natural counterpart of this policy position would be a program of research and study aimed at *identifying potentially useful government interventions in trade.*

3. *Cautious nonactivism.* This position would argue that the uncertainties and political risks of any immediate change in the philosophy of U.S. trade policy outweigh the benefits. A program of research and study would, however, be indicated. In particular, one might advocate careful monitoring of the possibility of harm to the United States from other countries' trade policies even while arguing for a maintenance of a basic U.S. policy of free trade.

4. *Strong nonactivism.* This final position would argue that the potential gains from activist trade policy are probably small, the appropriate policies are highly uncertain, and the risks are high because increased flexibility will be abused for domestic political reasons and lead to a deterioration of international economic relations. In this view free trade is still overwhelmingly likely to turn out better for the United States than any actual program of intervention.

I have tried to make all of these positions sound reasonable. The proponents of these views are all honorable men (more accurately, there are honorable men in each group). Let us hope that the issue will in the end be decided as it ought to be, on the basis of evidence.

An Overview of the Volume

The papers in this volume are organized around the theme of the role of new thinking in our approach to trade policy. Four principal issues are considered. First is the theoretical foundation for changes in trade policy. Second is the question of what the content of new trade policy might be. Third is the evaluation of actual trade policies. Fourth is the implications of new thinking for the future.

In the first group of papers, we begin with James Brander, one of the founders of the new school of academic thinking about trade policy. Brander provides a stimulating discussion of the rationale for "strategic" trade policies, relating this rationale to both traditional economic analysis and recent developments in the study of game theory. His paper is complemented by a paper by Gene Grossman, one of the most influential skeptics about the feasibility of activist trade policy. Grossman provides a clear exposition of the complexities and ambiguities that would hamper the implementation of any excessively ambitious attempt to put Brander's theories into practice.

In the second group of papers we begin with Barbara Spencer, another of the founders of this new area. Spencer poses the following question: Suppose that a government were to try to formulate an international competitive strategy in the same way that a corporation does; what would be the content of that strategy? The answers Spencer provides illustrate both the power of new ideas and the difficulty of translating them into practice. Following this paper is a discussion from a quite different tradition: Michael Borrus, Laura Tyson, and John Zysman, drawing on the massive case study material being developed at the Berkeley Roundtable for International Economics, present an incisive discussion of the role of policy in international competition in high-technology sectors. Finally, Jonathan Eaton addresses a question particularly relevant to the organization in whose honor the conference was organized: the role of credit policies in a world where trade is often limited by financial constraints.

The third part of the conference turns to the actual experience of policy. Kozo Yamamura's discussion of Japan shows that a "strategic" point of view has indeed informed Japan's policy and guided her development. Yamamura points out, however, that the policy experience of the credit- and foreign-exchange-constrained Japanese economy of the 1950s and 1960s is a poor guide to both Japan's future and our own. Geoffrey Carliner takes a broader view of strategic policies and emphasizes the mixture of motives that actually determines policy. William Cline then examines the record of our own trade policy for troubled industries. He finds that although adjustment and a restoration of competitiveness are often the expressed aims of policy, political power dominates the actual policy choice, and few protected industries actually are restored to competitiveness.

In the final section of the volume the authors look ahead. J. David Richardson considers the implications of new thinking for the international system. Reiterating the concerns of Brander, he focuses on the problems of interaction of national trade strategies. William Branson and Alvin Klevorick review the experience of an effort to bring policymakers and academics together on a sustained basis, showing how the new theories of trade policy can enrich discussion of the real world. Finally, and appropriately, Avinash Dixit concludes with a cautionary note. He warns us not to discard hard-won insights too quickly for the glamour of new ideas, especially when the new ideas can be used to serve political ends.

It should be apparent from this brief description that this volume does not espouse a single viewpoint, or arrive at any single conclusion. That was not its purpose. Instead, it was meant to promote an exchange of views among the most innovative theoretical thinkers and the most thoughtful doers—and in that aim I believe it has succeeded.

2

Rationales for Strategic Trade and Industrial Policy

James A. Brander

Professional economists remain, on the whole, opposed to the use of what might be called "strategic" trade and industrial policies, such as export subsidies. There are several sources of this opposition, including simple mistrust of government, but possibly the most important source, at least in academic circles, is a certain view of the world incorporated in the dominant theories of international trade. The orthodox position of international trade theory is that trade and investment patterns are determined by comparative advantage, and that free markets are the best way of exploiting comparative advantage. The best government policy, then, would involve a strict noninterventionist stance. This paper presents some counterarguments and shows that a modest departure in the direction of realism from standard theory can create a rationale for interventionist policy.

Before any reasonable discussion of policy tools and tactics can begin, however, it is necessary to establish what the objectives of policy are. If two people disagree over policy objectives, it should not be surprising if they disagree over policy tools as well. For example, if some people believe that an objective of trade policy should be to retain a strong domestic steel industry for military reasons, these people are likely to favor protection or subsidization of the steel industry. Those who do not regard promotion of a domestic steel industry as an important defense objective, on the other hand, probably would oppose such policies. The important point of course is to distinguish clearly between disagreements over objectives and disagreements over method.

Economists normally concern themselves with two objectives: economic efficiency and the distribution of income. Roughly speaking, pursuit of economic efficiency involves maximizing the size of the pie to be divided. As far as distribution is concerned, economists usually like to imagine that some overall government policy (mainly the tax-transfer system) can be used to pursue equity objectives and that other economic policies should be concerned mainly with efficiency. Finally, it is always necessary to be clear about who the reference group is, about whose welfare it is that we (or policymakers) care about. In policy discussions it is normal to assume that promotion of national welfare (as opposed to world welfare) is the objective.

This paper is concerned exclusively with the economic rationale for certain trade policies; economic objectives are the only objectives considered. This is not to deny that there are legitimate noneconomic grounds for trade policy. Export subsidies, for example, might well have a role in helping to provide key exports to countries with friendly governments, whereas export restraints might be used to inhibit technology transfer to unfriendly countries. Such policies are undoubtedly important, but they are not taken up here.

The noninterventionist stance of trade theory is really a slight extension of one of the most important themes in economic thought, first articulated by Adam Smith (1776). This theme is that competition between private producers promotes the efficient use of resources. A precise statement of the theme is contained in a theorem known as the first theorem of welfare economics: "Perfect competition is efficient." In other words, private markets do about as well as could be hoped for in promoting efficiency, and intervention can only reduce efficiency. Furthermore the second theorem of welfare economics and the associated policy statements assert that any distributional objective can best be met by reallocating wealth or income and then just leaving private competitive markets to do their job of enforcing efficiency.

Needless to say, there are a number of important conditions underlying these theorems, including the absence of externalities and public goods, the free availability of relevant information, and the presence of markets for all goods and services. As the statement of the first theorem suggest, however, the central condition is that markets be perfectly competitive. Perfect competition means that individual firms believe they have no influence on market price. Each firm takes prices as exogenously given by the market and believes it can sell all it wants at the going price. Furthermore free entry and exit into and from industries ensures that there will be no economic or "pure" profits. Firms earn just enough to cover costs, including enough payments to the owners of the firm to keep them in business. The assumption of perfect competition is a good approximation for some industries; it may even be a good approximation, for some purposes, in describing whole economies. The problem with assuming perfect competition is that it simply rules out or ignores many aspects of the real world that are important when considering trade policy.

In particular, in a world of perfect competition there is no room for one firm to be concerned that expansion or price-cutting by another firm will lower the price it can command or impinge on it in any way. There are no strategic interactions between firms. Furthermore perfect competition cannot very easily handle cost structures that involve large start-up or overhead costs, nor can it easily handle learning-by-doing and research and development.

In short, the assumption of perfect competition, as incorporated in the dominant theories of international trade, fails to address the issues raised by firms and policymakers. I do not intend to argue that consideration of imperfect competition creates a general presumption in favor of policy intervention. I would, however, assert that it makes sense to analyze trade policy using models that are at least capable of capturing the phenomena that businessmen are concerned about.

As indicated, there are many conditions necessary for application of the first theorem of welfare economics. Failure of any of them to hold can lead to a failure of markets to be efficient, a situation referred to as market failure. The particular type of market failure to be focused on here is imperfect competition. Specifically, there is an international market for some good or closely related set of goods, but there are relatively few firms in the market. As a consequence it is possible for firms to earn profits above the rate of return earned in purely competitive industries. Trade policy then emerges as a national attempt to obtain as large a share of these international profits as possible. In effect trade policy by other countries might enable them to capture returns that would otherwise accrue to the United States, or U.S. policy might allow the United States to capture returns that would otherwise go elsewhere.

There are several variations on this basic structure that will be discussed. It should be emphasized, however, that this paper does not constitute a laundry list of possible motives for trade policy arising from market failure, or even just from imperfect competition. Relatively well-known arguments, such as the "optimum" or "monopoly" tariff argument, are not discussed. The cases examined here are drawn mainly from recent and comparatively little-known contributions to the theoretical literature.

Profit-Shifting Subsidies

The first case of welfare-improving policy to be examined involves the use of subsidies to enhance the strategic position of a domestic firm engaged in competition for world markets with a foreign rival. (This discussion corresponds to a more formal analysis presented in Brander and Spencer 1984.) As the heading suggests, the basic idea is to shift profit from foreign to domestic firms, so a short digression on describing exactly what is meant by profit might be useful.

Everyone knows what he or she means by the term "profit". The problem is that different people often mean different things. When an economist says (or writes) "profit" he usually means "pure profit," sometimes called "excess profit" or "above-normal profit." This means profit above the minimum amount necessary to keep the owners of the firm in business. This profit is therefore what is called a "rent" to owners of the firm. Rents of this sort may also go to the firm's workers in the form of wages and salaries above the minimum amount necessary to keep these workers with the firm. It is often alleged, for example, that workers in the U.S. auto and steel industries earn large rents. Even the government may take some rent from firms in the form of taxes. All these rents are a bonus to the domestic economy: the domestic economy as a whole is better off if the total of rents earned from foreign sources rises, for this expands national command over goods and services. The argument presented here really applies to all rents, not just to profits. If some policy makes it possible for domestic workers to earn higher rents, then that policy is very little different from a policy that generates higher profits. In describing the case for strategic subsidies I shall refer only to profits. We should keep in mind, however, that some of the profits may be channeled into other rents, but that this does not affect the logical structure of the argument.

The argument is presented in a very stylized environment, so as to make the central points as clearly as possible. Imagine that there are two firms, one domestic and one foreign, serving a world market contained entirely in other countries. With only two firms in the market, neither is likely to act like a perfect competitor. Each firm seems sure to recognize that its profit depends in part on what its rival does.

Such situations are often referred to as "strategic games." The problem for the analyst is to predict how firms will behave in such a situation. They might form a cartel and maximize combined profits. Experience suggests, however, that cartels, especially international cartels, are very unstable and that a theory based on the assumption that firms are able to maintain cartels would not generally be a good theory.

There is, unfortunately, no single empirically supported theoretical structure that describes all or even most oligopolies well. The first plausible theory, suggested by Augustin Cournot in 1838, remains the most widely used. Cournot's idea is that equilibrium will occur when each firm is doing the best it can, in the sense of maximizing profit, through the choice of its own output level, given the output level of its rival. It is not necessary that firms assume their rival's output is fixed out of equilibrium, the idea is just that when firms are simultaneously responding as best they can to each others' output level, we would expect some stability and could reasonably refer to the situation as an equilibrium.

The Cournot model does have some drawbacks. It does, for example, rely on the idea that firms do in fact choose output levels and are prepared to allow prices to change as necessary to sell this output. This might be appropriate if quantities are set by physical capacity constraints but is inappropriate if firms choose prices and can easily adjust outputs as required.

Cournot's theory has the desirable feature that output and price end up somewhere between the monopoly and perfectly competitive outcomes. If more firms entered the industry, output would rise and price would fall, approaching the perfectly competitive limit as the number of firms grew very large. With only two firms, however, each firm can generally earn relatively large profits.

Each firm could of course earn even greater profits if it could persuade its rival to cut back output. One firm might try to induce contraction of the other by threatening to produce a larger output. For that matter, one firm might threaten to produce a ruinously high level of output unless the other firm left the industry.

If firms are on an equal footing in the marketplace, however, it is difficult to see why one firm should be intimidated by the other. If one firm simply aggressively expanded output, the other firm might well match the increase, inducing a price war. The point is that once the Cournot equilibrium market shares are reached, no aggressive threat by one firm need be believed by the other. Each firm has good reason to believe that it can hold its ground in the face of temporary expansions by the rival firm. Expansions are likely to be temporary because these aggressive threats violate the firm's own self-interest unless the other firm acquiesces and reduces output. Bluffs and kamikaze-like aggressiveness may play a role in some industries, but it is hard to give them a systematic role in analysis, and certainly economic analysts tend to dismiss them.

Now consider a different experiment. Suppose one firm discovers how to produce output more efficiently and is able to lower its costs, and in particular, the cost of producing additional output. What will happen to industry structure? Now it is actually in the self-interest of the fortunate firm to expand output. This threat to expand is credible because, even given the output of the other firm, it is optimal to expand. The new Cournot equilibrium will involve a higher market share and output for the firm with lower costs and a smaller output and market share for the other firm. This is how industries evolve: some firms innovate, lower their costs, and are therefore able to increase their market shares.

One important feature of the structure described here is that not only will the lower cost firm expand output, but the rival will actually contract. The reason is as follows. When one firm expands output, supported by a credible threat, the other firm has no reason to believe the increased competitiveness is only temporary. The best it can do is respond to the lowered leftover demand that it sees by reducing output. This in turn helps the lower cost firm. In effect this firm benefited twice from lower cost. In the first instance, it simply gained directly because costs fell. In addition the lowered costs improved its strategic position in the market and indirectly induced the rival to contract. This contraction by the rival increases the price that the expanding firm can obtain for any given output level and causes profit to rise through that channel. Thus the firm with lowered costs benefits by more than the amount of the cost saving.

This paper of course is not about cost savings; we all agree that firm and country are likely to be better off if the domestic firm is able to lower its costs through more efficient methods of production. The point to be made is that as far as the domestic firm is concerned, an export subsidy (or a production subsidy) has the same effect as lowered costs. A subsidy to the cost of producing extra output makes it in the firm's interest to expand output, even taking the other firm's output as given. Therefore the firm's expansion of output is credible. The rival firm can best respond by contracting output. In effect the subsidy makes it possible for the domestic firm to stake out a larger market share of a profitable international market than it otherwise could.

This policy is obviously good for the firm. It saves that part of costs that is now covered by the subsidy, so its profit certainly will rise. But these subsidized costs are paid for from the domestic treasury; the subsidy itself is just a transfer from taxpayers to shareholders of the firm. How is such a policy in the national interest?

The key is to think carefully about the example of lower costs again. Just as in that case, there are two effects of the subsidy. One effect is the apparent cost saving, which is really just a transfer. There is, however, the second effect to consider. Because subsidized costs make it credible or believable (to the rival) that the domestic firm will expand, the rival's best response is to contract, and this in itself raises the domestic firm's profit by an additional amount. This second effect is sometimes called the "strategic" effect because it owes its existence to the nature of the strategic game played by firms. It implies that profits to the domestic firm rise by *more* than the amount of the subsidy. The benefit to the firm exceeds the cost to taxpayers.

If one then goes back to the economist's criterion for policy: expansion of the (domestic) economic pie, we find that this subsidy policy looks good. Provided shareholders of the firm are domestic nationals, then total domestic command over goods and services rises as a result of the subsidy policy, since profits rise by more than the subsidy cost.

We might of course be concerned about the distributional consequences of the subsidy policy since the benefits accrue to shareholders of the firm (or possibly in rents to workers). Some of the cost will be recovered from income taxes on shareholders. It is even possible that this extra tax could fully offset the subsidy cost, but this is unlikely. Relying on the tax/transfer system to take care of the distributional issues is perhaps not fully justified in this case.

As for the international distribution of income, it should be clear that this policy is predatory in its effect on rival producing countries; the gain to the domestic economy comes completely at the expense of this rival, and this is true regardless of whether the other country is itself using a strategic subsidy or not. It might, however be argued that such policies are more acceptable if they are in retaliation than if they are "first strikes." I will have more to say about this point later. One additional important point to recognize is that consuming countries will benefit from the subsidy policy because part of the subsidy will be passed on in the form of lower final prices. In fact the combined benefit to consuming countries and the domestic country will exceed the cost to the other producing country. From the world point of view this policy is actually welfare improving. The welfare improvement comes about because the subsidy acts to reduce the monopoly distortion in this imperfectly competitive industry.

As is normally the case with economic theory, the simplified environment that is assumed in order to make an argument clear or to isolate a particular economic effect is not the environment encountered by real policymakers. The real environment is much more complicated. The question then becomes: How robust is the basic idea? Do slight changes or complications undermine it completely? Gene Grossman, in chapter 3, suggests a series of modifications that tend to weaken the force of the argument for strategic subsidies that I have presented. These qualifications draw chiefly on recent work by Grossman, Avinash Dixit, and Jonathan Eaton, all of which is, as far as I know, logically correct. Changing the form of oligopolistic competition can certainly alter the results, as does increasing the ratio of domestic to foreign firms.

I believe, however, that the basic point is more general than the specific model presented in Brander and Spencer (1984) and just described. This point is that government action can alter the strategic game played by foreign and domestic firms. In profitable markets domestic firms are made better off if foreign firms can be induced to contract (or to expand more slowly than they otherwise would). Firms themselves try to deter rivals of course, and such actions are part of what leads to industry equilibrium. The main element in the argument is then that governments have access to tools, such as subsidies, which the firms do not have access to, that can further deter rivals. Such government policies can lead to a national advantage. This effect corresponds to the complaint of American firms that they can compete against Japanese firms but not against Japanese firms and government combined, or to the complaint by non-American firms than they have a hard time competing against American firms supported by large defense contracts.

Even this more general statement applies only to a few industries of course. Barbara Spencer's paper (chapter 5) discusses those industry characteristics that are necessary for the argument to apply, so I will not duplicate that here. I will just emphasize that this case for subsidies is not an argument for general subsidization of exports; it would not work for most industries. The policy would have to be one of targeting particular industries, of "picking winners," which is not easy.

Perhaps concluding this section with an example would be the best way to reinforce the basic point being made. The wide-body jet aircraft industry comes as close as any industry to being a classic oligopoly. Industry analysts suggest that the market can probably accommodate only two firms producing the next generation of wide-body jets. The industry is of interest because subsidies from France and other European countries have enabled a European entrant to gain a foothold in the market by producing the Airbus, a contender in the current generation of jet aircraft.

The two firms that are able to dominate the next generation will likely make substantial profits, but it is unlikely that three firms could all make profits from the market. Boeing will probably be one of the "winners"; the other contenders are McDonnell-Douglas, Lockheed, and the European entrant. Subsidization of the European entrant gives that firm an edge. If those subsidies persuade McDonnell-Douglas and Lockheed not to try to enter the market, then the subsidies will have had the effect described in this paper. To the extent that subsidies persuade rival firms to produce less or to stay out of the market altogether, it is possible that the subsidy can more than pay for itself in the form of profits or other rents.

It does not follow of course that this particular subsidy policy is necessarily successful by economic criteria. If, for example, the European entrant turned out to be an inefficient producer, then the subsidies might never be offset by earned profits: a large market share alone does not necessarily imply that the policy is a good one. The point remains, however, that this example illustrates the way a strategic subsidy might work.

Protection and Home Market Effects

Trade policy is traditionally more concerned with protection of domestic import-competing industries than with export promotion. The main, but not the only, tools of protection are the tariff and the quota.

The tariff arose, not as a strategic policy, but simply as a way of raising revenue. There is, however, a very old argument for protection that does have a strategic interpretation: the infant-industry argument. The idea was that temporary protection of an industry that could not currently compete with foreign rivals might be justified if the industry, because of the protection, would have a chance to grow, become more efficient, and eventually compete with foreign firms. This argument is well known, and I will not describe it in detail here. One weakness of the argument is that it must rely on either the idea that firms in an industry generate positive externalities among themselves or the claim that firms are unable to make efficient long-term investments through capital markets. Otherwise, the firms would always have an incentive to themselves go through the necessary period of losses in order to make long-run gains without requiring protection. The only industries that would require protection would be those that were not worthwhile.

In recent years some arguments have arisen that are related to the infant-industry argument but which do not require capital market failures or externalities to apply. I shall describe a few of those arguments here. The first such argument is based on Krugman (1984). Krugman analyzes formally an idea that is often discussed in the business press but is inconsistent with standard trade theory. The idea is that restricting a particular market, or subset of a market, to certain firms helps those firms in other markets. For example, protecting the domestic market from foreign firms helps domestic firms not only in the protected market but in export markets as well. If the domestic firms can earn extra profits from these export markets, then such protection may be in the national interest.

The important element in Krugman's analysis is the presence of some form of advantage of size or "economy of scale." The simplest case is simply when incremental or "marginal" cost, which is the cost of producing an extra unit of output, falls as total production by the firm rises, and when there is, once again, a single domestic firm and a single foreign firm. In the absence of protection, one would expect both firms to operate in all markets, even if the firms produce identical products (as analyzed in Brander 1981). If the domestic market is then closed to the foreign firm, the domestic firm would normally raise its output in the domestic market. The marginal cost of production would fall, since marginal cost falls as output rises, and the domestic firm would then find itself able to expand its market share credibly and to profit in foreign markets.

Cases of declining marginal cost are probably rare, but Krugman's second case seems more relevant empirically. This case is based on the idea of learning by doing. Learning by doing is similar in structure to the declining marginal cost case except that the role of time is made explicit. The idea is that as a firm produces more it learns how to undertake further production more efficiently. The firm is said to move down its "learning curve." Having a protected home market can allow a domestic firm to produce more in its home market than it otherwise would and therefore to learn more quickly than foreign rivals. As before this will allow the domestic firm to compete more successfully and earn higher profits in export markets than it otherwise would. Krugman calls this policy "protection as export promotion."

No welfare analysis is undertaken in Krugman's paper. The policy is good for firms but bad for domestic consumers, who have access to a less competitive domestic market as a result. If, however, one is prepared simply to add up the dollar benefits to firms and subtract the dollar costs to consumers, an aggregate welfare effect can be calculated. The extra costs to consumers are mainly just transfers to the domestic firm, although not entirely. The firm, however, also benefits in the form of enhanced profits from foreign markets, and these benefits can more than tip the balance. As with export subsidies this policy is predatory with respect to other producing countries but may serve to help any net consuming countries. The world welfare effect is ambiguous.

One industry where home market effects interact in an interesting way with policy is the high-technology communications product market. Most countries that have such industries offer implicit protection to domestic producers because the principal users are regulated firms. Often in fact production of communications equipment and communications services are carried out by the same firm. For example, until very recently AT&T produced such equipment through Western Electric and was the principal buyer through its operating companies. The trade argument being made with respect to AT&T is that divestiture of the operating companies is equivalent to trade liberalization because foreign firms will now have the opportunity to sell products to the independent operating companies. If the Krugman argument applies here, then AT&T will lose profits because it will lose the advantages of having a protected home market. Furthermore, and more interestingly, this could be against the national interest if it gives foreign rivals an advantage in earning profits in other markets.

A different and comparatively subtle case in which protection improves domestic welfare is examined in Venables (1984). As with Krugman's argument, consider a world in which foreign and domestic firms compete in their own markets and possibly in other markets as well. This time, however, instead of international duopoly with just one foreign firm and one domestic firm, the market is large enough to accommodate quite a few firms, and entry is free enough that profits are always driven to their "normal" level. Furthermore, instead of declining incremental cost, incremental cost is constant but there are substantial fixed costs. (This cost structure is often alleged to be empirically important.) The important property of this cost structure is that average cost, or cost per unit, falls as output rises. To complete the description of the environment, firms are not perfect competitors. Each firm faces a downward sloping demand curve for its product, and Venables uses Cournot's idea that industry equilibrium occurs when each firm is maximizing profit with respect to its own output level, given the output level produced by the rest of the market.

In this environment Venables argues that either import tariffs or export subsidies will improve national welfare. Consider a tariff first. The most obvious effect of the tariff is that it raises revenue, which counts on the plus side of the benefit-cost ledger. The second effect is that the relative disadvantage of foreign firms operating in the domestic market increases. Whereas before they had transport costs to contend with, they now have transport costs and a tariff. The effect of this will be to lower the share of foreign firms in the domestic market and, as a result, in the world as a whole. Each domestic firm meanwhile is able to expand both domestic and total output and move down its average cost curve. Domestic firms now have lower average costs, and foreign firms have higher average costs than before. Provided domestic firms are more important in the domestic market than foreign firms are, the net effect will be to cause domestic price to fall and consumer welfare to rise. Free entry keeps profit at precisely its normal level, so there is no welfare effect there, leaving a net welfare benefit to the domestic economy.

Meanwhile in the foreign country firms now earn less from export markets and are forced to charge a higher price at home as they move up their average cost curves. Foreign welfare therefore falls. The maximum difference between foreign and domestic prices is equal to transport costs, so this policy can only be important to the extent that transport costs are large.

The reasoning with subsidies is similar. Subsidies allow domestic firms to export more and move down their average cost curves, which causes domestic prices to fall and domestic welfare to rise. The similarity between the Krugman and Venables arguments is that both rely on the mechanism that producing more is good for domestic firms because there is an advantage of size that allows firms to have lower average or marginal costs. Effects such as these are ruled out by standard neoclassical trade theory because, by assumption, there are no economies of scale. The difference between Krugman and Venables is that Krugman has limited entry so that benefits appear mainly as extra profits to firms. In the Venables case, on the other hand, the economies of scale are less pronounced, allowing relatively free entry which keeps profits at the competitive level. Benefits then come in the form of lower prices to domestic consumers.

One final example of what might be described as a "neo-infant-industry argument" is drawn from Brander and Spencer (1981). As coauthor of the idea, however, I can safely say at the outset that this particular argument is probably of minor empirical significance. In any case the reasoning runs along the following lines. As an initial situation, imagine a domestic market in which no domestic firms are operating but which is served by a foreign firm. The foreign firm is aware of the possibility that a domestic firm might enter the market but prices in such a way as to deter domestic entry. A tariff in this situation can extract rent from the foreign firm because, up to a point, the foreign firm will just absorb the tariff and not raise domestic prices for fear of enticing domestic entry. A sufficiently high tariff will eventually force the foreign firm to give up this practice of entry deterrence; domestic prices will rise, and domestic entry will occur.

Domestic consumers are harmed by the price rise, but the treasury is earning revenue. Therefore profits are shifted from the foreign firm to the new domestic firm. Furthermore the domestic firm may earn profit from foreign markets. Overall, such a policy can be welfare improving for the domestic economy, but to be a good policy, the domestic firm must have relatively low costs once it enters. It does not pay to induce domestic entry if the entrant's costs are high. However, even if domestic costs are high, the domestic government can still take advantage of fact that there is a potential entrant around, and use tariffs to extract rent from the foreign firm, but the optimal policy in this case would be to stop increasing the tariff short of the level required actually to induce domestic entry.

The argument for using a tariff to extract rent is made attractive by the possibility of domestic entry, but potential entry is not required for a tariff to be attractive. If there is a foreign firm earning profits in the domestic market, it will normally be in the domestic interest to extract some of those profits or rents by using a tariff. The tariff is in effect a tax on the foreign firm.

Government–Government Interaction and Retaliation

A skeptical reader who began entertaining nagging concerns about policy retaliation upon reading the first few pages of this paper might by now be getting rather distraught. Surely other governments cannot be expected to sit (or stand or whatever governments do) passively by and let one government get away with the polices described so far.

The task now is to consider the strategic game played by national governments. The simplest possibility is that national governments aside from the domestic government really are passive and adopt a completely noninterventionist stance. A noninterventionist stance would, for example, arise from the view of the world implied by the standard models of international trade for countries that were small in world markets. A more interesting and more likely possibility is that the national governments involved see the world in more or less the same way. Thus I assume that each national government is out to maximize national welfare, as measured by command over goods and services, and that each government recognizes the strategic possibilities present in the formation of international trade policy.

The structure of the strategic environment faced by governments is similar to the environment faced by oligopolistic firms themselves. The payoff to each player or participant depends on its own action and on the action of its rival. In the case of governments, national welfare in Japan, for example, depends on Japanese trade policy and on American trade policy. Just as there is no generally accepted single

Country *E*

		Cooperate	Defect
	Cooperate	400, 400	50, 500
Country *A*	Defect	500, 50	100, 100

Figure 2.1

theory of oligopoly behavior, there is no generally accepted theory of policy interaction.

We can, however, easily imagine three sorts of policy outcomes. Consider the Krugman policy of protecting home markets. One policy outcome is that one country protects its home market and enables its home firm or firms to gain an advantage in international markets, which translates into a national advantage for this country, while other countries do nothing. A second possible outcome is that all countries try to help domestically based firms through protection, with the result that no firm is able to do well in export markets. No firm is able to realize advantages of size, and all countries end up with both low levels of competition and high costs. This is perhaps the worst of all possible worlds. The third outcome is that countries agree not to use protection, in which case all countries do better than in the full protection regime but each must resist the temptation to try to gain unilateral advantages by being a lone defector.

There is a simple theoretical structure that captures the incentive structure of this foreign policy environment. Suppose that there are two countries called, imaginatively, country *A* and country *E*. Each country has access to an interventionist policy that is in national interest but that reduces the welfare of the other country. Cooperating means refraining from using the policy; defecting means adopting the policy. To illustrate the point, let us imagine that we can represent the net benefits to the countries of the different policy regimes using numbers. These benefits or payoffs can be summarized most easily using a box or payoff matrix, as shown in figure 2.1.

The first element in each small box represents the payoff to country *A*; the second element represents the payoff to *E*. Along the top, country *E*'s strategies are represented, and along the left, country *A*'s strategies are listed. Thus if both countries defect from the cooperative noninterventionist policy, each country gets a return of 100. If country A defects, and the other country does not, then A gets a return of 500 and country E gets only a small net benefit of 50 from this industry. If neither country defects, each country gets a net benefit of 400.

The actual numbers are not important. What is important are the relative magnitudes. These relative magnitudes reflect a common situation in international policymaking. Unilateral predatory policy is attractive if the other country is passive, but mutual nonintervention would give the highest combined total return, in this case, 800.

Consider the decision problem faced by country A if it has to make a once and for all policy decision. If country E chooses a strategy of nonintervention, then A can make gains by intervening because 500 is greater than 400. Furthermore, even if E chooses to intervene, A's best strategy is still to intervene because 100 is better than 50. Defection or intervention is a dominant strategy: no matter what the other country does, intervention is best. If governments only make decisions once, then the outcome in which both countries intervene is compelling as an equilibrium. Thus each country gets 100, which is clearly much worse than the 400 each could get if only the two countries could agree to open their markets to each other.

This particular strategic structure is known as the "prisoner's dilemma," since it is usually described using prisoners rather than countries, and was first formalized by Tucker (1950). It is the most widely studied structure in the theory of strategic interaction, or game theory. The problem of choosing subsidy levels in the profit-shifting context has a structure similar to the prisoner's dilemma. It really does not matter whether the other country has a strategic subsidy or not; the best response for either country is to use a subsidy also. The actual benefit of the subsidy is much higher if the other country does not use a subsidy also. Both producing countries would be better off if neither used the subsidy, but the unilateral incentive to use the subsidy is clear.

One might ask at this point why countries do not get together and do the sensible thing, which would be to agree to avoid the use of these subsidies altogether. International treaties are usually attempts to do precisely that sort of thing. The General Agreement on Tariffs and Trade (GATT), for example, is an attempt to get countries to agree multilaterally to have low tariffs. The problem with such agreements is that individual countries have incentives to cheat or defect. Cooperative outcomes are fragile at best because there is no international court that can force countries to abide by the treaties they sign. In the case of GATT, success in getting tariff reductions has occurred simultaneously with major increases in other forms of trade intervention.

On the other hand, the prediction that noncooperative outcomes always occur is clearly too pessimistic. A major problem with the theory of the prisoner's dilemma as presented so far is that it is restricted to the case of once and for all strategy choices. In reality a decision to use subsidies or to close home markets is not irrevocable and will usually be reviewed at regular intervals. In effect the prisoner's dilemma game is repeated indefinitely. Repetitions of the decisions make the game much more complicated in that relatively complex strategies become possible. One strategy might be to always play the noncooperative move of defection. Another strategy might be to always play the cooperative move. More interesting are contingent strategies, such as the strategy of cooperating if the rival cooperated last time but defecting if the rival played the noncooperative move last time. This approach, combined with a first move of cooperation, is known as the "tit for tat" strategy. Much more complicated contingent strategies are also possible. A strategy that economists have devoted considerable attention to is the "trigger strategy," which is to cooperate until the rival defects, and then play the noncooperative move forever thereafter.

What is likely to be the outcome of such an environment? One approach to answering this question is to try to draw inferences from observed strategic interaction between governments. Though most analysts would agree that it makes sense to keep in the mind the conduct of actual policymakers, it is fairly obvious that this approach is limited by several factors. First, the world is not a laboratory in which experiments can be repeated. Consequently the simple quantity of useful data is much smaller than one would want. Second, it is very hard to disentangle the many effects that contribute to real policy outcomes. Any particular policy action is normally the product of several factors. It is difficult therefore to isolate the effect any one factor, such as a particular strategic stance, has on the outcome. Yet it is precisely the ability to isolate the consequences of different factors that constitutes real understanding.

A second possible approach is to confine oneself to purely theoretical investigations and ask what rational decision makers would do in particular stylized situations. The obvious problem with this approach is that it relies too heavily on the analyst's idea of what constitutes rational or reasonable behavior. A third style of analysis is to construct experiments. This suffers from the problem that one cannot be sure that people will behave in real situations as they do in manufactured environments, but I would argue that the results are at least worth looking at.

A University of Michigan political scientist named Robert Axelrod has recently published the results of some very interesting experiments. Axelrod invited a group of game theorists from several academic disciplines and several countries to submit strategies for a repeated prisoner's dilemma game of the following form. Each entered strategy would confront each other strategy 200 times. (In addition to the entered strategies Axelrod also included a random strategy that cooperated or defected on a purely random basis.) After this series of round robin repeated prisoners dilemma games, the scores would be added up to determine the winner.

In this game Axelrod received 14 entries, including some relatively complex strategies. The winning strategy, however, submitted by psychologist and philosopher Anatol Rapaport of the University of Toronto, was "tit for tat," which happened to be the simplest strategy submitted. (Recall that tit for tat cooperates as its first move, then does whatever the rival did last time.) This strategy requires only four steps in a Fortran computer program. The second place strategy was relatively complicated, requiring 41 computer steps. (This strategy was submitted by economists Nicholas Tideman and Paula Chieruzzi.) The "trigger strategy," submitted by economist James Friedman, finished seventh in the field of 15 strategies consisting of the 14 entries and the purely random strategy included by Axelrod. The random strategy finished last.

Axelrod wrote up the results of this competition, including an analysis of why certain strategies did well, then advertised in computer magazines for entrants in a larger-scale replay of the experiment. In the second experiment there were 62 entries plus the random strategy. Whereas the first game had been restricted to professional game theorists from academic disciplines like economics, psychology, and political science, the second game attracted most of its entries from computer buffs, although most of the original entrants also submitted entries for the second game. This time the entries were more complicated: the third place finisher had 77 computer steps, and one strategy had 152 steps (and finished 43rd). The Tideman and Chieruzzi strategy, slightly modified, which was a very close second in the first game, fell to ninth place. A modified Friedman entrant fell to 52nd place. On the whole the second game was much tougher, with second through sixth places being taken by fairly complex strategies, all submitted by computer buffs.

The winning strategy, however, was "tit for tat," submitted again by Anatol Rapaport. Once again tit for tat was the simplest strategy submitted, and was the only simple strategy to do well. The other strategies of comparable simplicity (six steps each) finished near the bottom. The random strategy finished 62nd (second to last).

What does all this have to do with policy? The point is that if experiments are any guide, strategies that cooperate if the rival cooperates and quickly but briefly punish noncooperative behavior are remarkably successful. Tit for tat strategies are widely used in practical situations of course, and they have a certain intuitive appeal. Unqualified cooperation is, in experiments, a poor strategy, but strategies that involve defecting first to get a temporary gain do not do well either when compared to tit for tat. To be successful, a strategy must have two characteristics: it must be able to acquiesce in long periods of cooperation with other relatively friendly strategies, but it must punish noncooperation.

One strategy that is related to tit for tat is "tit for two tats." This strategy cooperates unless the rival has played the noncooperative move twice in a row. Interestingly, this strategy would have won the first game, played only by professional game theorists, had it been entered. However, it was entered and did relatively poorly in the second game. The weakness of tit for two tats is that it can be exploited by really devious strategies.

This can be interpreted in a world of real policymaking. If a national government faces what it believes is a tit for tat strategy from another government, there is little it can do but cooperate, provided there is always a next period. Predatory strategies just do not pay against tit for tat. Against tit for two tats, on the other hand, there is a strong incentive to get away with the occasional predatory action.

It is very tempting to apply the results of this experiment directly and advocate the use of tit for tat trade policies. Drawing inferences from experiments like this for policymaking is, however, not straightforward. One problem is that there are many policy areas, not just one, which means that it is hard to be clear about the correspondence between the policies of different countries. For example, it is sometimes argued that the United States should place import controls on Japanese exports in retaliation for Japanese protection from American exports. The Japanese can respond, however, by saying that certain protective policies are a response to the advantage the U.S. firms have in having preferential access to defense contracts, or in drawing on a heavily subsidized research establishment in the U.S. university system. In other words, in the real world it is not easy to identify clearly which policy is "tit" and which policy is "tat."

I do not believe that this problem of identification is insurmountable, but it does introduce extra considerations. If a country is trying to follow a tit for tat strategy, it has to select policy responses that are easily communicated as reasonable responses to the perceived predatory action by the foreign country.

A second problem in trying to use the prisoners dilemma experiment as an input to policy analysis is that trade policy is conducted in an explicitly multilateral environment under GATT, whereas the prisoners dilemma is a purely bilateral kind of interaction. Trying to carry out tit for tat policies of a multilateral sort is not only difficult but probably very foolish as well. One example of the problem with multilateral tit for tat strategies that is in the news as of this writing is the possibility that the United States might impose quotas and or tariffs on steel imports to counteract Japanese and European subsidies. Such policies would, however, also apply to Canadian exports of steel to the United States. Needless to say, this is not popular in Canada and could give rise to Canadian retaliation. (My current understanding is that President Reagan has decided to refrain from imposing such quotas.)

There are those in the United States who lament the deterioration of multilateralism. It is, however, hard to see how to avoid bilateral interactions if a tit for tat strategy is to be used. The whole advantage of a tit for tit approach is its bilateral nature. In other words, country-specific policies must be targeted to specific policies used by other countries. There are aspects of U.S. policy that have a tit for tat character. In particular, some actions of the Export-Import Bank can be interpreted in this way. If project-specific or industry-specific export subsidies from other countries are matched by Eximbank subsidies and if other countries believe the bank's commitment to a tit for tat policy, then this should be a factor tending to inhibit predatory or "first strike" subsidies from other countries.

Synthesis and Concluding Remarks

I would now like to review and draw together the two main themes in this paper and to distinguish these themes from conventional reasoning. The sections of this paper entitled "Profit-Shifting Subsidies" and "Protection from Home Market Effect" are set against a background of unresponsive or unchanging policies from foreign governments. What these sections demonstrate is that there is a unilateral economic motive for interventionist trade policy in certain cases. This conclusion is in sharp contrast to the standard results and received wisdom of mainstream international trade theory. The difference comes about by allowing a more varied and more realistic role for individual firms. Instead of insisting on perfect competition and ruling out learning by doing, economies of scale, entry barriers, high profit rates, R&D races, and other phenomena normally excluded by international trade theory, the arguments presented here draw on a body of research that focuses explicitly on these phenomena.

This notion of a richer role for the individual firm is of course very familiar to industrial organization economists. The research used as background for this paper can be viewed as a marriage of industrial organization and international trade. Along with a more satisfying view of individual firms, this research also inherits from industrial organization theory some problems, particularly a proliferation of cases, and a lack of general easy-to-follow policy guidelines. Policy becomes a series of special cases. My view is that this is only delayed recognition by international trade economists of a principle long understood by economists in the fields of public finance and industrial organization and by policymakers: different industry structures give rise to different policy incentives. There is no point in trying to maintain, for example, that the policy-relevant characteristics of the jet aircraft industry are just like those of the textile industry.

While on the subject of imperfect markets, it would be remiss not to draw attention to a fact supported by a lot of theory and brought home most forcefully in a recent empirical study by Richard Harris. Specifically, though economies of scale and imperfect competition give rise to incentives for interventionist unilateral trade policy, they also greatly expand the gains from trade. The reasons are obvious: international trade expands market size, allowing realization of economies of scale and increased competition in imperfectly competitive industries. From any one country's point of view, however, the gains come about much more from having access to other country's markets than from allowing foreign firms to have access to domestic markets.

The second major theme of the paper, contained in the section entitled "Government–Government Interaction and Retaliation," builds on the first theme that there are unilaterally attractive interventionist policies. The step it takes is to consider how other governments might respond to policy initiatives. What is a sensible policy stance in a world of strategic governments? A naive answer might be that the possibility of retaliation completely undercuts any case for strategic policy. Such a response fails to address the question of what to do in the face of existing predatory policies by other countries, and fails to take account of the basic incentive structure of the international environment.

It would, I think, be foolish to suggest that there is any one best policy stance that is appropriate for international trade issues. What I have done is to present some experimental evidence based, admittedly, on a very artificial environment that nevertheless suggests that tit for tat policies can be very effective strategies. In other words, policy regimes that promise retaliation for predatory actions but otherwise cooperate seem to be attractive strategies.

There are of course a host of practical problems in actually implementing tit for tat strategies. One problem is that it may be very difficult or costly actually to make a commitment to tit for tat policies. For example, in order for the Eximbank to act as a credible deterrent to predatory subsidization of the European entrant in the wide-body jet aircraft market, it would need more financial resources than its already substantial budget allows. A second problem is that sensible application of tit for tat strategies involves explicit bilateralism, which would be a departure from a multilateral approach to trade policy that many observers feel has served the United States and the other western democracies well with respect to both economic and political objectives. My only point is that it is at least possible to put forward a sensible case for interventionist policy in a world of policy interaction between governments. Furthermore such a policy should probably shy away from predatory first strikes but might reasonably have a retaliatory role.

It is worth emphasizing at this stage what the paper is not. First of all, if does not provide a rationale for a broad-based policy of subsidization. The rationale it provides is for targeting of a few industries, even when the policy is purely retaliatory. The informational requirements in formulating such policies are substantial. (Krugman 1983 is one of many to express skepticism about the ability of governments to undertake successful targeting.) My own view is that governments might do a better job of targeting if they knew what they were looking for.

A second thing the paper does not do is to justify the policy of providing a "level playing field" for foreign and domestic firms. As predatory strategies, the policies described here are explicitly intended to give domestic firms an advantage. As retaliatory strategies, they are intended to get other countries to stop their predatory actions.

The case for interventionist trade policy presented here is limited and narrow. There are certainly other economic rationales for intervention, rationales that are neither predatory nor retaliatory. Credit subsidies might be appropriate if financial markets are incomplete, subsidies and taxes or tariffs might be good policies to deal with various positive and negative externalities, and so on. I have also not dealt with some of the major general criticisms of interventionist policy, including the argument that policy institutions, however well intentioned initially, are too easily influenced by special interest groups.

The research underlying this paper is not likely to bring academic trade theorists and industry lobbyists into agreement. Its value is that it addresses some of the issues that industry lobbyists regard as important, rather than dismissing such issues by assumption. The paper undoubtedly does not go so far as actually to get academic economists, policymakers, and industry representatives all talking the same language. I hope, however, that we are at least recognizably talking about some of the same subjects.

References

Axelrod, Robert. 1984. *The Evolution of Cooperation*. New York: Basic Books.

Brander, James A. 1981. "Intra-industry trade in identical commodities." *Journal of International Economics* 11, 1–14.

Brander, James A., and Barbara J. Spencer. 1981. "Tariffs and the extraction of foreign monopoly rents under potential entry." *Canadian Journal of Economics* 14, 371–389.

Brander, James A., and Barbara J. Spencer. 1984. "Export subsidies and international market share rivalry." *Journal of International Economics*, forthcoming.

Cournot, Augustin. 1838. *Recherches sur les principes mathematiques de la theorie des richesses*. Paris: Hachette.

Cox, David, and Richard Harris. 1984. "Trade liberalization and industrial organization: some estimates for Canada." *Journal of Political Economy*, forthcoming.

Dixit, Avinash K. 1984. "International trade policies for oligopolistic industries." *Economic Journal* 94, Supplement.

Dixit, Avinash K., and Gene M. Grossman. 1984. "Targeted export promotion with several oligopolistic industries." National Bureau of Economic Research Working Paper No. 1344.

Dixit, Avinash K., and Albert S. Kyle. 1983. "On the use of trade restrictions for entry promotion and deterrence." Woodrow Wilson School Discussion Paper No. 79, Princeton University.

Eaton, Jonathan, and Gene M. Grossman. 1983. "Optimal trade and industrial policy under oligopoly." National Bureau of Economic Research Working Paper No. 1236.

Grossman, Gene M., and J. David Richardson. 1984. "Strategic U.S. trade policy: a survey of issues and early analysis." NBER Research Progress Report.

Harris, Richard G. 1984. *Trade, Industrial Policy and Canadian Manufacturing*. Toronto: Ontario Economic Council.

Harris, Richard G. 1984. "Applied general equilibrium analysis of small open economies with scale economies and imperfect competition." *American Economic Review*, forthcoming.

Krugman, Paul R. 1983. "Targeted industrial policies: theory and evidence." In *Industrial Change and Public Policy*. Symposium sponsored by the Federal Reserve Bank of Kansas City, Jackson Hole, Wyoming, pp. 123–156.

Krugman, Paul R. 1984. "Import protection as export promotion." In H. Kierzkowski, ed., *Monopolistic Competition and International Trade*. Oxford: Oxford University Press.

Spencer, Barbara J., and James A. Brander. 1983. "International R&D rivalry and industrial strategy." *Review of Economic Studies* 50, 707–722.

Tucker, A. W. 1950. "A two person dilemma." Mimeo. Stanford University.

Venables, Anthony J. 1984. "International trade in identical commodities; Cournot equilibrium with free entry." Centre for Economic Policy Research Discussion Paper No. 9, London.

3 Strategic Export Promotion: A Critique

Gene M. Grossman

In recent years, as the competitive pressure on the United States has increased, and the perception has developed that governments abroad are at least partly responsible for the inroads made by foreign corporations, the case for U.S. government support of domestic firms in their international struggles has broadened in appeal. Popular observers note that our trade partners are "targeting" profitable industries, and question whether allowing them do so can possibly be in the national interest. Would it not be better, they ask, to match subsidy with subsidy, or even to preempt with targeting practices of our own, so that the high returns in the sunrise industries of tomorrow will be won (or at least shared) by American companies? Should we "allow our industrial structure to be determined by foreign governments," or should we strive to "choose those industries in which our producers will develop comparative advantage"?

Such questions almost inevitably evoke a stock retort from international economists, who have long opposed export promotion of any kind. They will point out that subsidies distort the allocation of resources from market-determined to less productive uses, and that they lower the price that our country's exports command on competitive world markets. They will then cite a well-known result from the theory of trade policy—that the nationally optimal intervention for a large country is a *tax* on exports—and conclude therefore that any argument to the contrary is surely self-serving sophistry. Unfortunately this orthodox response fails to meet the issue head on and is in fact based on a model of world production and trade that is quite inappropriate for doing so. Whereas the proponents of industrial targeting point to potential above-normal profits as the prize for successful policy, the textbook model of international trade precludes the existence of such profits by assumption. The advocates speak of "strategic trade policy," which would seek to alter the competitive balance in industries where small numbers of progressive firms vie to establish their shares of an evolving world market, while the opponents draw on an analysis in which competition is assumed to be atomistic, market shares are infinitesimal, and strategy can have no role. Evidently a serious response to recent proposals for aggressive and strategic export promotion requires a fresh analytical approach to trade policy, one that does not presuppose an answer in its very formulation.

The starting point for recent theoretical treatments of strategic trade policy is a world of imperfect or oligopolistic competition. In such a world, the number of participants in some particular industry is small, and profit opportunities above and beyond the "normal" return to scarce factors of production are not ruled out, at least in the short run. Here it is reasonable to ask whether there is anything that a national government can do to ensure that its own participants in the competition win a large share of these profits, and if so, whether implementing such a policy would be in the national interest. The insight first provided by James Brander and Barbara Spencer (see Brander and Spencer 1983 and Spencer and Brander 1983) is that in some circumstances, a policy of export promotion can serve exactly this purpose and that the extra profits that would accrue to domestic firms if this course were pursued would exceed the budgetary cost.[1]

The Brander-Spencer finding has received much attention from academic researchers and policy analysts because it seems to provide theoretical support for a targeted industrial policy. But as with all theory, the conclusion is only as strong as the assumptions that serve as its foundation. Further inquiry reveals that the results are not robust and that great care is needed in translating them into policy prescription. Treating the case for strategic export promotion on its own terms, I will argue that we do not now (and may never) have sufficient knowledge and information to merit the implementation of a policy of industrial targeting. My argument will be based on the introduction into the simple, Brander-Spencer framework of a number of realistic considerations that render the policy conclusions ambiguous. Thus I will not deny that strategic export promotion could in principle be beneficial, but I will suggest instead that it is equally possible that it would be economically harmful and that the policymaker has no systematic basis for identifying instances where the former is true rather than the latter. In other words, the efficacy of any targeting policy ultimately rests on its criteria for selection and the information that would be required to implement a successful policy of strategic export promotion along the lines suggested by the Brander-Spencer analysis is well beyond what economists or industry analysts could reasonably hope to provide.

The Argument for Strategic Export Promotion in Imperfectly Competitive Industries

In a world of perfect markets and perfect competition, prices reflect the scarcity value of all goods and provide appropriate incentives for economic decision makers. Each consumer purchases units of goods until the value to him or her of the last of these is exactly equal to the price. Firms take product prices as data, being themselves too small in the overall market to influence them, and hire resources until the cost of producing the marginal unit is equal to the revenue that is realized by doing so. In this way the market equates marginal benefit in consumption with marginal cost of production.

In this idealized world there is no reason for a government to prefer one industrial structure over another. All industries are equally "profitable," profit being the normal return to such scarce factors as managerial ability and entrepreneurship. "Strategy" (by which is meant actions that are taken to induce favorable responses by rivals) plays no role, since all actors perceive themselves as being too small to influence market outcomes and behave as if the market environment were a given. The only valid reason for a country to intervene in international trade on aggregate welfare grounds is to improve its terms of trade, the rate at which its exports exchange for imports in the world market. If, for example, it restricts the quantity of its exports by taxing them, it can create an artificial scarcity of these goods that drives up their world price. But, as well known, such gains are achieved at the expense of one's trade partners, and thus policies to manipulate the terms of trade invite retaliatory measures that leave all worse off than under free trade.

Although this depiction of the economy is useful as a benchmark, it does not correspond well with the competitive circumstances that many businessmen describe, or that by casual observation would seem to characterize some of the glamour industries to which industrial targeting presumably would be aimed. A number of industries have only a small number of participants, either because economies of scale and exclusive patent rights limit entry or because government regulatory policies dictate market structure. Prices in these industries may exceed marginal production costs, and profit opportunities, at least temporarily, may be quite large. Firms in such industries, guided by their strategic planning departments, do consider the possible effects of their actions on those of their competitors and on the market variables that determine their profit performance. And market shares in such industries evolve over time and, in principle, are subject to the influences of government policy.

The simplest possible imperfectly competitive market environment in which we can reconsider the efficacy of export subsidies is one where two firms, one American firm and one foreign competitor, sell substitutable products in (and only in) a third-country market. Each firm is assumed to have a single decision variable that it sets in this competition, namely the quantity of output that it produces and offers for export. It is further assumed that either firm could, if it so desired, expand its output to any level that might be relevant (though not necessarily at a constant per unit cost), by drawing on resources that otherwise would be employed in competitive (i.e., zero-excess profits) uses elsewhere in the economy. Once the two firms have selected the quantities to place on the market, the prices of the two goods are determined according to demand conditions, so that the entirety of what has been produced is sold. The two firms are assumed to be aware of the relationship between market prices and their own and their rival's quantities at the time that they choose their production levels.

In this setting it is unreasonable to suppose that the firms will take the market prices as data in making their production decisions. Each will realize that its own decision, as well as that of its rival, will influence the realized price. Each must make some conjecture of how its competitor will behave, and possibly may try to influence that behavior, in determining its own optimal course of action. In the parlance of game theory, the firms are in a situation that calls for them to act "strategically."

What would be the outcome of this duopolistic competition in the absence of government policy? This is a difficult question, and depends on what each thinks the other will do, and what each thinks the other thinks it will do, and so on. One solution that has a long history in the theory of oligopoly is to suppose that the industry will eventually settle down to a stable or "equilibrium" situation in which each firm takes the behavior of its rival as *given* and chooses its best response to that action.[2] If each firm has selected the level of output that is optimal given the output of its rival, and each believes that it no longer has any ability to affect the choice of its rival, then neither will have any incentive to change its behavior, and the outcome can be self-sustaining.

Now suppose that this stable market outcome were to emerge, and consider the following thought experiment. Imagine that the chief executive officer of the U.S. firm were to announce an intention to expand aggressively sales in the export market. If the foreign firm were to believe this threat, it would expect a fall in prices there. Its best response would then be to cut its own output. This would leave the domestic firm with a slightly lower price than before (but not as much lower as would occur if the foreign firm were to maintain its output level) but with an increased market share. The increase in market share could easily outweigh the fall in price, and the domestic firm could prosper as a result.

There is a problem with this strategy, however. Given the situation that I have described, the foreign firm would have every reason to believe that the chief executive officer's threat to expand sales was merely a bluff. It would know that the U.S. firm's initial level of output was optimal given its own decision, and that as long as it did not alter its own actions, the U.S. firm would have no incentive to deviate from the initial stable situation and actually carry out its stated intentions. Thus the U.S. company would have no way of making its threat credible, so long as the foreign company remained firm in its resolve.

Here is where trade policy, and in particular export promotion, has a potential role to play. Suppose the U.S. government were to implement an export subsidy. Then this would change the market environment, and the initial situation would no longer be an equilibrium. Now the domestic firm's "threat" to produce more, even if unspoken, must be taken seriously by the foreign competitor. Indeed, with exports subsidized, the U.S. firm would find it in its own interest to expand sales relative to the prepolicy level, even if the foreign firm were to maintain its original level of production. But once the foreign firm realizes this, it can no longer treat the threat as a bluff, and will respond to the new, higher level of U.S. sales by reducing its own offering. The export subsidy alters the competitive "rules of the game" by lending credibility to the home firm's aggressive intentions.

This induces a favorable response by the foreign firm (in this case, a retrenchment), so that the U.S. firm's profits increase by more than the amount of the subsidy. Thus the national interest is served by export promotion.

In real world situations firms may indeed be less inclined to enter new markets, or to expand their sales efforts in existing markets, if they know that their foreign rivals have the backing of their governments. Strategic export promotion can also alter the nature of oligopolistic competition if, by enabling the domestic entrant to expand its sales in one market or at one point in time, the government allows its national firm to gain experience and slide down its "learning curve." Then it will be in a better competitive position in other markets or at later dates. In fact many would claim that MITI has pursued exactly this policy for both of these reasons and that Japanese firms have prospered as a consequence. However compelling as the argument might seem at first blush, there are many caveats that bear discussion.

The Benefits of Export Promotion: Caveats and Modifications

For an economist to argue the case for a particular policy intervention, it is not enough that he or she establish that in some theoretical model the policy is preferable to laissez faire. It is also necessary that he or she show that the conclusion is robust to slight changes in the assumptions of the model, especially when the assumptions are not based on well-established empirical regularities. In cases where theoretical results are found to lack robustness, with perhaps one policy being indicated in one set of circumstances and another under alternative conditions, an activist stance can only be justified if the analyst is confident in the ability of the policy authorities to match policy measure to situation, and thereby improve on the market outcome.

Next, in each of six subsections, I will relax one of the basic assumptions of the Brander-Spencer analysis and show how doing so modifies the conclusion. The intent is to show how difficult it would be in practice to identify those industries for which the argument for strategic export promotion is valid and to distinguish them from those for which theory indicates that free trade, or even a tax on exports, would be warranted.

How Do Firms Behave?

The strategic interaction between firms is an essential part of the story that supports export subsidies for imperfectly competitive industries. That large firms do behave strategically, taking into account the effect of their behavior on that of rivals and on market variables, seems self-evident. Exactly how they behave—for example, what tools of competition they can invoke in various circumstances, what rules they follow, what conjectures they entertain, what implicit promises they can make, and what threats they find credible—is less obvious. Given that we know little about these aspects of corporate behavior, and that the Brander-Spencer assumptions in this regard were selected to be simple and illustrative, it is imperative that we entertain several alternative possibilities.

One such alternative would be to suppose that, instead of choosing output levels and letting market prices adjust accordingly, the two firms competing in the third-country export markets set the prices for their products and then satisfy the demands that emerge at the pair of selected prices. We could again describe a stable, equilibrium situation in the absence of policy as one where, given the price chosen by each firm, the other's price is its best response. Again, as long as each believed that it could influence the other no further, each would have no incentive to alter its price.

The story proceeds as before. The U.S. firm might contemplate an attempt to alter the outcome, only in this case it would not want to "threaten" but to "promise." In other words, it might promise to keep its price high in the export market as long as the foreign firm did not try to undercut. If the home firm were to raise its price, and the foreign were to follow suit, then both could earn higher profits at the expense of consumers in the third-country market. But note that the initial (more competitive) situation had the property that each firm was behaving optimally given what the other was doing. At any other pair of prices at least one firm would have an incentive to change. At the higher (more collusive) prices, profit margins would be large, and each might try to shave its price to steal a few customers from its rival. The other might then respond, so that the high price situation would not be stable. In fact the foreign firm, forecasting these events, and knowing that the prepromise price of the U.S. firm was its optimal choice, would probably dismiss the promise as empty. Again the problem would be one of credibility.

And once again, government intervention can solve the credibility problem. The home government can lend substance to its firm's promise to maintain a high price by implementing a policy that in fact makes it in the firm's own interest to do so. Then the foreign firm would recognize this and would respond by raising its own price to a mutually more profitable level. But what policy would ensure a higher delivered price of U.S. exports on foreign markets? In this case the optimal strategic trade policy is an export *tax*.

Other characterizations of oligopolistic behavior are also possible. We have thus far assumed that each firm acts on the belief that once the market situation has settled, it will no longer be able to induce changes in its rival's actions. In other words, each firm was assumed to take its rival's behavior as given and immutable. But markets are always evolving, and action is often met by response and counterresponse. Firms may continue to conjecture that any deviation in their behavior will induce a reaction on the part of their rival, and their conjectures may be borne out by reality. How do such conjectures affect the market outcome, absent policy? Consider again the case where firms compete by choosing their levels of output. Suppose that each believed that if ever it tried to increase its sales, its rival would respond vigorously by increasing its own; then its optimal behavior would be to keep its output relatively low, less than if it did not believe that expansion would induce an aggressive response.

Alternatively, if each conjectured that its opponent was not very committed to the market in question, so that it would respond to any increase in its own sales by reducing output, then each would find it optimal to produce more than when the competitor's output is instead treated as constant. For each pair of beliefs we usually can find an industry equilibrium (different in each case) whereby neither firm would want to change its behavior given its rival's current action and its own conjecture of how the rival would respond to any change. The market equilibrium for an oligopolistic industry, if it exists, thus depends crucially on what firms believe to be true about their competitor's modus operandi.

What is the role of trade policy in this more general depiction of duopolistic competition? It is possible to show that for each parameter value representing the conjecture of the U.S. firm as to the response that its rival would take to its own initiatives there is a different optimal U.S. trade policy. For a range of parameter values (including the conjecture of no response as a special case) the national interest is served by a policy of export promotion. But for another range of possible conjectures on the part of the U.S. firm, optimal policy calls for an export tax, and any export subsidy would be harmful. Indeed, there is one borderline set of beliefs, known in the industrial organization literature as the case of "consistent conjectures," for which free trade is best.[3]

Still more real-world complexity could be introduced into our models. After all, firms do not compete only by altering prices or quantities offered by sale. Other tools of strategic competition in oligopolistic industries often include product quality, breadth of product line, post-sale service, research and development, and advertising. Industrial organization economists are just now beginning to understand more about how competition in these realms affects the equilibrium industry outcome or the dynamic course of industry growth and development. But no one has yet considered what the effect of export subsidies would be on firms' use of these alternative instruments of corporate strategy, and whether such policies would be nationally beneficial once these induced effects have been taken into account.[4]

How Many U.S. Firms Are in the Market?

The second modification of the Brander-Spencer result concerns the number of domestic firms active in the export market. Suppose there is not one but several American competitors. Then each will not take into account the effects of its own actions on the profits of other domestic firms. From the point of view of the country as a whole, there exist pecuniary externalities. In particular, firms will invest too much in capacity, offer too much of their products for export, and charge too low a price relative to the actions that would maximize their collective returns. This is because each competes with the others for market share, whereas aggregate U.S. welfare is at a maximum when they coordinate their actions.

How can trade policy be used to offset the pecuniary externality? An export tax would induce the American firms to reduce their outputs, to behave less aggressively toward one another. This policy would effect an improvement in the U.S. terms of trade (an increase in the price of exports) but could cause a loss of some sales to foreign competitors. However, we know that on balance an export tax must be beneficial if the number of domestic firms is large and the market is nearly competitive; this is simply the textbook argument for protection to exploit national monopoly power when firms are too small and too competitive to do so themselves. Even if the number of firms is relatively small, and if we consider an imperfectly competitive market situation where the Brander-Spencer profit-shifting argument for export promotion would be valid in a duopoly, an export tax could be called for in an oligopolistic situation if the externality effect dominates.[5] In fact, depending on industry conditions, it could even be so when there are as few as two American firms in the market.

Conditions of Market Entry

The argument for strategic export promotion rests on the existence of above-normal profits or excess returns in a given industry. If such situations arise, they are not likely to persist indefinitely. The existence of large profit opportunities provides incentive for new firms to enter a market. As entry proceeds and the industry matures, profits are dissipated and usually approach a "normal" or competitive level. Thus, even if export promotion could be beneficial, it would only be so temporarily.

But consideration of market entry clouds the issue even further, because the presence of an export promotion scheme affects who will choose to enter and when they will elect to do so. When export subsidies are in place, new entrants into an oligopolistic export market abroad are more likely to originate in the subsidizing country. This can have adverse consequences on national welfare for two reasons. First, subsidies can easily induce excessive entry from the point of view of achieving economies of scale. This can mean higher average costs of production in the long run than would result without the subsidy. Second, when a subsidy induces a large number of domestic firms to enter an export industry, they may ultimately engage in excessive competition among themselves and thus drive down the long-run price of the export good. Thus any short-run gain from export promotion could be lost in the long run, when the terms of trade for the subsidizing country (the price that its export good commands on world markets) become permanently worsened. Similarly, if an export subsidy causes entry to occur sooner than it would otherwise, it will mean that oligopolistic profits in the third-country export market evaporate more quickly, possibly to the detriment of both the subsidizing country and its rival suppliers.

Furthermore it may even be difficult for the trade authorities to identify situations where above-normal profits are being earned. Often what appears to be an especially high rate of profit is just a return to some earlier, risky investment. Research and development expenses, for example, can be quite large, and many ventures end in failure. Firms will only undertake these large investments if they can expect to reap the benefits in those instances where they succeed. Once the market is in operation, we will of course only observe those companies that have succeeded. We may then be tempted to conclude that profits rates are unusually high. But industry profits should be measured inclusive of the losses of those who never make it to the marketing stage.

In fact we should expect the high after-the-fact rates of profit in many imperfectly competitive industries to be normal, risk-adjusted rates of return to success at some earlier stage of competition. This is because few economic activities have natural barriers to entry so large at *every* stage as to preclude, for example, even efforts at product or process development, or the establishment of capacity, when profit opportunities are in evidence. Most industries that are oligopolistic would seem to be so because there are relatively large fixed costs to production, R&D, or advertising or because patent rights legally limit further entry. In each of these cases there would have been an earlier round of competition to establish capacity, conduct the research, undertake the advertising campaign, and win the patent that would have proceeded until (approximately) the extra benefit from further participation or greater intensity of effort was equal to the extra cost of doing so.

What is the implication of this for strategic trade policy? It means that it will be misleading for us to form our view of the opportunities for profit-shifting in supposedly above-normal return industries at the ex post stage when part of the competition has already been played out. If we choose to subsidize such industries on a regular basis, the primary effect of the policy once it comes to be anticipated will be to shift resources into the earlier stages of competition in the target industries, since the rates of return to success will be augmented by the amount of the expected subsidies. This creates a distortion of resource allocation akin to that ascribed to export subsidies in a fully competitive world, because the appropriate long-run view of the industry would indicate that the excess profits to be captured by one country or the other by means of strategic policy are nonexistent. The Brander-Spencer argument for export promotion applies only to truly "natural oligopolies," where the opportunities for entry at all stages of competition are limited. The number of such industries may be small.

What about Domestic Consumers?

Until now I have assumed that the only competition between U.S. exporters and foreign firms takes place in third-country markets. But most goods that are exported by American firms are also consumed at home. In such instances a further implication of an imperfectly competitive market structure besides those that have already been mentioned is that consumption in the home market will be suboptimally low. This is because firms with oligopoly power mark up their prices above marginal cost so that, when consumers purchase the good until their personal valuation of the last unit is equal to the price, the marginal benefit in consumption remains above the marginal social cost of production.

Export subsidies provide incentive for firms to divert their supply from the home market to markets abroad. This generally drives up domestic prices and discourages home consumption. Thus export subsidies can exacerbate an existing market distortion associated with imperfect competition, with correspondingly adverse implications for national economic welfare. In fact, if antitrust policy is imperfect or unavailable, an export tax can work as a partial substitute by causing domestic firms to divert supply from the foreign to the domestic market, thereby driving prices at home closer to their competitive levels. The clear-cut Brander-Spencer finding becomes theoretically ambiguous as soon as the welfare of domestic consumers is taken into account.

Which Oligopoly Should We Choose?

The central issue concerning industrial targeting is which industry should be chosen for targeting. This question does not arise if export promotion is based on strategic considerations and if there is only a single imperfectly competitive sector in an otherwise perfectly competitive economy. If resources can be made to earn above-normal returns in the oligopolistic sector, this represents a clear improvement over their earning a competitive return elsewhere. But this may not be a realistic description of the situation in the progressive, high-technology sectors most frequently mentioned as candidates for targeted export promotion. Many of these industries draw on a common pool of resources, and one that may be in relatively inelastic supply in the short to medium run. In particular, the supply of scientists, engineers, and skilled workers, necessary as inputs to production in the high-technology sectors, might not be able to respond very quickly if an industrial targeting effort were to be undertaken. If it did not, then expansion in one or several of these sectors could only occur at the expense of the others.

To consider this issue more carefully, let us suppose that there are a number of duopolistic industries, each of the Brander-Spencer variety (i.e., with one foreign and one domestic firm, and potential opportunities for profit-shifting via targeted export promotion) but each requiring some amount of input per unit output of a particular scarce factor of production. For simplicity, assume further that this scarce input is not used at all in the competitive sectors of the economy. Now imagine that one specific industry is selected for promotion. The American firm in this industry will have a credible threat to expand, which will cause its foreign competitor to yield market share, as discussed earlier. The domestic firm will earn extra profits relative to the situation without the export subsidy, and these directly contribute to an increase in U.S. well-being. But as this firm seeks to expand its output, it will bid up the market wage of the scarce factor needed by all of the other firms engaged in duopolistic competition. Each of these will see their cost of production rise, and their foreign competitors will realize that they are no longer in a position to compete quite so vigorously. Thus in each of these other industries the domestic participant must cut back production (as is necessary to release resources for the targeted industry to expand), and the foreign rival will respond by increasing its output and expanding its market share. The profits of the American firms in all of the nontargeted duopolies will fall, offsetting the gain in the targeted sector.

What is the net effect of the export promotion policy, once the direct gain and the indirect losses have been added together? In a situation where all of the industries are symmetric (i.e., they face similar demand conditions in the export market and have similar production technologies and face similar degrees of foreign competition), it can be shown that the losses outweigh the gains when any one sector (or more) is singled out for subsidization.[6]

This leaves us with the question of how to choose which sector to promote in situations that are not symmetric. Contrary to what might be expected, it is not the industries that offer the highest returns that should be selected. Rather, the criterion for selection is how much extra profit could be shifted to the American firm from its foreign rival per unit of the scarce resource expended in doing so. This depends in a complicated way on the technologies of the domestic and foreign firms, on the degree of substitution between their products, on the price-responsiveness of demand in the export market, and on the nature of oligopolistic competition. Needless to say, the selection criterion identified in the theoretical model would be difficult to implement in practice.

A simple alternative would be to promote all of the high-technology industries by an equal rate subsidy. However, in the case where all industries are similar, a subsidy to all is like a subsidy to none, and only has the effect of increasing the return to the scarce factor.[7] If the industries are not identical, then the rise in the wage of the scarce factor would affect them differentially. Some of the U.S. firms would find themselves in a stronger competitive position vis-à-vis their foreign rivals, while others would find that the rise in the factor cost more than offsets the direct benefit of the subsidy. On net, the export promotion policy would be in the national interest only if it happened that the industries that use the scarce factor unintensively are also those where a great deal of profit shifting occurs when an extra unit of the scarce factor is applied there. Unfortunately there is no reason to believe a priori that this is the case.

The Criterion for Success and the Cost of Raising Revenue

A final issue concerns the criterion for success that should be used in evaluating strategic trade policy. It is common in the theory of trade policy to assume that issues of income distribution should be downplayed (since these are better dealt with using other economic policies) and that any revenue required to finance trade policy could be raised in a nondistorting manner. Under these two assumptions the proper criterion for evaluating any trade policy is "aggregate economic surplus," or the sum of (1) the excess of consumer valuation over the price of commodities, (2) the excess of producer revenues over the opportunity costs of the factors of production, and (3) the revenue collected (or disbursed) by the government. This sum is a measure of economic efficiency, and it presumes that a dollar is a dollar, whether in the hands of consumers, producers, or the government.

There are two reasons why this measure may systematically overstate any gains that might be attainable under a policy of strategic export promotion. First, the income distributional implications of such a policy are in fact likely to be unfavorable. Export industries in the United States, and particularly those that have been suggested as candidates for strategic promotion, are skilled-labor and technology intensive. Subsidies to these industries will raise the wages of currently well-paid workers, possibly to the detriment of unskilled workers in import-competing sectors. Furthermore, since strategic trade policy is predicated on the idea of transferring rents to firms already earning supernormal profits, shareholders in these firms are the other potential beneficiaries of such policies. And although it is true that other policies do exist that are superior to trade policy as instruments of income redistribution, these policies (e.g., the income tax, the corporate profits tax) are far from costless in terms of their effect on economic efficiency.

The second reason why the gains from export promotion may be overstated in economic models such as those employed by Brander and Spencer is that in reality there are substantial costs to raising the revenue needed to finance subsidy schemes. The nondistorting lump-sum taxes of economic textbooks do not exist in practice. Instead, governments must use fiscal tools that impose deadweight efficiency losses on the economy. Thus a policy that generates slightly more than a dollar of extra profits for an American company, but requires the government to expend a dollar in doing so, may not be in the national interest. This problem seems particularly acute in the context of the currently astronomical Federal budget deficits.

To recapitulate, the theoretical question of whether or not an export subsidy targeted to some particular industry can be used strategically to effect a shift of profits from foreign to domestic enterprises, and if so, whether the aggregate national interest is served as a result, hinges on a number of industry-specific factors. These include the nature of oligopolistic competition (what tools of competition are available to firms, what does each conjecture about the response of its rivals to its own initiatives, etc.), the number of actual and potential domestic firms in the industry, the amount of domestic consumption of the output of the industry, and whether resources for the industry's expansion can be drawn from competitive uses elsewhere in the economy. These in turn interact with demand conditions in the home and foreign market and aspects of the home and foreign firms' production technologies, as well as general economic factors such as the cost at the margin of raising another dollar of government revenue and the elasticity of supply of skilled laborers. Other factors may also turn out to have a bearing (the degree of economies of scale, the rate of technological advance, etc.) as we further complicate our models to bring in further aspects of reality.

There is a limit, however, to how far economic theory can take us in formulating policy. Theory can be used to help us to understand how markets work and how they may fail to work perfectly. For each carefully specified imperfection, theory can identify the ideal tool of correction. But ultimately there is the question of whether we have enough information to implement the type of policy identified by the theory. In some policy situations the information issue is not so central, since all of the relevant economic factors point in the same direction. For example, it is clear that the existence of highway congestion indicates a road tax and not a subsidy, and only the size of the appropriate toll is really at issue. But in the case of strategic intervention in international trade, this is not so. And in this instance the information requirements seem particularly severe, calling on industry characteristics that have not been measured in the most detailed industry studies undertaken to date. For this reason alone a trade policy initiative based on strategic considerations seems, at the least, premature.

Practical Issues in Implementing Strategic Export Promotion

Besides the ambiguities raised by economic theory regarding the strategic promotion of exports, there are a number of practical issues that should be discussed in relation to any trade policy initiative. In this section I will consider two: the prospects for foreign retaliation and the political economy of trade policy formation.

The Threat of Foreign Retaliation

Trade policies that seek to confer domestic gains at the expense of trade partners, and even those that harm other countries incidentally, invite foreign retaliation. When retaliation does occur, each country can be left worse off than it was before the policies were implemented. Thus cooperation in the trade policy realm is often mutually beneficial, and unilateral action can be self-defeating.

It is necessary therefore to consider for each trade policy that is being contemplated what the likelihood is that it would evoke an undesirable response from one's trade partners. In the case of strategic export subsidies by the United States, that probability would have to be rated as fairly high. Most of our trade partners are anxious to claim stakes in the very sectors that are being mentioned as possible targets for strategic promotion. In most of these industries the United States is already a leading competitor, and foreign governments are not likely to remain passive if the United States adopts policy intended to strengthen the advantage of its companies there. Subsidies are likely to be met by countersubsidies, with the consequence being that relative positions are left roughly unchanged, and all of the exporters suffer from an excessive buildup of capacity in the industries in question.

It might be argued in response that foreign governments are already undertaking a policy of industrial targeting, so that the issue of retaliation is not relevant. However, even if the premise of this oftheard contention is accepted, the conclusion may be a non sequitur, and the issue requires considerably more subtle analysis. On the one hand, a legitimate argument for an activist U.S. policy would be that it causes foreign countries to enter into negotiations to end practices that injure the United States, where otherwise they would not be inclined to do so. On the other hand, there is no guarantee that if the United States were to retaliate against foreign practices, a process leading ultimately to cooperation would be the outgrowth; another possibility is that a war of export subsidies would result.

Relatively little is known about the use of trade policies as a means to threaten foreign countries and as punishment for practices that we deem objectionable. When are such policies likely to achieve their goals, and when will they lead instead to costly escalation of trade frictions? Must retaliation be taken in the same industry, as was implicitly assumed in much of the proposed "reciprocity" legislation, or can measures in other industries serve the same purpose? Is it necessary to use similar instruments to the offending policies, or will any aggressive actions suffice? And perhaps most important, how can a country develop a reputation for "toughness" so that it will not actually need to invoke the mutually harmful policies? These are the types of questions that should be answered before a policy of systematic retaliation is put into effect.

What seems clear is that the criteria for choosing sectors in which to intervene and policies for doing so when deterrence and retaliation are the objectives are different from those identified in most popular and academic writings on industrial targeting. Policies that are most effective for achieving the former aims are those that are automatic (rather than discretionary), since these entail precommitment and thus cannot be viewed as empty threats or "waited out" in expectation of their being removed. The theory of games suggests further that incentives to negotiate are determined by "threat points"—outcomes that obtain in the absence of an agreement. A favorable threat point is achieved by a policy that causes the most damage to one's opponent relative to the harm that is inflicted on oneself. This may involve intervention in an import-competing industry, or in a traditional competitive sector, or perhaps even in some totally unrelated area of foreign policy. Finally, it is important to remain clear on what the objective of any such policy would be: success would be gauged not by the achievements of American firms in certain contested industries but rather by whether or not foreign governments are induced to cease their intervention.

The Political Economy of Trade Policy Formation

Most academic analyses of economic policy implicitly introduce a fundamental asymmetry between the workings of economic markets and those of political markets. At the same time that it is recognized that actors pursuing their own interest in the economic realm may interact in such a way as to cause an inefficient outcome, it is often then assumed that so long as the inefficiency can be identified by the technocrat, a political solution can be invoked to correct the market failure. But recent writings on the political economy of policy formation have pointed out the inherent illogic and lack of realism of this assumption.[8] Economic actors are likely to pursue their interests in political as well as economic markets by lobbying their representatives, contributing to candidates that support their positions, filing at administrative and regulatory hearings, and so on, with the implication that once a procedure for market intervention has been established, it may be used to achieve outcomes that were not foreseen by, and certainly not the intention of, the policy analyst.

Historically this problem has been particularly acute in the area of trade policy. Experience has shown that the trade policy apparatus is susceptible to the political pressures of special interest groups, and that the outcomes often fail to take adequate account of the interests of consumers. Import protection often is awarded not based on the demonstrated merits of the case but rather in response to a particularly intense lobbying effort. Even administrative mechanisms that were designed to deal with particular identifiable foreign practices or domestic market failures have been manipulated to serve a more general protectionist function.[9]

The risk that any scheme of targeted export promotion would fall prey to much the same sort of special interest pressures is cause for grave concern. If an apparatus for discretionary industrial policy of this type were to be erected, each and every export sector would have ample incentive to argue the (alleged) merits of its own case for subsidization. And even if the policy analyst could somehow solve the difficult technical problems of identifying industries worthy of promotion, there could be little guarantee that these would be the ones to emerge from a politically influenced process of selection. In all likelihood established industries would win out over emerging ones, those in politically contested regions of the country over those in areas clearly in the camp of one party or the other, and those that could most easily overcome the free-rider problems associated with industrywide lobbying campaigns over those that could not. In short, the market failures in the political realm might easily outweigh those in the economic realm, leaving us with a set of strategic trade policies that would serve only the interests of those fortunate enough to gain favor.

Conclusions

Recent studies by international economists seemingly offer a theoretical basis for implementing a MITI-style targeted industrial policy in the United States. I have reviewed some of the difficulties that would arise in applying this theory in practice. My reservations fall into two broad categories: those that are inherent to the nature of the theoretical argument and those that go beyond the theory to question what real-world outcomes would most likely be observed.

On the theoretical side, it is well established that an ideally designed targeting policy would improve aggregate economic well-being in the United States. Markets are not perfect, and the "invisible hand" can push resources in the wrong direction. Government policy that corrects for the market's failings is bound to be beneficial. In the international context there is the further issue of "us" versus "them." As soon as we leave the world of perfect competition where all resources earn their opportunity value (the amount they would earn in their next best alternative use), we can no longer be indifferent to our country's industrial structure. There are some industries that provide greater national benefit than others, and all the countries in the industrialized world would prefer to be active and successful in these. Government policy can, in principle, help to ensure that this comes about.

Thus there is a firm basis for an ideal industrial targeting policy. But how close could economists and policymakers come to identifying this ideal? In general, this depends on a number of factors, including whether or not the guidance provided by the theory is relatively clear-cut and whether the information needed by the policymakers is readily available and of sufficient quality. And here the answers are not encouraging. Not every sector should (or can) be targeted, but choosing the right ones involves subtle and complicated analysis. The existence of imperfect competition is not enough; there must be sustained supernormal profits and no hidden forms of competition that dissipate these. There must not be excessive competition between the various domestic firms engaged in the industry struggle, but there should be enough competition in the home market so that oligopoly prices do not seriously injure domestic consumers. The targeting of one industry should allow it to expand but not at the expense of other industries with equal potential. Competition between rival firms in the industry should be of a sort that leads the U.S. participants to be insufficiently aggressive rather than excessively so. In short, the theory is replete with ambiguous policy conclusions that can only be resolved on the basis of very detailed data and a relatively complete understanding of how a particular industry competition is played out and about how the industry in question interrelates with other sectors of the economy.

And, if these impediments to a successful targeting policy are not enough, it must be recognized that analysis would not take place in a vacuum. Valid arguments and accurate data would be mixed with self-serving claims and misleading evidence. The larger the stakes, the greater would be the incentive for spokesmen of special interests to argue their case and bring pressures to bear. The invisible hand of the economic market would be replaced by the even less visible hand of the political market. It seems unlikely, indeed, that what would emerge from an actual process of selecting industries for promotion would approximate the prescriptions of the objective analysis, no less the ideal regime alluded to here.

Does this mean that there is no role for policy in support of American industry in international competition? I would argue not. Policy should seek to create a fertile environment for innovation and entrepreneurship and to offset evident market failings. Government support of education and industrial R&D could be justified on these grounds. So too could an effective adjustment policy that would foster an efficient redeployment of resources released from declining industries. Macroeconomic policies are also important, as overvalued exchange rates and excessively high interest rates hamper U.S. firms in their attempts to compete abroad. Devising sensible broad-based policies offers challenge enough; choosing the industrial structure that would best serve the country is another question entirely.

Notes

1. For further work along these and related lines see Krugman (1984), Dixit (1984), and Dixit and Kyle (1983).

2. This concept of equilibrium for an oligopoly was first developed by Cournot (1897) and was generalized in the seminar work of Nash (1954). It is referred to as a Cournot-Nash equilibrium.

3. For further discussion and proof of these results, see Eaton and Grossman (1983).

4. Brander and Spencer (1984) did show that an export subsidy continues to be welfare improving in their model when a simple form of R&D competition is introduced.

5. For given market parameters an export tax is more likely to constitute an optimal policy, rather than an export subsidy, the greater the number of domestic firms. See Dixit (1984) and Eaton and Grossman (1983).

6. This result is derived in Dixit and Grossman (1984).

7. If some substitution for the scarce factor is possible in the production of high-technology goods, or if some extra supply of the factor can be drawn from the economy at large as its return rises, then an equal rate subsidy would yield some benefit. For more detail, see Dixit and Grossman (1984).

8. See, for example, Baldwin (1981, 1982) and Brock and Magee (1978).

9. See Finger, Hall, and Nelson (1982).

References

Baldwin, Robert E. 1981. "The Political Economy of U.S. Import Policy." Unpublished manuscript.

Baldwin, Robert E. 1982. "The Political Economy of Protectionism." In J. N. Bhagwati, ed., *Import Competition and Response*. Chicago: University of Chicago Press.

Brander, James A., and Spencer, Barbara J. 1983. "Export Subsidies and International Market Share Rivalry." Unpublished manuscript.

Brock, William A., and Magee, Stephen P. 1978. "The Economics of Special Interest Politics: The Case of the Tariff." *American Economic Review* 68, 246–250.

Cournot, A. A. 1897. *Researches into the Mathematical Principles of the Theory of Wealth*. New York: Macmillan.

Dixit, Avinash K. 1984. "International Trade Policies for Oligopolistic Industries." *Economic Journal* 94(supplement), 1–16.

Dixit, Avinash K., and Grossman, Gene M. 1984. "Targeted Export Promotion with Several Oligopolistic Industries." Woodrow Wilson School Discussion Papers in Economics No. 71, Princeton University.

Dixit, Avinash K., and Kyle, Albert S. 1983. "On the Use of Trade Restrictions for Entry Promotion and Deterrence." Woodrow Wilson School Discussion Papers in Economics No. 56, Princeton University.

Eaton, Jonathan, and Grossman, Gene M. 1983. "Optimal Trade and Industrial Policy under Oligopoly." Working Paper No. 1236, National Bureau of Economic Research.

Finger, J. Michael, Hall, H. Keith, and Nelson, Douglas R. 1982. "The Political Economy of Administered Protection." *American Economic Review* 72, 452–466.

Krugman, Paul R. 1984. "Import Protection as Export Promotion." In H. Kierzkowski, ed., *Monopolistic Competition International Trade*. Oxford: Oxford University Press.

Nash, John F. 1954. "Equilibrium States in N-Person Games." *Proceedings of the National Academy of Sciences*, 36, 48–49.

Spencer, Barbara J., and Brander, James A. 1983. "International R&D Rivalry and Industrial Strategy." *Review of Economic Studies* 50, 707–722.

4   What Should Trade Policy Target?

Barbara J. Spencer

Recent developments in international trade theory have shown that there may be domestic gains from trade policy targeted to particular industries facing foreign competition. Governments and firms are seen as being engaged in a strategic game to gain profits in world markets. The theory indicates that policies such as export subsidies can affect the underlying structure of the game so as to allow domestic firms to achieve extra profits from exports that exceed the amount of the subsidy. If this is the case, the policy will have resulted in a net gain to the domestic economy.[1] In theory some of the additional profits could be redistributed by taxation so that the general taxpayer does not lose from the cost of the subsidy and still allow the owners and workers in the targeted industry to be better off.

In policy circles there has been a perception that some foreign governments such as the French and Japanese have chosen to target certain sectors of the economy.[2] This has led to a current debate about whether the United States should also join the targeting game. There are many difficult issues that arise from this debate, including philosophical questions about the appropriate role of government. Supposing this issue were decided in the affirmative, there is also a considerable difference of views as to which types of industries should be targeted. For example, should the government attempt to revitalize declining industries, support existing profitable high-technology industries, or somehow pick the winners of the future? This paper is not concerned directly with the first major issue. Rather it has the more limited objective of addressing some aspects of the second question as to the types of industries to be targeted. In particular, the aim is to describe the implications of the recent trade theory for the broad characteristics of industries most likely to lead to a national benefit from targeting.[3]

Identification of these characteristics is a preliminary step toward translating theory into practical policy proposals, but there remain serious practical problems of implementation. For example, some characteristics indicated by the theory require information that is not readily available, such as the nature and level of costs in both domestic and foreign firms. Furthermore accurate prediction of the behavior of foreign firms and governments, which is important for some of the characteristics, is likely to be extremely difficult to obtain. These problems and others may well make a policy of targeting particular export industries undesirable. Nevertheless, even without domestic implementation of an industrial targeting policy of this sort, it seems useful to see what economic theory has to say on the subject. This should lead to more informed debate as well as perhaps to some better understanding of the effects of foreign industrial policies.

In this paper I take a broad view of what is meant by trade policy targeting. In some discussions the word targeting is restricted to policies that promote some narrow group of products within an industry or even a single firm. Although trade theory does indicate some of the issues that might arise in deciding on how specific to a firm, product, or group of products a targeting policy should be, this question is very much affected by the particular nature of the industry or group of industries being considered and would require both more theoretical analysis and detailed industry studies. I also take a broad view as to the nature of the targeting instruments. Clearly export subsidies and tariffs are two possible instruments. However, other policies such as subsidization of R&D and plant and equipment could well have a greater long-run impact on profits earned from export sales and would need to be considered as part of any policy to promote industrial exports.

Industry Profitability and Barriers to Entry

The argument for export subsidies found in the recent theory is based on extracting additional profits from foreign producers and consumers. For an export subsidy to be domestically welfare improving, it must increase the profits to be earned by the industry on export sales by an amount exceeding the cost of the subsidy to the taxpayers. Apart from dynamic considerations of product innovation and development, and the possibility of extreme economies of scale, a net gain requires that the sale price exceed the opportunity cost of inputs determined without the subsidy. This cannot be the case unless there is some barrier or cost of entry to the industry, both to make subsidization initially beneficial and to preserve the gain in profits for a reasonable length of time. Common barriers to entry would include high capital or R&D requirements as well as legal barriers such as patent laws.

Traditional trade theory assumed that there were no barriers to entry so that an industry would consist of a large number of small firms earning only the normal profit required to remain in business. In such a purely competitive industry, price is equal to each firm's private marginal cost of production, so an export subsidy of, for example, $1 per unit, would lead to a price that is $1 less than the real marginal cost of production. In this situation an export subsidy can only reduce domestic welfare, at best acting as a gift to foreign consumers.

This requirement for profitability would appear to rule out subsidization as a method to "save" unprofitable or so-called declining industries and still benefit the country as a whole. This is generally the case, although some seemingly unprofitable industries might earn above-normal returns from exports if the hidden returns in the form of wages and salaries above their opportunity cost are counted.

The first requirement for an industry to be appropriate for targeting is summarized as characteristic 1:

Characteristic 1 The industry or potential industry must be expected to earn additional returns (expressed in profits or greater returns to workers) sufficient to exceed the total cost of the subsidy. This requires that at least for a period there be substantial barriers to entry.

Restrictions in Sales of Foreign Firms

For an export subsidy to be appropriate, increases in domestic exports must lead to a reduction in the output levels of rival foreign firms. Indeed, an export subsidy is more likely to improve domestic welfare, the greater is this effect or the more the domestic expansion is at the expense of sales of foreign rivals. Without a loss in sales by foreign firms, the increased domestic exports induced by a subsidy would normally result in a fall in price sufficient to make the additional sales unprofitable. A reduction in foreign output mitigates the price fall from domestic expansion, allowing the possibility that domestic profits will increase.

This requirement clearly rules out intervention in the case of a true monopoly where a domestic firm does not face competition or potential competition in export sales. A true monopolist will be in a position to price and make investment choices so as to maximize its own profits.

Whether an export subsidy will cause foreign firms to cut back output depends on the nature of the oligopolistic rivalry between firms and on the nature of the response, if any, by foreign governments. The effect of oligopolistic rivalry in pricing decisions has been explored in Eaton and Grossman (1983). They show that the opposite industry response, often associated with tacit collusion models, is certainly possible. If one firm raises price by cutting back output, this may cause other firms to follow suit and also cut back output, increasing prices closer to the joint profit-maximizing monopoly level. Conversely, a rise in exports by domestic firms brought about by an export subsidy could lead to an increase in output by other firms and a further fall in prices, reducing the profitability of the domestic industry. Such would be the case under what is called Bertrand competition, in which each firm assumes that if it changes its own price, other firms will maintain their price even in the face of loss of sales. In this case an export tax rather than a subsidy would increase domestic profits from exports.

On the other hand, the Eaton and Grossman (1983) analysis applies most easily to short-run pricing decisions after capital is in place. In the earlier stages of product development, there may well be a prior game between rival firms as to the level and timing of capital investments. In highly capital-intensive industries, capacity decisions will condition the nature of future price rivalry, exerting an important influence on overall profitability and market share at the future production stage. For example, if an industry has a large and inflexible capital requirement, once the foreign firms are at capacity, an expansion of domestic output cannot induce an immediate expansion in foreign output as is implied by Bertrand price behavior. Theoretical work by Kreps and Scheinkman (1983) supports this view.[4]

In such industries it would seem likely that an early and large domestic investment would tend to preempt the foreign competition leading to the lower foreign investment and output in the long run, which is required if targeting is to be domestically beneficial. Government policies that increase domestic capacity are likely to serve as signals to foreign governments and firms that domestic ouput will be higher so that the return on investment to foreign firms will be lower. Such policies are likely to be most effective in reducing foreign capacity if they occur relatively early in the product life cycle before plans for foreign capacity have been finalized.

This discussion should make clear that one of the problems in implementing targeting is that the nature of the reaction of the foreign firms and governments may not be known. Further study of this complicated question would be needed on an industry by industry basis. In effect, this discussion implies the following requirements for successful use of targeted subsidies:

Characteristic 2   The domestic industry must be subject to serious foreign competition or potential competition. Subsidy of the domestic industry should lead foreign rival firms to cut back capacity plans and output. Although they are not necessary, large and inflexible capital requirements are likely to increase the chances of this type of behavior.

Industry Concentration

As indicated in the previous section, an export subsidy will increase domestic welfare only if the enhancement of domestic exports from a subsidy is not "too large" in relation to the reduction in sales or rival foreign firms, so the fall in price associated with the subsidy is kept to a minimum. Assuming that the industry satisfies characteristics 1 and 2, some factors are likely to magnify the tendency for domestic expansion to be at the expense of foreign rivals, making the industry a better prospect for domestic targeting.

Dixit (1984) and Eaton and Grossman (1983) have shown that the price fall associated with an export subsidy is likely to be lower, the more concentrated is the domestic export industry relative to the foreign competition. Hence this consideration tends to favor subsidization of those industries or parts of industries that consist of fewer domestic than foreign firms. The exact form of this result does require some special assumptions on the nature of the industry, but the direction of effects should still remain.[5]

Considering the foreign industry first, a given increase in domestic output tends to reduce foreign output more, the greater the number of foreign firms or the less concentrated the foreign industry. With a greater number of foreign firms each firm may tend to cut back less, but the total reduction in output tends to be higher for a given expansion in domestic output induced by a subsidy.

Also declining marginal costs, both short and long run, magnify the tendency for foreign output to fall in response to domestic expansion. In the short run a cutback in output then raises marginal costs, reducing the profitability of output at the margin so that output is reduced more than if marginal cost were constant. In the long term foreign firms would move to plants designed for a lower level of output, raising their average costs because they are able to take less advantage from economies of scale.

Turning to the question of concentration in the domestic industry, for any one domestic firm the response of rival domestic firms to an industry subsidy is just as important for profits as the response of rival foreign firms. As expressed by Eaton and Grossman (1983), there is a kind of pecuniary negative spillover between domestic firms, in the sense that each firm in choosing its output considers only the effect of that output choice on its own price and profits and does not take into account the way its actions may affect other firms in the domestic industry. An increase in sales by any one domestic firm tends to reduce the price and profits received by other domestic producers. One normally applauds this effect, which leads to more competitive pricing as being in the best interest of domestic consumers, but if sales are mainly to foreigners, the country's best interest lies in keeping monopoly profits high. This negative effect of the expansion of other domestic firms on the price and profit earned by any one domestic firm tends to be smaller the more concentrated is the domestic industry, since there are then fewer firms to which the externality applies. Of course, as indicated earlier, even if there are a large number of domestic firms, the existence of an equally large number of foreign firms can offset this effect, so that an export subsidy can still be advantageous.

Assuming that firms have Cournot behavior and each firm produces the same product at the same cost of production, the effect of industry concentration on whether a domestic export subsidy would reduce foreign sales sufficiently to raise welfare is summarized in characteristic 3:

Characteristic 3 The domestic industry involved in exporting should be more concentrated or equally as concentrated as the rival foreign industry.

This advantage from domestic concentration points toward an argument for relaxation of antitrust laws for firms that are heavily engaged in export sales. This could facilitate the internalization of the negative spillovers from independent pricing of export sales by domestic firms. The cost of all this, of course, is that the same cartel-like pricing behavior could carry over to the domestic market.

Factor Price Effects

The rent extracted from export sales includes rents received by workers as well as total profit. Workers receive rent if they earn more than the opportunity cost of their labor. As explained by Krugman (1984), if an export subsidy results in an increase in employment so as to increase the total rent earned by workers in industry, this is a benefit to the economy just as much as an increase in industry profit. On this basis the existence, for example, of high worker rents due to unionization might be used as an indication that the industry could be a candidate for targeting by the government.

However, the existence of a union brings an additional player into the strategic game between firms and governments, and government subsidy policies rather than just increasing employment would under normal conditions result in an increase in the union wage.[6] This increase in the wage with the same or higher employment level would increase the total rent earned by workers. However, this is not just a transfer of profit from shareholders to workers, leaving the total surplus earned by the industry unchanged. An increase in the wage by increasing marginal costs affects the result of the strategic game, reducing the level of exports as well as the total rent earned by the industry. To the extent that a subsidy is reflected in a higher wage level, this undoes the strategic effect of the subsidy, making each subsidy dollar less effective.

Of course the impact of a union on the effectiveness of targeting depends on both the nature of the union bargain and the nature of the subsidy or protection tool. If the union contract depends partly on profit sharing, then the union will have an incentive to raise wages less in response to a subsidy, increasing the bonus payments of workers from profit sharing. In the extreme, if the union set wages at the competitive level so that all transfers of rent to workers comes from profit sharing, then the union would have no effect on the total domestic rent earned from government intervention.

Also certain means of subsidization are more likely to result in an increase in the union wage than others. My conjecture here is that a subsidy tool that reduces the negative impact of a wage increase on employment more than other tools is likely to lead the union to be more aggressive in raising wages. For example, direct and permanent wage subsidies would likely have the least restraining effect on the union. Wages would have to increase by more than the subsidy per worker in order to reduce employment. In the case of a capital or R&D subsidy an increase in the wage bill equal to the total amount of the subsidy would tend to lead to a substitution of capital for labor and intensify the search for labor-saving innovations. This prospect may lead a union to be more moderate in its wage demands.

If inputs are not easily substitutable in production, a production subsidy or subsidy per unit of output would affect the union wage in the same manner as a wage subsidy. This effect would be reduced if the subsidy were restricted to export sales, as is the case with the current interest rate subsidy to purchaser financing which is provided by the Export-Import Bank. Most exporting firms also produce for the domestic market, and the union wage bargain covers both domestic and export sales. The prospect of a reduction in domestic sales and employment from a wage increase should mitigate the tendency for wages to rise.

A further factor price effect to be considered is the possibility that there is a fixed amount of some critical input used in a group of exporting industries. Dixit and Grossman (1984) show that in this case an export subsidy to one of the exporting industries would increase production of that industry, but mainly at the expense of the profits and sales of other exporting industries. Dixit and Grossman suggest that such an input might be scientists or engineers of a particular kind. It is clear that this could be a problem, particularly in the short run. In the long run, inputs are not generally fixed in supply. Given the demand, more engineers and scientists would be trained in the United States, and additional skilled workers would emigrate to the United States from other countries.

These considerations lead to characteristic 4 of industries most likely to be suitable for targeting:

Characteristic 4   Factor prices should not increase much in response to domestic targeting. This is more likely if

i. the industry does not have a strong union;

ii. worker incomes are at least partly based on profit sharing;

iii. no key input is in fixed supply.

Cost Advantages

Another question is whether subsidy money is better directed toward those industries where a country already has an initial advantage, such as cheaper raw materials or better-trained workers, or whether the money would be better spent in some way compensating for higher costs of production relative to the foreign competition.

If the nature of the industry is such that an export subsidy is beneficial, it can be shown that the lower the initial domestic cost relative to foreign marginal cost, the greater is the domestic gain from a given amount of subsidy. There is a greater return in increased profit from each subsidy dollar if the domestic industry already has a natural advantage relative to the foreign competition.

In addition the very nature of imperfect competition leads it to be associated with scale economies, which provide a barrier to entry and thus maintain the industry profitability. In this case government intervention, particularly in the form of subsidies to capital, can lead to a lowering of marginal cost sufficient to create a domestic advantage where otherwise it might not have existed. Of course it does not follow that such a policy is necessarily in the country's best interest. Rather, this consideration indicates that if an industry has a natural cost advantage in production such as cheaper raw materials or location advantages, and if in addition it is subject to learning economies or other scale economies, then it is a better candidate for targeting than otherwise. This idea is expressed as characteristic 5:

Characteristic 5   Targeting is more effective if

i. the domestic industry has a fundamental cost advantage relative to the foreign competition;

ii. there are substantial scale or learning economies from increased production.

More fundamentally, innovation in products or processes can lead to the creation of an initial absolute advantage in the production of a product. It has been argued that because of spillover effects of R&D or transfer of technology to other firms, an innovating firm will be unable to appropriate fully the return from R&D. Patent protection can help to overcome this problem, but it has proved less than fully effective, particularly in the international arena. In those industries where there are major problems from appropriation of returns from R&D, private incentives can lead to too little R&D from the viewpoint of the best resource allocation within a society.[7] Transfer of technology to other firms confers benefits to society that are not taken into account by the innovating firms.

This traditional argument for government subsidization of R&D arising from the existence of substantial spillover effects of R&D depends on taking a world view of welfare, rather than the more national view in which the gains and losses of other nations are not taken into account. From a domestic viewpoint it is important whether the externalities are conferred on domestic or foreign firms. If there is oligopolistic rivalry between foreign and domestic firms, any spillover of domestic R&D to the foreign firms is likely to reduce the rents earned by domestic firms in international markets. This effect could lower the domestic benefit from R&D subsidies. Domestic policies can be designed to reduce the extent of spillovers of domestic R&D to foreign firms. For example, the law could be amended to reduce the ease of licensing of U.S. innovations to foreign firms.

Even if a firm is not first in innovating a product, it may still do well if it is in a position to copy and improve on major innovations being made elsewhere. If there is international rivalry, this means that a domestic industry will be better off if it is in a position to take maximum advantage of spillovers of R&D from foreign firms. For example, it has been suggested (e.g., Weinstein et al. 1984) that the Japanese semiconductor industry has benefited substantially from U.S. R&D in basic technologies. By concentrating on process technology, the Japanese were able to replicate or adapt U.S. designs at low cost. This enabled them to capture in a relatively short time a large share of the market in consumer products using semiconductors. Government support of activities that speed the transfer of foreign technology to domestic firms can be domestically beneficial. These considerations lead to characteristic 6:

Characteristic 6 A domestic industry will be a better candidate for targeting by R&D subsidies if

i. there is a minimum of spillover of new domestic technology to rival foreign firms;

ii. the government intervention aids the transfer of foreign technology to domestic firms.

On the other hand, if there are no spillovers of R&D so that domestic firms can appropriate the full return from R&D, an increase in domestic R&D due to government subsidies can set the stage for an increase in profits from export sales, which more than exceeds the cost of the R&D subsidy. Just as in the case of capital subsidies, this policy is effective to the extent that it leads foreign firms to reduce their R&D levels (see Spencer and Brander 1983). Domestic firms alone may not be in a position to achieve such a response. If a domestic firm announces that it is substantially increasing its expenditure on R&D, this may not be entirely convincing or credible to foreign firms who may decide to continue with their R&D plans, making the domestic increase in R&D unprofitable. On the other hand, increased domestic expenditure on R&D would be expected as a natural response to a domestic subsidy to R&D and could well indicate to foreign firms that their research in this area is less likely to pay off. Hence supporting R&D-intensive industries could be one way of obtaining a greater share of future winning industries.

There also may be a connection between government support of R&D and capital investment in the early stages of a product's development and the future structure of the industry in terms of the eventual number of firms in the industry and the timing of their entry. In the early stages of a product's life cycle, an initial innovating firm may have a temporary monopoly of the product. After a time imitators enter, reducing the profits of the innovating firm and bringing the industry into what is often called its "mature phase." Government subsidies to investment by the original firm can allow it to enjoy greater economies of scale, making entry by other firms less profitable. There may be a domestic gain if such policies reduce the number of foreign entrants or delay the entry of foreign firms. These ideas are summarized in characteristic 7:

Characteristic 7 If a domestic industry is involved in rivalry with foreign firms, it will be a better candidate for targeting by R&D and investment subsidies if

i. R&D and capital costs form a significant proportion of industry costs, indicating they are important factors in firm rivalry;

ii. a likely winning product is in the early stage of development or production and R&D, and capital subsidies will raise entry barriers to foreign firms.

Targeting and Import Protection

Tariffs and quotas can also be used to target domestic industries. If there are significant scale economies or dynamic learning economies from moving down the experience curve, the closing or partial closing of the domestic market to foreign competition can in theory lead to a lower marginal cost of production which then promotes success in exports (see Krugman 1984). Indeed, it has been argued that the existence of a closed domestic market in Japan allowed Japanese firms to gain sufficient experience in modern technology so as to become a force in international competition. Also, if the domestic market is large, protection, by taking away potential sales by foreign firms, may inhibit foreign entry in industries with high entry cost. This would leave the market clear for a domestic firm to enjoy maximum scale economies (see Dixit and Kyle 1984).

However, this method of promoting exports is rather indirect and can easily lead to the reverse result. For example, in economies such as Australia and Canada, high tariff walls in certain industrial fields have led to the development of too many small plants which do not have sufficient scale economies to compete successfully on the world market.

Even if tariffs and quotas allow achievement of some scale economies by domestic firms, commonly they will still have the effect of raising prices in the domestic market, to the detriment of consumers. In comparing protection with subsidy measures of industrial promotion, one must always keep in mind that protection normally reduces world trade, whereas subsidies are generally trade enhancing. Broadly speaking, subsidy measures have a better chance of improving world welfare (including consumer benefits) than do protection measures.

This is not to say one should accept foreign subsidization of rival firm production as a gift. Foreign subsidies may help domestic consumers, but if they reduce the profits earned by domestic producers, in many cases the economy will lose as a whole. Tariffs in the form of antidumping duties can therefore be an appropriate measure to offset the effects of foreign targeting practices on the domestic economy.

Targeting by Other Governments

An important question is the way targeting by other governments might affect the criteria for domestic targeting. It has been argued that the U.S. government should match foreign subsidies so that U.S. industry is not put at a disadvantage by foreign governments. This is the so-called "level playing field" argument.

It should be clear from the criteria for targeting that have been presented that such a policy is not likely to be generally advantageous. In the first place the very fact that an industry or product group has been targeted by a foreign government reduces the expected rent to be earned by other firms in the industry (see characteristic 1). Even if the domestic return from subsidization is still positive, if foreign targeting has been successful in reducing foreign marginal cost, the domestic return from a subsidy will be lower than otherwise (see characteristic 5). In other words, although matching foreign subsidies may make a "level playing field," the playing field is now at a lower level than before. Prices and profits in each country are likely lower after subsidization by both governments than if there had been no government intervention (see Brander and Spencer 1984).

Also the industries that are most suitable for targeting by foreign governments may not always satisfy the criteria for a national gain from domestic targeting. For example, if the industry is highly concentrated in the foreign country but not in the United States, this asymmetry will tend to favor a foreign subsidy but will make the optimal U.S. subsidy low or perhaps even negative, implying that an export tax would be appropriate.

On the other hand, a domestic government should not necessarily be dissuaded from supporting certain industries that meet the required characteristics, just because a foreign government has decided to target the same industry. An important consideration is the nature of any foreign subsidy program. For example, it is important whether the foreign subsidy program and the proposed domestic program are directed toward a broad or a very narrow group of products and whether the foreign subsidy program is fully committed in the sense that it cannot be changed by domestic actions.

If a foreign government targets a narrowly defined product such as the 250K semiconductor chip, then similar domestic targeting of the same product is not likely to be beneficial. The domestic government would be better off being first to promote some other likely growth product, although even this is a highly risky policy. If one basically believes in private enterprise, a domestic response to foreign subsidization in the form of subsidization of a broad group of industries such as the semiconductor industry as a whole would have the advantage of allowing private domestic firms to continue to choose the specific products to be developed, presumably taking into account the likely foreign developments. Unless a product promoted by a foreign government had exceptional potential, the domestically chosen products are likely to be significantly different from those of their foreign rivals, making the foreign subsidization of the industry less relevant.

Some types of foreign subsidies can more easily be reduced by negotiation and other domestic actions. A foreign subsidy program that has already resulted in increased R&D and capital expenditure in specific products will have long lived effects on the distribution of any rents earned on those products, even if domestic government pressure reduces future subsidy levels. On the other hand, subsidies such as those that reduce the cost of export financing have less of a long-lived effect on the profitability of exporting industries and may also be more amenable to bargaining tactics. A domestic policy of matching such a subsidy set by a rival producing nation could in the short run allow domestic firms to achieve a major sale and, by nullifying the advantage from the foreign government action, could be an important bargaining tool to reduce subsidy levels. This appears to be the situation with the type of help to export financing which is provided by the U.S. Export-Import Bank.

Targeting of Export-Oriented Industries versus Purely Domestic Industries

The question has been raised as to why subsidize exports when the tax money could equally be spent on subsidizing domestic sales. For example, Baron (1984, p. 79) argues that both policies could help the industry achieve economies of scale, lowering prices, but a subsidy to domestic sales would have the advantage of being kept at home rather than becoming a gift to foreign consumers.

First, the reasons for subsidizing exports or export-oriented industries imply very different policies from those associated with helping the domestic consumer. If it is the domestic consumer the government has in mind, targeting policies could well include efforts to increase entry of new firms into the industry, reducing the degree of industry concentration, which tends to lower prices and profits. This policy is just the opposite of those implied by the theory of export targeting. The logic of targeting of exports is based on raising the profits of domestic firms at the expense of the sales and profits of foreign rivals. Consumers will not necessarily benefit much, since an increase in domestic profits depends on prices not falling too far.

Also, if there is but one monopoly or oligopolistic industry within an otherwise perfectly competitive economy, one can say that the output of the monopoly is too low relative to the optimal product mix from the viewpoint of consumers. This is not the case in an economy with a large number of monopoly and other types of distortions. The theory of the second-best indicates that unless all distortions are undone by domestic policies, an attempt to remove a few distortions by subsidizing domestic sales of some oligopolistic industries may not result in a net improvement in consumer welfare. Some industries may expand too much, relative to other monopolistic industries that are not subsidized or do not respond in the same way to the subsidy program.

For both the preceding reasons, the direct inclusion of consumer preferences in a targeting program is likely to distort and complicate the application of such a program, making it less likely that increased domestic benefits would be achieved. However, if domestic consumer preferences are not taken into account, then the same kind of argument that has been presented in support of subsidies to exporting firms would also apply to domestic sales. Because of imports, domestic firms may well face competition from foreign firms at home as well as abroad. To the extent that a subsidy will increase sales of domestic firms at the expense of imports, the country can gain from the transfer of profits from foreign firms.

This does not mean, however, that whenever it is advantageous to subsidize exports, it will also be advantageous to subsidize domestic sales. If, as we have been assuming, the domestic and foreign markets are separate in the sense that different prices can be charged in the two markets, the structure of competition could well be different at home than abroad. For example, there may be a higher proportion of domestic to foreign firms serving the domestic market than foreign markets, which reduces the chances that a subsidy on domestic sales will be socially beneficial. Some types of policies, such as subsidies to capital and R&D or encouragement of research joint ventures, naturally apply to both foreign and domestic markets. Since these types of policies could well be particularly helpful in the long-run strategic game between firms, consideration of their effects on both the domestic and foreign markets would be required.

An Example

One example of targeting of an industry that broadly fits the criteria of this paper is provided by the development of the European Airbus consortium. Indeed, government support of the European Airbus consortium may be one case in which a government subsidy program has proved effective. The consortium is approximately 70 percent government owned and enjoys substantial subsidies from the French and German governments, which on some calculations amount to about 20 percent of the airplane price. Airbus has managed to capture a substantial portion of the commercial wide-body jet aircraft market at the expense of sales of U.S. competitors, such as Boeing and McDonnell-Douglas. It seems clear that government subsidization has allowed the airbus to obtain a larger share of the world market than it otherwise would. Indeed it is rather unlikely that an unsupported private European firm would have entered the market at all.

Whether government subsidization will translate into economic success in the sense that the additional profits earned from the airbus are more than sufficient to pay for the subsidy is not yet clear. However, the aircraft industry does satisfy a number of the criteria that theory indicates are likely to be important for a successful targeting program. The industry has substantial barriers to entry because of large capital and R&D requirements increasing the chances of good returns on investment. From the European perspective there is substantial foreign competition (from the United States) so that European sales are at the expense of the sales and profits of foreign firms. Indeed, since the European Airbus consortium is the only European contender in the wide-body aircraft market, subsidization is particularly effective since additional sales cannot reduce sales of other domestic firms.

Apparently the Japanese are also interested in targeting their aircraft industry, although the Japanese are not yet a major force in this industry. Whether the Japanese can also be successful remains to be seen. As indicated in the previous section, the theory of industrial targeting indicates that as more governments subsidize the same industry, the possible gains from subsidization are reduced. Countries could benefit from mutual agreements not to subsidize.

Conclusion

Fundamentally the possibility of a domestic gain from a government subsidy program targeted to a particular industry depends on the way in which government intervention affects the strategic interplay between foreign and domestic firms. This argument therefore depends first on the existence of imperfect competition in the targeted industry and on the nature of that competition. There is general agreement that many industries are not perfectly competitive, but it would be much harder to get agreement that any particular industry fit the somewhat abstract requirements indicated by the theory. Nevertheless, theory in industrial organization and trade does give some guidance as to the broad characteristics one would need to look for in developing a targeting program of a type that might have some chance of conferring a net domestic benefit.

For example, one should look toward those industries in which the domestic country is likely to have a natural advantage relative to the foreign competition even if there were no government intervention. Lower existing domestic marginal costs tend to increase the impact of each dollar spent on a subsidy program in raising domestic export profits (characteristic 5, part i). Also factor prices in the industry should not tend to increase much in response to targeting. This is more likely to be the case if the industry does not have a strong union or, if the industry is unionized, that worker incomes be at least partly based on profit sharing (characteristic 4, parts i and ii). Furthermore no key input should be in fixed supply (4, part iii).

More important, a number of the conditions for profitable targeting of export-oriented industries point toward industries that have large capital or knowledge requirements. Such requirements provide barriers to entry that help to ensure that domestic firms at least have a potential for earning substantial profits from export sales (characteristic 1). Commitment to heavy expenditures on capital and R&D can play a central role in the strategic game between firms (characteristics 2 and 7, part i). This strategic game in capital and R&D which naturally occurs in the early stages of a product's life cycle has a major influence on the eventual profitability of the product in the mature production stage of the industry (see characteristic 7). Among other things this game also affects the eventual concentration of the domestic industry relative to the foreign industry, which is a factor in the effectiveness of any continuing government promotion of the industry (see characteristic 3). Finally, we associated decreasing average costs of production and dynamic learning economies with heavy capital and knowledge requirements for production. As indicated in characteristic 5, part ii, these scale economies tend to magnify any advantage from a government subsidy program.

This emphasis of the economic theory on large capital and knowledge requirements strongly point toward the encouragement of the development of new products and processes as part of any targeting program that might hope to lead to a national benefit rather than just favor some special interest group. The enhancement of the ability of domestic firms to pick up quickly on new advances being made elsewhere could also be important.

However, even if it had been decided that a targeting policy of this kind were desirable, many more theoretical as well as practical issues remain. For example, it should be clear from this paper that an advantage from targeting can depend not only on the right choice of industry to target but on the nature of the targeting instruments themselves. Although we know that a direct production subsidy is likely to have different effects than a wage subsidy or certainly than a capital or R&D subsidy, very little study has yet been done on this question.

In particular, given that the creation and maintenance of high profits is a key requirement of the theory, more information is needed on the likely effects of various methods of targeting on both foreign and domestic entry into a targeted industry. For this purpose the question as to whether a targeting policy should be narrowly focused toward a single firm or product, or broadly focused toward an industry as a whole, is also important. The answer to this can partly depend on the nature of the targeting instruments. For example, an industrywide export subsidy may create entry of domestic firms, reducing the domestic advantages from the subsidy, but a broadly based R&D subsidy applied to the same industry may lead to the creation of new products for which the innovating domestic firm has at least a temporary world monopoly. Even if it is decided that an active U.S. industrial targeting policy is not appropriate, research on the likely effect of various targeting policies within different industries could help us understand foreign targeting practices and the best methods to counteract them.

As a final concluding remark I would like to emphasize that I believe it is important that policy discussion on industrial targeting proceed so far as possible from facts concerning particular industries and the likely effects of targeting policies, rather than from preconceived notions arising, for example, from the traditional competitive trade model, which may not be very relevant in many real industrial situations. Also it would appear that the tax code in the United States already has many provisions that have the effect of promoting some industries relative to others. For example, rules for depreciation of commercial real estate tend to promote real estate development. One would hope that a better understanding of which types of intervention are more likely to improve rather than worsen overall domestic welfare could at least modify the distribution of government expenditure and tax relief in the right direction relative to the present somewhat haphazard system.

Notes

1. See Spencer and Brander (1983, 1984) for the basic theoretical argument.

2. See, for example, USITC publications No. 1437, October 1983, and No. 1517, April 1984.

3. This paper should not be viewed as an overall survey of the literature on industrial targeting. Other criteria as to which industries should be targeted have been suggested. Krugman (1983) provides an excellent discussion and critique of some of these.

4. Kreps and Scheinkman (1983) show that if firms play a two-stage game in which capacity is chosen prior to output and if capital requirements are inflexible, then under some mild assumptions on demand, the unique outcome is a Cournot equilibrium. Under this structure a higher domestic capacity should reduce the equilibrium levels of capacity and output of the foreign firms.

5. This result does depend on some specific assumptions concerning the

nature of the industry. For example, firms are assumed to have Cournot behavior, implying that in equilibrium each firm will have chosen the level of output that maximizes its own profits given the level of outputs of the other firms. Also it assumes that each firm produces the same product at the same cost of production.

6. See Brander and Spencer (1984) for a model of the strategic interplay between firms and a union in a partially unionized industry. It can be shown that a subsidy on exports of the unionized firm would be substantially absorbed in higher wages, reducing the effectiveness of the subsidy.

7. There is an opposite argument: that excessive duplication of research effort by competing firms will lead to an excessive use of resources for R&D. If this is the case encouragement of research joint ventures by domestic firms could solve this problem by allowing R&D dollars to be spent more effectively (see Grossman and Shapiro 1984).

References

Baron, David P. 1983. *The Export-Import Bank: An Economic Analysis.* New York: Academic Press.

Brander, James A., and Barbara J. Spencer. 1984a. "Export Subsidies and International Market Share Rivalry." *Journal of International Economics*, forthcoming.

Brander, James A., and Barbara J. Spencer. 1984b. "International Markets with Asymmetric Labor Commitment and Union Power." Mimeo.

Dixit, Avinash K. 1984. "International Trade Policy for Oligopolistic Industries." *Economic Journal* 94, supplement, forthcoming.

Dixit, Avinash K., and Gene M. Grossman. 1984. "Targeted Export Promotion with Several Oligopolistic Industries." Discussion Paper # 71. Woodrow Wilson School of Public and International Affairs, Princeton University.

Dixit, Avinash K., and Albert S. Kyle. 1984. "On the Use of Trade Restrictions for Entry Promotion and Deterrence." Discussion Papers in Economics No. 56. Woodrow Wilson School of Public and International Affairs, Princeton University.

Eaton, Jonathan, and Gene M. Grossman. 1983. "Optimal Trade and Industrial Policy under Oligopoly." NBER Working Paper No. 1236.

Foreign Industrial Targeting and Its Effects on U.S. Industries, Phase 1: Japan. U.S. International Trade Commission Publication No. 1437, October 1983.

Foreign Industrial Targeting and Its Effects on U.S. Industries, Phase 2: The European Community and Member States. U.S. International Trade Commission, Publication No. 1517, April 1984.

Grossman, Gene M., and David J. Richardson. 1984. "Strategic U.S. Trade

Policy: A Survey of Issues and Early Analysis." Prepared for the NBER Research Program in International Studies.

Grossman, Gene M., and Carl Shapiro. 1984. "Research Joint Ventures: An Antitrust Analysis." Discussion Paper #68. Woodrow Wilson School, Princeton University.

Grossman, Gene M. 1984. "Foreign Industrial Targeting Practices in the Telecommunications Equipment Industry." Mimeo.

Krugman, Paul R. 1983. "Targeted Industrial Policies: Theory and Evidence." In *Industrial Change and Public Policy*. Symposium sponsored by the Federal Reserve Bank of Kansas City, Jackson Hole, Wyoming, pp. 123–156.

Krugman, Paul R. 1984a. "Import Protection as Export Promotion: International Competition in the Presence of Oligopoly and Economies of Scale." In H. Kierzkowski (ed.), *Monopolistic Competition and International Trade*. Oxford: Oxford University Press.

Krugman, Paul R. 1984b. "The U.S. Response to Foreign Industrial Targeting." Manuscript prepared for the Brookings Panel on Economic Activity.

Kreps, D. M., and J. A. Scheinkman. 1983. "Quantity Precommitment and Bertrand Competition Yield Cournot Outcomes." *The Bell Journal of Economics* 14 (Autumn).

Richardson, David J. 1983. "International Trade Policies in a World of Industrial Change." In *Industrial Change and Public Policy*. Symposium sponsored by the Federal Reserve Bank of Kansas City, Jackson Hole, Wyoming, pp. 267–312.

Shapiro, Carl. 1984. "Strategic Behavior and R&D Competition." Mimeo.

Spencer, Barbara J., and James A. Brander. 1983. "International R&D Rivalry and Industrial Strategy." *The Review of Economic Studies* 50 (October).

Weinstein, Franklin B., Michiyuki Venohara, and John G. Linvill. 1984. "Technological Resources." In Daniel I. Okimoto, Takuo Sugano, and Franklin B. Weinstein (eds.), *Competitive Edge, The Semiconductor Industry in the U.S. and Japan*. Stanford: Stanford University Press.

5 Creating Advantage: How Government Policies Shape International Trade in the Semiconductor Industry

Michael Borrus,
Laura D'Andrea Tyson,
and John Zysman

By the early 1980s the Japanese semiconductor industry had become a major competitor on world markets, achieving significant gains in global market share, largely at the expense of the U.S. industry. By 1984–85 the Japanese industry dominated certain product and market segments, and fierce competition between Japanese and American producers resulted in dramatically falling prices, depressed profits, and growing excess capacity.

In our view the rapid emergence of the Japanese industry as a world-class competitor was not an unexpected outcome of the forces of free trade but rather a planned result of a concerted policy effort. The Japanese government employed a variety of policy tools to nurture its domestic industry and to shield it from foreign competition—mainly from U.S. producers—until it had reached a scale and a level of product quality and sophistication that made it competitive on world markets. In this paper we present a brief history of the evolution of the U.S. and Japanese semiconductor industries during the 1974–84 period to support our interpretation. In our discussion we focus on the roles of the U.S. and Japanese governments in shaping industry dynamics in their own countries and in international markets as well.

As a prelude to our analysis we begin with a brief overview of how our work on the semiconductor industry relates to the new theory of international trade. We also identify some critical analytic issues that must be addressed by trade theory and policy when there are significant spillover effects between performance in one or more high-technology industries and performance in the rest of the economy. The semiconductor case illustrates both the nature and the importance of the effects we have in mind and indicates that in the presence of such effects, government targeting of a single sector can have profound effects throughout the economy.

The Semiconductor Case and the New Trade Theory

Our analysis of the evolution of the semiconductor industry provides empirical support for the view that government policy, even temporary government policy, can have an enduring effect on the competitive position of national firms in international competition, when such competition occurs in imperfectly competitive markets and involves research-intensive, high-technology products. This view is consistent with the conclusions of the so-called "new" trade theory that focuses on the determinants of trade patterns and on the resulting distribution of national welfare under such conditions.[1] Although this theory clearly demonstrates that strategic government policy can permanently influence trade patterns and can produce a national welfare outcome superior to the free-trade outcome, most of the scholars credited with developing the theory treat their results as logical possibilities rather than as empirical realities with policy implications. The mounting evidence in our work on the semiconductor industry led us to accept these results as empirical realities even before they had been derived as formal possibilities in the new trade theory literature.[2] Among the new trade theorists the prevailing view is that the case where strategic government action can radically shape market outcomes in international trade has not yet been demonstrated empirically. A basic objective of this paper is to provide such a demonstration from our analysis of the semiconductor industry.

A second objective of the paper is to indicate how the character of technological development in the semiconductor industry has important spillover effects throughout the rest of the economy. The new trade theory examines how government policy can create enduring effects on competition and trade in a given sector or for a given product. If government targeting of one of several sectors has spillover effects on other sectors, then the overall effects on the economy and on its competitive position in a whole chain of related sectors can be widespread and profound. If spillover effects are important, then the national welfare implications of strategic government policy will be very sensitive to whether such policy is targeted at industries whose spillover effects are nonexistent or limited or at industries whose spillover effects are large. Successful strategic targeting of sectors with significant spillover effects will have a much more dramatic influence on national economic well-being.

Although the notion of spillover effects is a somewhat imprecise one, our work in the semiconductor industry suggests the kinds of effects we have in mind. Technical developments in the industry are at the heart of the electronics revolution. If the United States loses its ability to compete effectively in semiconductors, it may lose its ability to innovate in both the semiconductor industry and in related electronics industries and its ability to diffuse electronics-based product and process innovations in a whole variety of actual and potential user industries.

The innovation literature indicates that there is usually a substantial degree of interdependence or connectedness between a particular technological change and prior developments in the same technology and complementary or facilitory activities in related technologies.[3] As a consequence of this kind of interdependence successful innovation usually requires that firms be plugged into a whole range of past and contemporary technologies that are related to their R&D efforts. As our case study illustrates, this kind of interdependence has been critical to the ability of U.S. semiconductor firms to stay on the frontier of technological change.

To some extent, of course, the flow of technological information across national or international markets through product sale and purchase can keep individual firms abreast of the latest technological developments. But our work also suggests that a new product often does not embody the entirety of a new technology. The know-how, the understanding of how the technology was developed, and the potential ways it can be used or modified, extends beyond the product into the network or community of people who developed the technology and who help to apply it. Moreover it is often the case that potential users of a new technology require knowledge of products in development months and even years before such products are available on the market if their own research and innovation activity is to be successful. Often the only way to acquire such information is to be involved actively in related research areas and to participate in the related scientific communities.

Under these circumstances, if the United States loses a substantial portion of its semiconductor industry to foreign competitors, it may lose the domestic scientific community on which the ability to innovate in semiconductors and related electronics industries depends.

Because business and scientific communities, despite their international character, remain more tightly knit on a national than on an international level, it is unlikely that the international exchange of scientific information can be a complete substitute for the erosion of a domestic research base. This is especially unlikely in the electronics field where the Japanese are an increasingly important force in innovation and technological change. Japanese scientific and business communities in this and other fields are quite closed, certainly when compared with the United States and Western Europe.[4] As a result technological information, especially the kind of information that does not flow through simple product market channels, is likely to move much more rapidly within Japan than between Japan and the rest of the world.

Overall the potential spillover effects of an erosion of the U.S. semiconductor industry on the pace of innovation in electronics and on the diffusion of microelectronics technologies through a broad range of sectors in the United States seem to be significant enough to warrant serious attention by theorists and policymakers alike. In critical sectors, like semiconductors, on which the competitive positions of numerous other activities depend, a country's gain or loss in competitive position can result in a cumulative gain or loss across a whole spectrum of connected industries. Under these circumstances the long-run welfare consequences of strategic government policy may be much greater than currently anticipated by even the most radical findings of the new trade theory.

The Evolution of Competition in Semiconductors

To explore the role of government in shaping competition in the semiconductor industry, we begin with an analysis of the development of the industry that led to the current state of U.S.-Japanese competition.[5] Then we turn to the analytic economic issues posed in the first part of this paper.

The U.S. Industry

The U.S. semiconductor industry has passed through three distinct phases of development. In the earliest period, from the invention of transistors in 1948 through the commercial introduction of the integrated circuit in 1962, the U.S. military played the role of "creative first user." Military R&D programs, emphasizing miniaturization, high performance, and reliability, set the direction for early product design, and military and space agency procurement provided an initial market for the integrated circuit. The existence of strong government demand contributed to the entry of new firms and accelerated the pace of diffusion of the integrated circuit into nonmilitary markets. Also, particularly critical in this phase for the industry's longer-term development, was the role of Bell Laboratories. Bell Labs innovated much of the basic research and process technologies that led to the development of the integrated circuit. Government anti-trust policy (the 1956 Consent Degree) assured that Bell Labs' know-how diffused cheaply to small new firms, which took the technology to market. This first development phase was, in short, critically dependent on government policy which established the industry's technological trajectory, made initial markets through procurement, and ensured that the technology was widely available at low cost.

The second stage of the industry's development, from the mid-1960s to early 1970s, rested on its synergistic relationship to the computer industry. Advanced integrated circuit design moved from the implementation of basic logic circuits to the implementation of entire computer subsystems on a single chip of silicon. In turn the growth of the mainframe and minicomputer markets both was fueled by and contributed to the rapid expansion of domestic digital integrated circuit production. During this period the computer industry emerged as the creative first user and volume procurer of components, and as a consequence government influence on the U.S. industry's development waned.

The third stage of the industry, roughly until the early 1980s, rested on the shift to MOS (metal oxide on silicon) technology, the emergence of large-scale integrated (LSI) circuit designs, and the appearance of the microprocessor. This stage saw a wave of new merchant entries and a broadening of the final systems markets that the integrated circuit producer served. Large-scale integration brought with it new markets in semiconductor memories, in consumer products, in telecommunications, and, most important, in a wide variety of applications markets for the microprocessor and microcomputer. In turn the strategies of firms changed as the markets for the more complex LSI circuits became more segmented and as the microprocessor, the third generation of computation equipment, offered new market development opportunities and challenges.

As the industry moved through large-scale integration, the nature of the products it produced changed and therefore so did its status as a "components" industry. As chips became increasingly more complex, with entire electronic subsystems beginning to be embedded in their structure, major merchant firms in the industry leveraged their strengths in integrated circuit technology to integrate forward into systems production. This was necessary to capture increased value to offset rapidly rising R&D and capital investment costs associated with putting so much complex circuitry on chip. Also "captive" production—either through acquisition or in-house start-ups—steadily increased as a variety of final electronic systems producers recognized the strategic nature of the integrated circuit to their future product development and market growth.

Although the industry's evolution has been shaped by changes and by growth in the final product markets for semiconductor devices, it is important to recognize that these market opportunities were a direct result of continuous product and process R&D spending which generated successive innovations in semiconductor technology. In the early years, semiconductors were simply replacements for vacuum tubes; they performed the same functions more effectively, but they did not fundamentally change the products into which they were incorporated. In the second stage of the industry's development, advances in semiconductor technology made possible the substitution of electronic circuits for many types of electrical mechanical functions. In the third phase of the industry's development, the advent of the microprocessor opened up new market opportunities beyond those substitution uses for which semiconductor technologies had proved cost-effective and performance enhancing. In essence the microprocessor and the growing range of complex large-scale integrated circuits opened the development phase of the industry.

Despite drastically increasing costs of R&D and capacity expansion, the U.S. semiconductor industry has not settled into the kind of stable oligopoly characteristic of mature industries. A constantly shifting set of merchant firms (i.e., there is almost constant entry and exit) whose primary business is the design, manufacture, and open-market sale of advanced integrated circuit devices has over time been complemented by the emergence of a rapidly increasing number of systems firms engaged in custom IC fabrication and design. With the addition of the two giants of the domestic electronics industry—IBM and AT&T—the structure of the domestic sector exhibits a diversity and dynamism unique in the world community. As we have argued elsewhere, however, the merchant segment of the industry has been the critical stimulus to commercial market diffusion of integrated circuits: by making the most advanced integrated circuits available at low cost on the open market, merchants have lowered technological and capital barriers to entry in existing electronic systems markets and led the development of new markets for the application of microelectronics technology. This competitive dynamism has spurred technological advance and until recently has sustained the international competitiveness of the American electronics industry as a whole.

The Japanese Industry

Where the U.S. semiconductor industry led, Japan, by contrast, was a follower industry, the latecomer. As a consequence its evolution was different. During the 1970s the Japanese industry moved from a consumer product orientation and a technological position of relative inferiority in components, toward a state-of-the-art capability in components, computers, and telecommunications. Critical to our story is the role of government in assisting and promoting catchup. Indeed, state policies helped to protect, promote, and rationalize the industry. High-volume production of commodity components manufactured with U.S.-licensed technology by U.S.-made production equipment to U.S. design standards characterized the successive stages of this transformation. Stable sources of plentiful capital for expansion in a closed domestic market served finally to allow Japanese export penetration of the U.S. market by the late 1970s. Such structural characteristics also served to cushion the Japanese industry from technological or market errors: Japanese firms could compensate for the consequences of a misjudgment or new U.S. innovation by returning to their domestic market insulated from foreign competition.

In other papers we have explored in detail our interpretation of the Japanese system, the strengths of the business community and of the effects of Japanese policy.[6] We do not reproduce here our full discussion of the evolution of the Japanese industry. Rather, we emphasize the elements of policy that proved critical.

We have characterized the Japanese economic system as one of "controlled competition" in which intense competition between firms in key industrial sectors is partly directed and at times limited by both

state actions and the formal and informal collaborative efforts of industrial and financial enterprises. The precise rules guiding the system evolve over time with the structure of the economy, the financial
and market strength of the companies, and the political position and
purposes of the bureaucracy.

The state bureaucrats do not dictate to an administered market, but
they do help in a detailed way to establish conditions of investment
and risk that promote the long-term development and international
competitiveness of Japanese industry.[7] Government industrial strategy assumes that the market pressures of competition can serve as an
instrument of policy and often induces the very competition it directs.
It induces competition by creating the market for products and making cheap investment capital readily available, thus seemingly ensuring a profit and attracting the entry of many competitors. The
competition is real, but there are limits, including product specialization agreed on within a set of competing firms and the often-cited
cartels to regulate capacity expansion in booms and cutback arrangements in downturns. In semiconductors during the 1970s, as in steel a
generation before, collaborative arrangements were central to Japanese international success.

In particular, the government's promotion objectives were pursued
through two sets of policies: those controlling the links between the
Japanese market and international markets, and those manipulating
the domestic firms to stimulate expansion. Let us look at both sets of
policies as they bear on our case story.

Controlled Access

T. J. Pempel once characterized the Japanese state as an official doorman determining what, and under what conditions, capital, technology, and manufactured products enter and leave Japan.[8] The
discretion to decide what to let in (and at the extreme what to let out)
of Japan, permitted the doorman to break up the packages of technology, capital, and control that multinational corporations represent.
Until recently the Ministry of Finance also operated selective controls
over inward foreign investment. MITI controlled technology imports
in order to force foreigners to sell raw technology in the form of
patents, licenses, and expertise.

Limits on foreign entry and forced transfer of technology were
critical to the early development of microelectronics in Japan. The
story of Texas Instruments' entry to Japan, in which it traded licenses

that could have blocked Japanese development for a share of the market, is really exemplary. As we have written before:

Thus, during the 1960s and the early 1970s the Japanese government, principally through MITI, sought to build a competitive semiconductor industry by limiting foreign competition in the domestic market and acquiring foreign technology and know-how. Foreign investment laws created after World War II required the Japanese government to review for approval all applications for direct foreign investment in Japan. The government consistently rejected all applications for wholly owned subsidiaries and for joint ventures in which foreign firms would hold majority ownership. It also rejected foreign purchases of equity in Japanese semiconductor firms. Simultaneously, the government limited foreign import penetration of the home market through high tariffs and restrictive quotas and approval-registration requirements on advanced IC devices in particular. For example, until 1974, ICs that contained more than 200 circuit elements simply could not be imported without special permission. Penetration was also managed by exclusionary customs procedures and "Buy Japanese" procurement and "jawboning" policies.

The price to U.S. firms for limited access to the Japanese market was their licensing of advanced technology and know-how. This too was regulated closely by the Japanese government, whose approval was required on all patent and technical-assistance licensing agreements. Since MITI controlled access to the Japanese market and its approval was required for the implementation of licensing deals, it was in a powerful monopsonist's position of being able to dictate the terms of exchange. Its general policy was simple and effective. It required foreign firms to license all Japanese firms requesting access to a particular technology. It limited royalty payments by Japanese firms to a single rate on each deal, thereby preempting the competitive bidding-up of royalty rates among Japanese firms. In line with the characteristic emphasis on export strategy, MITI often linked the import of particular technologies to the acquiring firm's ability to develop export products using that technology. MITI also conditioned approval of certain deals on the willingness of the involved Japanese firms to diffuse their own technical developments, through sublicense agreements, to other Japanese firms. The total result of these policies was a controlled diffusion of advanced technology throughout the Japanese semiconductor industry. Tilton gives a convincing measure of the extent of Japanese firm dependence on the acquisition of U.S. technology: by the end of the 1960s Japanese IC producers were paying at least 10 percent of their semiconductor sales revenues as royalties to U.S. firms—2 percent to Western Electric, 4.5 percent to Fairchild, and 3.5 percent to Texas Instruments.

Royalty income may have been substantial for a number of U.S. firms, but market access was ephemeral indeed. The one successful entry into the Japanese market by a U.S. firm came when Texas Instruments reached an agreement with Sony on a joint venture in 1968. Texas Instruments petitioned the Japanese government for a wholly owned subsidiary in the early 1960s, and was offered a minority-share joint venture which it rejected. Its chief bargaining chip during these negotiations was its continuing refusal to license its critical IC patents to Japanese firms without gaining a substantial production subsidiary in Japan in return. NEC and the other firms sublicensed to it were in fact producing ICs based on technology developed by TI and Fairchild through an NEC-Fairchild licensing agreement. However, because the TI-Fairchild patent accord explicitly excluded Japan, those Japanese firms were not protected, as Fairchild licensees in Europe were, against patent-infringement suits brought by TI. The Japanese government stalled approval of TI's patent application in Japan, and this enabled NEC and the other firms to play domestic technology catch-up, thereby forcing TI to negotiate for quicker access. The Japanese government then held up Japanese exports of IC-based systems to the United States because TI threatened infringement action. A compromise was finally reached in which TI got a 50 percent share of a joint venture with Sony, and agreed further to limit its future share of the Japanese semiconductor market to no more than 10 percent. TI bought Sony's share of the joint venture in 1972, and though 1980 remained the only U.S. merchant firm with a wholly owned manufacturing subsidiary in Japan.

We concluded then that "the strategy of technological diffusion and limited market access, implied in the TI story . . . enabled Japanese firms roughly to mimic technological developments in the United States." Thus in the early phase the market space to permit firms to grow in the face of foreign advantage was generated by government.

Such a closed market yields a substantial advantage. It permits the possibility of gearing up to reach world-scale production at home and then very aggressively pursuing foreign markets. Foreigners are unable to exploit a technological advantage and turn it into an enduring market presence. Cooperation between firms aimed at excluding foreigners, tight relations with domestic customers, and lock-up distribution channels, all endure to preserve the domestic Japanese market—and the production volumes gained serving it—for Japanese firms even after formal government restrictions on entry are removed.

Indeed, since the early 1980s access to Japanese markets has eased. Continuing negotiations of the High Technology Working Group have resulted in a staged reduction of tariffs. Pressures have been brought to accelerate domestic purchase of American products. Closure appears to endure, however.

"Controlled access" is the term that best captures what we believe occurs in semiconductor and related systems markets in Japan. We believe that Japanese semiconductor firms can concertedly control the composition and extent of U.S. semiconductors sold in Japan because the largest Japanese producers are also the largest consumers of semiconductors and are directly tied to other major consumers through the *keiretsu* structure of affiliated industrial groups. The ten largest Japanese semiconductor-electronics firms account for almost all of Japanese semiconductor production and for about 60 percent of domestic semiconductor consumption, but on the average, only about 20 percent of production is captively consumed by each producing firm. Another set of aggregate figures suggests that 80 to 90 percent of semiconductor output is consumed within the *keiretsu* of the major semiconductor producers.

Two possible arguments have been offered to account for these aggregate figures. First the figures illustrate trade among the major Japanese firms and their *keiretsu* based on a pattern of component and systems specialization. The evidence for this is that joint research and development programs encouraged existing product specialization. This argument has been criticized because it allegedly "fails to answer why one Japanese firm would sacrifice profits by purchasing from another rather than from cheaper foreign supply."[9] When the Japanese industry was technologically backward and facing technologically advanced foreign competitors, collaborative interfirm trade would be a perfectly rational response: profits would be sacrificed simply to prevent the low-cost foreign competitors from overrunning the Japanese domestic market. There is little doubt that this in fact occurred.

A second explanation is that the data show extremely high intra-*keiretsu* consumption. In effect there may be a captive market operating at the level of the *keiretsu*. In either case, the vestiges of past policies endure in the current structure of demand in the domestic Japanese market. They make that market very hard to penetrate even today.[10] The result is that the competitive advantage of a closed market, detailed earlier, continue to assist the international position of Japanese producers.

Collaborative R&D and Japanese Manufacturing Advantage
The collaborative promotional policies referred to previously and considered here are the R&D programs, not the broader industry development programs. The programs such as the VLSI project in the mid-1970s were aimed at developing generic technologies—those with wide application but common production techniques—and refining mass production processes, not product-specific tech-

nologies. The government reduced the cost of the riskiest and least predictable phase of the R&D process. The government also encouraged the diffusion of the generic technologies among the several firms. It only influenced specific product choices indirectly, by forcing specific company groupings and choosing the technological directions of its projects.

Because these projects came at the beginning of a technology cycle, they did not cost huge sums. The much larger sums for actual product engineering and for the application of jointly developed process techniques to commercial manufacture came through company coffers, though often subsidized by the government through preferential, low-interest loans and outright grants, and through premium-price procurement by government agencies like NTT. The research investments, however, proved critical. They permitted Japanese firms to develop production refinements (of the collaboratively acquired generic and process technologies) that have vaulted Japanese firms into a world-class competitive position.

Indeed, by leveraging off of these programs and the stable, growing demand in their closed home market, Japanese firms created characteristic innovation in semiconductor production processes that have led to real competitive advantage on international markets, particularly in commodity memory. By 1984 Japanese firms dominated the production of Random Access Memories (RAMs) worldwide—a product U.S. firms had pioneered and held the lead in until 1980. In 1984 Japanese firms captured between 60 and 90 percent of the market for state-of-the-art dynamic and static RAMs. In short, Japanese producers have established an international advantage in these market areas chiefly with production strategies that focus competition on cost and quality of commodity products, rather than with the entrepreneurial strategies characteristic of U.S. firms that focus competition on diffusion and advance of new technologies.

Such Japanese dominance of commodity memory through continuous heavy capital investment in manufacturing refinement places severe competitive pressure on U.S. merchant producers for two closely related reasons. First, commodity memory devices like RAMs have historically generated the operating *margins* necessary to allow U.S. merchant firms to reinvest and attract additional capital for R&D and growth. Second, and equally important, successive generations of RAMS have been the simplest of increasingly complex integrated

circuits; experience gained in their production has heretofore provided U.S. firms with the manufacturing know-how to move through
successive iterations to the competitive production of more complex
devices. Hence, U.S. firm margins, and thus their capacity to innovate, are squeezed at the same time that their abilities to acquire
critical production know-how are threatened. This bluntly represents
a shift in the terms of competition in established semiconductor
markets.

Government Policy and the Current Competition

The U.S. industry is now entering a fourth stage of development,
which is loosely associated with the move to even greater levels of
complexity in integrated circuits that is characteristic of very large-
scale integration (VLSI). In part this fourth phase represents an
intensification of some of the major trends of the industry's previous
phase. The production of more systemslike components, forward integration into systems markets by merchant firms, the increasing
penetration of markets such as factory and office automation (in
which electronic intelligence has had up to now only limited or no
application), and the rising presence of captive production are all now
ingrained features of the industry's evolution that find their roots in
the era of LSI. To these should be added a number of new structural
trends that are beginning to take shape and will dramatically influence the nature of competition in the latest phase of development.
The most important of these can be roughly characterized according
to whether they tend to preserve the dynamic, innovative character of
the industry or whether they cause it to settle down toward a more
mature structure.

Pushing toward innovation are four factors: (1) the emergence of
potentially large markets for nonstandard application-specific (custom and semicustom) integrated circuits made possible by the design
capabilities of VLSI, (2) the latest wave of new merchant firms, (3) the
identification of new standard systemlike commodity components
(e.g., telecommunications processing chips), along with the emergence as commodity products of certain formerly low-volume market
niches (e.g., erasable-programmable memories), and (4) closer
strategic cooperation between merchant producers and final systems
manufacturers. Pushing toward maturity are two other factors: (5) the

enduring presence of Japanese competition, with the heavily capital-intensive, manufacturing-based strategy described earlier and (6) high and rising capital costs of R&D and production.

The Case against Industry Maturity

As an industry matures, product design parameters become standardized and the focus of competition shifts toward incremental manufacturing refinement and marketing. Such maturity is delayed, however, by technological innovation that upsets established design parameters and refocuses the search for competitive advantage on new products and processes. VLSI, as we shall explain, has the effect of upsetting established semiconductor design parameters. It represents continuing technological innovation that cuts directly against arguments that the semiconductor industry is "maturing." Indeed, the firms that succeed in implementing VLSI will set the terms of future competition in semiconductors.

VLSI rests on technological advances in semiconductor fabrication that permit dense packaging of extremely complex circuits, with a transistor count starting at roughly 100,000 per chip. Thus VLSI is both a process innovation and a product innovation that permits the ability to implement more complex and radically new systems architectures in silicon. The limit on the widespread diffusion of these complex large circuits is the great difficulty of design: the extremely high cost of VLSI design has generally precluded the widespread use of application-specific circuits. But a partial solution to this dilemma has been found in design automation—the use of computer-aided design (CAD) systems to simplify and reduce the cost of designing VLSI circuits.

Seizing on the capabilities of VLSI, existing U.S. firms and a spate of new entrants have accelerated the pace of innovation, developing new commodity components like digital signal processing chips, fragmenting mass commodity markets into high-value niches (like high-performance, complementary MOS nonvolatile memories), and pushing the development of new potential markets for custom and semicustom circuits. In particular, the continuing development of automated design for custom and semicustom circuits is drastically reducing the design costs associated with nonstandard VLSI. In turn broad new merchant markets are emerging for these application-specific circuits, especially among the vast majority of systems manufacturers that have no captive semiconductor production.

In past phases of the industry's evolution, new merchant firms have been the development vehicles by which major technological advances have been diffused into commercial use. In this regard application-specific VLSI is no exception. The entrenched positions of the captive and established merchant producers—the strategic focus of the former on keeping custom circuits proprietary and of the latter on standard commodity components—have militated against their developing and bringing the new technology to market as fast as its potential applications warrant. As a consequence many new merchant firms have entered the semiconductor business with the avowed aim of developing markets for application-specific circuits.

If the new strategic alternatives to the traditional commodity semiconductor strategy pan out, a growing segment of the U.S. industry will become, in effect, an engineering service business tied to silicon-foundry production strategies. The new entrants have fragmented the traditional commodity strategy of the merchant producers in order to pursue new potential markets in custom design. Indeed, the transfer of design technology is a new strategy for creating market demand by educating the user to the potential of VLSI custom design. In that sense the new merchants have taken a strategic page from the book of earlier generation merchant producers like Intel, who introduced microprocessor development and support systems to expand radically their markets by educating users to the virtues of the microprocessor. If users can be quickly educated to custom design, then the markets for applications-specific circuits will expand rapidly because the potential competitive advantages of the new approaches are numerous. Indeed, the growth of application-specific markets, and the market presence of the new merchant entrants seeking to push along the use of custom circuits, has created new dynamic instability in existing component markets. Virtually every major established merchant firm has committed resources to respond to the new opportunities and competitive challenges associated with custom circuits.

The Case for Maturity
Although the advent of custom capabilities associated with VLSI is an important competitive development that plays to American innovation strengths, standard commodity components will continue to dominate semiconductor production for the foreseeable future. This is so because VLSI permits the commodity production of increasingly

dense and versatile memories, microprocessors, and peripheral circuits that will open new markets in areas like factory and office automation and also because complex systems products will continue to use standard components in tandem with custom-designed circuits. Standard devices accounted for approximately 88 percent of the total market for semiconductors in 1984, a percentage that we believe is unlikely to undergo drastic deterioration before the 1990s.

Indeed, with the exception of recession years commodity component markets are continuing to grow at rapid rates. Even such memory subsegments as complex nonvolatile memories (EE PROMS) are becoming high volume. And any one commodity segment can be broken into subsegments and within each subsegment broken down further according to device density, access time, and other characteristics. Many of these segments and subsegments have now taken on a commodity character and are capable of generating sufficient returns to sustain merchant firm growth. There are limits, though, that hinge on the ability to gain production experience (as argued earlier with respect to the critical role played by RAMs).

If the Americans have pushed the innovation of custom devices and the expansion of subsegments into commodity products— thereby pursuing the strengths evident in the first development phases of the industry—the Japanese have pursued their partly policy-induced advantage in commodity component manufacturing.

The Japanese producers leveraged their entry to the U.S. market by engineering a system of commodity component manufacturing that allowed rapid entry with relatively simple components of high quality and low cost. By entering in this way, Japanese firms changed the terms of market competition by imposing new basic manufacturing parameters that favored Japanese strengths. By putting a premium on manufacturing in the context of rapidly escalating capital costs, Japanese firms speeded the maturation of the industry and further enhanced their own competitive position. Indeed, as suggested earlier, the formidable character of Japanese competition in semiconductors has been amply demonstrated since 1980.

As a result of coordinated research in the Japanese VLSI project (1976–1980), Japanese firms led their U.S. merchant competitors in more quickly introducing the 64K dRAM and moving it into volume production. This represented the first commodity IC device for which Japanese firms led U.S. merchants in new product and market development. Because the 64K dRAM required high capital investment, generated very high volume demand among a few large purchasers, was relatively less complex than other dense circuits, did not require much servicing or support, and involved production know-how and capacity that was fairly easily transferred to the manufacture of similar commodity devices (such as static-RAMs), it meshed perfectly with characteristic Japanese strengths and manufacturing strategies. Nevertheless, Japanese success at developing the product market and sustaining a leadership position in this device represents an important departure from the established Japanese strategy of being successful market followers. Indeed, Japanese firms have retained their leadership in RAMs, as the market share figures given earlier suggest, and have used it as a lever to challenge U.S. firms in other standard component areas.

In commodity memory Japanese producers have spent heavily to bring down production costs by automating production. They invested in highly automated capacity expansion (for 64K dRAMS during the 1981–1982 U.S. recession, and for 256K dRAMs since 1983) while U.S. firms delayed or cut back their expansion plans, given recurrent American recessions. The Japanese ability to spend heavily during rough economic times and the move to automation illustrate again the characteristic policy-induced, domestic-based strengths of the Japanese industry. The ability to spend was based on the stable access to cheap capital (which was undoubtedly much cheaper for Japanese firms, given the grossly high real interest rates that have obtained in the United States since 1980) afforded by the Japanese financial structure. The point to be made about automation is more complex.

First, automation implies high front-end manufacturing costs, which bring with them two kinds of associated vulnerabilities. One is vulnerability to product innovation, where automated production that is optimized for particular product or design is made obsolete by a new product or design that becomes an industry standard. Japanese RAM producers were helped in this area because no single 64K or 256K design became an industry standard as Mostek's 16K design had been in the previous generation. Moreover the Japanese financial structure and government policies generally decrease this kind of vulnerability by permitting cheap reinvestment combined with rapid tax write-offs and less concern about the impact of obsolescence and reinvestment on current earnings.

The related vulnerability is to fluctuations in demand because the higher fixed costs of automated production place a premium on the use of full capacity. If demand drops, but capacity is fully used, oversupply could eliminate profits on the device in question. This appears to have occurred. Indeed, excess RAM capacity has forced severe price-cutting in the market since late-1983, and it appears that very few Japanese firms—if any—are making a profit on RAMs. Some have outright losses. However, given the arguments earlier about an essentially closed market, Japanese companies face a sufficiently high level of stable demand to mitigate this second vulnerability, at least relative to their U.S. competitors.

The question remains whether the Japanese government still plays the same roles in this round of competition that it played earlier. Indeed, the government still plays a critical role in funding the generic research in device and production technologies, both through projects funded by MITI and by NTT. The details of these newest projects have not yet been translated into market products, so we do not review them here. Our conclusion, though, is consistent with that of several national panels charged with evaluating these issues. The programs appear significant and successful. It is less clear to us whether the Japanese market still is formally closed by government pressure or by internal corporate relations, or whether and to what degree the continuous political pressure from the United States has loosened access to the Japanese market. Access to markets and R&D remains terribly difficult. The answer is not crucial to this argument that government policy has mattered at least until now.

Maturity or Innovation?
The key question for the future of competition then is which way the industry will evolve, toward maturity and Japanese advantage or toward continuing innovation and U.S. advantage. The Japanese semiconductor firms have consolidated in their manufacturing-based strategy the international advantages afforded them by domestic Japanese industrial structures (themselves partly policy induced) and policies. That consolidation has permitted them to dominate RAM production and compete in other product areas. In tandem with rising capital costs, the Japanese strategy has pushed the terms of international competition in semiconductors toward heavy capital investment and manufacturing—signs of a "maturing" industry that play to Japanese strengths. U.S. firms have responded by diversifying their competitive strategies and flexibly positioning themselves to

take advantage of new market opportunities. Rather than abandoning their strengths in innovation in the face of signs of "maturity," U.S. firms have chosen to push the pace of innovation. Some large U.S. firms have chosen to compete head-on with the Japanese in RAM markets; other merchant firms have ceded RAMS to concentrate on the development of newer commodity component markets where the United States leads. Simultaneously new and old U.S. merchants as well as U.S. captive producers have begun to take custom and semicustom technology to market, creating new competitive opportunities. As these strategic maneuvers indicate, the diverse structure and flexible responses of the U.S. semiconductor industry enable U.S. firms to keep on the move as they respond to Japanese competition.

In our view policy actions taken by the U.S. (particularly in the trade arena) and Japanese governments structure the competition and will ultimately determine whether the nature of competition in semiconductors shifts to favor the Japanese or continues to preserve the dominant position of U.S. merchants and the U.S. industry. As argued, current and past Japanese government policies tend to slant the terms of international competition toward Japanese strengths. One could envision appropriate U.S. policy actions that could make a decisive difference. For example, the point of U.S. policies might be to ensure that the newly emerging strategies of the U.S. industry, and particularly of its merchant producers, have a fair chance to succeed in the market.

The Semiconductor Case: The Issues

What then can we conclude about our initial questions from this story? Our first question was how has government affected the evolution of the industry? In the early years in the United States, the military procurement and development policies ensured a launch market for the firms innovating the new technologies. The long-run development, though, was assured by the role of antitrust policy toward Bell Laboratories, which made the Labs a technology pump ensuring a constant flow of new technology and ideas into the industry. It meant that small firms could concentrate on product development, since much of the basic research was being done elsewhere. Government policy that structured the role of Bell Labs and the financial possibilities of the industry was therefore essential. In our view joint industry research programs such as MCC or SRC are useful, but not sufficient, substitutes for either government sponsorship of generic research projects or the prior role of Bell Laboratories before divestiture.

In the Japanese case government policy was an absolutely indispensable element in ensuring the competitive development of that nation's industry. Without active government policy in the 1970s the industry could not have climbed to international prominence. That policy largely consisted of two parts: market closure and financing of generic research projects. In the current period it is difficult to judge the precise extent and significance of government-promoted market closure, but government sponsorship of generic research at critical technology junctures remains essential. How widely such technology projects will be diffused is an issue. There appear to be limits on their international diffusion. In sum, government actions altered the resources available to firms and thus changed the character and ambition of their strategies. Shifting the set of possibilities available to firms, expanding their resources, and lifting constraints, does not guarantee market success. The Japanese firms acted effectively to capture the possibilities opened by the choices of government, in particular with their mastery of complex manufacturing. Japanese government policy depended on the strengths of the firms and exploited the market, but the policy was essential to the market outcomes.

The second question of course is whether those outcomes matter. Does the character of technological development in the semiconductor industry generate important spillover effects? Or, to put it another way, will the technologies of microelectronics diffuse differently depending on whether the origin of innovation is domestic or foreign? The density and the significance of the innovative interconnections in this industry are easy to underestimate. Four issues emerge from our story.

First, is a semiconductor more like a ball bearing or an electronic system? If it is more like a ball bearing, it can, for the most part, be simply imported. If it is more like a system, then crucial innovation occurs at the level of the chip, and losing the ability to design systems can affect a wide range of industries. Standard older generation chips are like ball bearings. Advanced chips are systems. Most important, knowledge about them transfers in the ties between design and marketing engineers in the producer company and the engineers in user companies. In some cases systems are designed in anticipation of semiconductor advances. Buying the product on the market puts user firms at substantial disadvantage. There are certainly policies to compensate for the absence of the most advanced firms, but they are second-best solutions if a viable and varied industry is a possibility—as perhaps Europe's deteriorating position in electronics demonstrates.[11] Information does not adequately diffuse by product.

Second, manufacturing and design expertise is largely embedded in the equipment supplier firms and only partly embedded in specific companies as learning experience. The most significant Japanese advances for the competitiveness of American firms may well be in the equipment end, and the greatest danger consequently is their potential domination of the manufacturing equipment business. Why? Because the equipment diffuses—by observed evidence—most rapidly in the country of origin.

Third, each current large segment of product demand represents a force for innovation—except, as our analyses suggest, military demand.[12] The critical segments are consumer electronic products, telecommunications products, and computer products. Japanese domination of the consumer electronics industries gave them a real advantage in new technologies of general importance, like CMOS, the emerging dominant processing technology.

Finally, the fact that the Japanese electronics industry is dominated by six large integrated firms poses quite significant issues. On the one hand, the firms depend for product advantage on innovation in semiconductors. In-house developments will diffuse within Japanese companies more rapidly than outside developments. Diffusion out from Japan of equipment knowledge and early product knowledge is likely to remain asymmetrical, to the disadvantage of American industry, for some time. In short, our answer to the second question is that critically important spillovers are indeed generated in this industry, and in Japan's case policy and industry structures combine to keep them isolated from diffusing internationally. The result is likely to be the generation of a substantial comparative advantage for Japan's producers of electronic systems, not just for Japan's semiconductor industry.

Overall, our analyses of the semiconductor industry suggests that strategic government policy has had a significant influence on the dynamics of industry competition. This conforms to the theoretical findings of the new trade literature. Our conclusions about the importance of spillover effects in the semiconductor industry suggest that future work in the literature must incorporate these effects if the broader influence of such policy across related sectors is to be understood.

Notes

1. The new trade theory examines the determinants and patterns of international trade under conditions that diverge from the stringent and unrealistic assumptions on which traditional comparative advantage theory is based. These assumptions, which include perfect competition, constant returns to scale, and the absence of externalities are clearly at odds with conditions in the markets for many manufactured goods, especially the high-technology goods that are the focus of this paper. In addition traditional comparative advantage theory cannot explain patterns of intrasectoral trade among the industrial countries, yet such trade is a substantial fraction of the total trade among them. Several of the papers in this volume contain contributions to the new trade theory.

2. Our first published analysis of the semiconductor industry appeared in Michael Borrus, James Millstein and John Zysman, *U.S.-Japanese Competition in the Semiconductor Industry* (Berkeley: Institute of International Studies, University of California, 1982).

3. See, for example, Richard Nelson, "Policies in Support of High-Technology Industries," mimeo, 1984, and Richard Nelson (ed.), *Government Support of Technical Progress: A Cross-Industry Analysis* (New York: Pergamon Press, 1982).

4. Our research into the Japanese semiconductor industry indicates that the Japanese community is organized around business groups with limited movement of personnel out of the groups. Microchip innovation within a group is used to advance final products within the group, and the final products serve, at least in part, a captive market.

5. This section depends heavily on the work of Michael Borrus. It is drawn from three sources, and in part paraphrases or quotes them: *U.S.-Japanese Competition in the Semiconductor Industry*, Michael Borrus, James Millstein, and John Zysman (Berkeley: Institute of International Studies, University of California, 1982); *Responses to the Japanese Challenge in High Technology*, Michael Borrus with James Millstein and John Zysman (Berkeley: Berkeley Roundtable on the International Economy [BRIE], 1983); and *Reversing Attrition. A Strategic Response to the Erosion of U.S. Leadership in Microelectronics*, Michael Borrus (Berkeley: [BRIE, 1985). Sections of these publications appear here without noted references.

6. See, in particular, Borrus, Millstein, and Zysman, *Responses to the Japanese Challenge*, and Zysman et al., *U.S. and Japanese Trade and Industrial Policies* (Berkeley: BRIE, 1984).

7. See Chalmers Johnson, *MITI and the Japanese Miracle* (Stanford: Stanford University Press, 1982).

8. T. J. Pempel, in Peter Katzenstein (ed.), *Between Power and Plenty* (Madison: University of Wisconsin Press, 1978), p.157.

9. William R. Cline, " 'Reciprocity': A New Approach to World Trade Policy?" in *Policy Analyses in International Economics*, No. 2 (Washington, D.C.: Institute for International Economics, September 1982), p.14.

10. This position is argued forcefully in the supporting documentation to "Petition of the Semiconductor Industry Association to the U.S. Trade Representative" under section 301 of the Trade Act of 1974, as amended. This so-called 301 petition was filed in August 1985.

11. This was a major conclusion of a recent BRIE conference on "Europe's Position in Telecommunications and Microelectronics," held at the University of California, Berkeley, in April 1985.

12. This position is argued in Leslie Brueckner, "Assessing the Commercial Implications of the Defense Department's Very High Speed Integrated Circuit Program" (Berkeley: BRIE, 1984).

6 Credit Policy and International Competition

Jonathan Eaton

In its fifty-year history the Export-Import Bank of the United States has provided a variety of financial services to U.S. exporters and buyers of U.S. products. Its purpose at its founding was to finance trade with the Soviet Union. During the Second World War it financed the war effort of our allies. In the immediate postwar era it provided long-term development finance to less developed countries, and provided balance-of-payments finance for Argentina and Brazil. In recent years its activity has focused exclusively on providing export credits, and insuring and guaranteeing private export credits, to buyers of U.S. products. With the establishment of the special facilities for lending to Brazil and Mexico in 1983 the Bank is once again providing finance for balance-of-payment reasons.

In many ways the Export-Import Bank (Eximbank) operates like a commercial bank. There are some significant differences, however. Eximbank does not compete for private deposits but receives loans directly from the U.S. Treasury. Eximbank's liabilities are backed by the U.S. government. The bank is exempt from many of the financial and reporting regulations imposed on private commercial banks. These differences place Eximbank at a competitive advantage in providing many types of export credits.

The existence of a government-supported bank providing commercial loans in a competitive capitalist economy requires justification. In fact many reasons have been given for such an institution. This paper provides a review of the rationale for government provision of export credits and government guarantees and insurance of private export credits. In providing these services the government acts indirectly to subsidize U.S. exports.

Export Credit and Export Subsidies

A Difficult Distinction to Draw

In discussing government provision of export credits to foreign buyers of U.S. products, it is useful to distinguish between the provision of credit and the subsidization of exports. The distinction is not a clear one, and discussions of the role of Eximbank have been contradictory in specifying whether or not the bank is to be in the business of subsidizing exports. On the one hand, a major tenet of bank operations is that bank activities "not compete with private sources of capital" (Feinberg 1982, p. 12). On the other hand, a stated objective of the administration is that "official export subsidies should be reduced, and eventually eliminated through international agreements" (Leland 1982).

To the extent that the government is providing a service that private markets are not supplying, at least some subsidy element is involved. Evidence of the removal of a subsidy element would be the emergence of private lenders competing directly with Eximbank in its lending activity, contradicting the tenet that the bank not compete with private suppliers of capital.

Although absence of active private competition is evidence of a subsidy element, it is not evidence that private markets would be unwilling to provide the services that the Eximbank provides if the bank did not exist. The presence of the Export-Import Bank and the export credit agencies of other countries is very likely to have discouraged the establishment of private institutions providing similar services, in particular, the provision of medium- and long-term export credits, especially to countries outside the OECD. Since these institutions have not developed, there is not the constituency to protest competition from Eximbank as there would be, say, if the bank were to begin to offer credit cards or checking account services. A government agency may so successfully compete with private competition that it drives it out altogether, and then it might claim that private markets are not providing the service rendered, thereby justifying its public provision.

The U.S. government, through its efforts to negotiate a multilateral agreement to reduce the subsidization of export credit through the OECD Export Credit Arrangement, has succeeded in reducing the subsidy element in such operations worldwide. Nevertheless, any argument in favor of a government agency to provide export credit at all must accept the notion that in economic terms such an agency is providing a subsidy. Arguments in favor of such a subsidy can be made, however, based on trade policy considerations, imperfections in international capital markets, and the pursuit of international political goals.

Identifying the Sources of the Subsidy

A number of studies have attempted to measure the subsidy element involved in the operations of Eximbank (U.S. Congress 1981, Boyd 1982, Baron 1983). Estimates of the total amount of the subsidy vary from $.2 to $.9 billion/year. This paper will not attempt to review the different studies or provide a critique of their methodology. But it is worth mentioning the various methods, some of them very indirect, by which the bank acts to provide a subsidy.

A distinction has been drawn between a financial subsidy, which exists when the bank receives a transfer of funds from the U.S. Treasury, and an economic subsidy, arising when the government treats the bank favorably relative to private commercial banks. Except for a few years in which it ran an accounting deficit (Baron 1983), the bank has shown an accounting profit, so a financial subsidy is not really an issue. Measuring the extent of economic subsidy is difficult, however. The fact that the bank can borrow funds from the Treasury at rates below that at which private commercial banks compete for deposits, and need not compete in equity markets, places the bank in a favored position vis-à-vis private lenders. (See Boyd 1982 for a quantification of the extent of subsidy from this source.) More difficult to quantify are the effects of the bank's exemption from many of the financial regulations imposed on private commercial banks by the Federal Reserve System, Federal Deposit Insurance Corporation, Controller of the Currency, and state financial regulators. Most important are (1) the bank's exemption from reserve requirements, (2) its exemption from standard procedures for writing off bad loans (Boyd reports that loans to the previous governments of Cuba and the People's Republic of China remain on the bank's books), and (3) its exemption from accounting requirements placed on commercial banks. In particular, the bank is not required to delay reporting income from nonperforming loans until it is collected. Boyd (1982) reports that accrued interest on delinquent loans constituted 84.5 percent of the bank's net income in 1980. The criticism of private commercial banks for their accounting treatment of loans to particular LDCs makes these last two points particularly sensitive, and their impact difficult to quantify.

The absence of the equivalent regulatory environment, as well as a lower cost of capital and debt, places Eximbank in a favored position vis-à-vis private commercial banks competing for loans to importers of U.S. products. This enables importers to borrow funds at below-market rates when they buy from the United States. The activity of the Export-Import Bank therefore subsidizes purchases of U.S. goods by foreigners. This is not to argue that the Export-Import Bank should be required to adhere to the same requirements for prudential lending as private banks. As argued later in this paper, various aspects of Eximbank activity make some of these requirements irrelevant. In particular, its explicit backing with the full faith in credit of the U.S. government makes the use of reserves unnecessary (although the recent case of Continental Illinois suggests that the liabilities of large commercial banks also have this backing).

Direct Credits versus Loan Guarantees and Insurance

As well as providing direct credit to foreign buyers of U.S. products, the Export-Import Bank guarantees loans made by private commercial banks and provides insurance for them. The once semipublic and now totally public Foreign Credit Insurance Association (FCIA), in particular, is the organ through which the bank provides loan insurance. Baron (1983) argues that almost all the reasons given in favor of government provision of export credit can be met by government loan guarantees and insurance to private lenders, as well as by direct lending.

Although shifting from direct lending to guaranteeing and insuring private lending eliminates one source of export subsidy, it does not eliminate export subsidization. Indeed, loans covered by FCIA arrangements, unlike direct credits, must be financed privately. Commercial banks must finance these loans at their marginal cost of capital, which will typically exceed the Treasury rate. As long as the government provides insurance and guarantees at below-market rates, however, the risk premium associated with these loans is reduced, and a subsidy remains. The absence of a private source of insurance at the same price as FCIA's implies that a subsidy element is involved. Baron (1983) argues why problems of moral hazard may lead to nonexistence of private insurance markets. He does not indicate how a government insurance and guarantee program will rectify these problems.

Other than to note the different nature of the subsidy involved in Eximbank's provision of loan guarantees and insurance as opposed to its direct credits, I will for the most part ignore the distinction between the two activities, treating them as alternative forms of subsidizing credit to buyers of U.S. goods.

Export Credits as Export Subsidies

U.S. government provision of export credits at below-market rates (and insurance and guarantee of private export credits) subsidizes U.S. exports by providing buyers of U.S. products abroad with a loan that they otherwise could obtain only at a higher rate, or else not at all. On the margin then potential buyers of U.S. exports have an added incentive to buy U.S. products.

Although government-subsidized export credits are a form of export subsidy, they are not the only way in which the government can subsidize exports. In fact the U.S. government has engaged in a number of programs that act to subsidize exports. The Domestic International Sales Corporations (DISCs) (ruled in violation of the GATT prohibition on direct subsidies) provide U.S. firms with the ability to defer tax payments on income from exports. (Hartman 1981 provides other examples in the tax code that treat export income favorably.) The Webb-Pomerene Act allows U.S. firms greater latitude in coordinating overseas sales than U.S. antitrust laws would allow in domestic activity. In assessing the role of Eximbank in providing a subsidy for exports, it is useful to consider how a subsidy via an export credit subsidy differs from other forms of subsidy.

It is useful analytically to use as a reference for comparison a hypothetical uniform *ad valorem* subsidy on the exports of all goods and services from the United States. Such a subsidy would treat all exports on an equal footing, raising the marginal incentive to buy from the United States or to sell abroad by the same percentage for all potential U.S. exports to all buyers in the world. In the nature of export credits, in general, and in the functioning of Eximbank, in particular, is an export subsidy that deviates from a uniform subsidy in both the type of products subsidized and the destination of the exports.

A comparison of the loans provided by Eximbank with those available commercially suggests that the subsidy element is greater for purchases of capital goods than for consumer goods and that the subsidy increases with the average lifetime of the product involved. The reason for this relationship is that export credit practices, both private and public, typically tie the term of the loan to the average lifetime of the product exported. Short-term export credits are available at reasonable rates to most borrowers, whereas the market for medium and long-term credits, most notably to borrowers outside the OECD, is very thin (Baron, 1983, p. 251).[1] Rates charged by Eximbank are relatively insensitive to term, and the bank is willing to provide credits to LDC's with up to five years maturity and, for purchases of aircraft and power generation equipment, much longer. Consequently the incentive provided to buy capital equipment with a relatively long lifetime is much greater than that to buy goods like replacement parts.[2]

Eximbank's policy of meeting the export subsidies provided by the government of competing suppliers generates a second source of bias. Relative to a situation of U.S. laissez faire (but not worldwide laissez faire) U.S. exporters whose competition abroad is more aggressively subsidized themselves receive a greater subsidy. Given the tendency abroad to subsidize high-technology exports, such exports from the United States also receive a greater subsidy.

A third source of bias that has been observed (Feinberg) is that Eximbank lending goes disproportionately to finance exports of U.S. products that are used in export-revenue-generating projects abroad, as compared with projects producing substitutes for imports or non-trade goods. Thus the export of U.S. goods used in such projects is favored over U.S. exports in general.

A fourth source of bias arises from the lower sensitivity of Eximbank lending to market assessment of country risk than the sensitivity of private lenders. While the bank has been criticized for the "regressivity" of its lending terms (charging poor country borrowers more), (Feinberg, 1982, p. 141) its regressivity in this regard is not as great as that of commercial lenders, who in fact ration credit to many LDC borrowers altogether.[3]

In summary, though Eximbank does provide an export subsidy, it does not subsidize U.S. exports uniformly. The subsidy provided to the sale of long-term capital equipment, especially to buyers outside the OECD, is large relative to that provided other sales.

Export Credits and Trade Policy

As argued in the previous section, export credits constitute a form of export subsidy. As such, they are a tool of government commercial policy. In this section I examine some arguments that have been given to justify a policy of subsidizing exports. Since in some cases these topics are covered by other papers in the conference, I will be somewhat cryptic.

Offsetting the Effect of Foreign Governments' Commercial Policy

Statements by officials in the past two administrations and by members of the bank's staff suggest that a major rationale for the operation of Eximbank is the operation of foreign government export financing schemes (e.g., see Baron 1983, Cruse and Whitsitt 1981, Schmidt 1981, Plaut 1980). I quote, for example, the testimony of the Assistant Secretary of the Treasury for International Affairs, Marc Leland, before the U.S. Congress:

> In a less-than-perfect-world, Eximbank still has a role, within available budgetary resources, to (1) support U.S. exporters against foreign predatory financing, and (2) help offset imperfections in the capital markets. Pressure should be maintained on other governments to negotiate reductions in export credit subsidies. Even if there were no foreign export credit competition, there would still be a role for Eximbank to play in facilitating access to adequate long-term financing. (Leland, 1982)

Offsetting the Effect of Foreign Distortions

The argument that foreign export credit subsidies justify U.S. subsidies has two strands. One version of the argument takes the existence of foreign programs as given. Since these foreign export subsidies distort the world allocation of resources, a role emerges for U.S. policy to offset these distortions.

Two objections can be raised. One is that it is not obvious that U.S. export subsidies in any relevant way offset the distortions introduced by the foreign subsidies. They do act to restore the share of U.S. firms in the relevant export market to their laissez-faire level. To the extent that foreign subsidies act to depress the price of U.S. exports, however, the addition of U.S. subsidies lowers the export price even further. In this sense U.S. subsidies move the equilibrium even further away from what would emerge under laissez faire.

The second objection is that even though foreign export subsidies and tariffs move the economy away from its laissez-faire equilibrium, pursuing national commercial policies to restore that equilibrium is not then in the national interest of the United States. Foreign commercial policies that affect the terms of trade of the United States are, from a U.S. perspective, no different from other changes in the world economy that affect world prices, including changes in foreign tastes and technologies. Such changes may work to the benefit or detriment of U.S. welfare, but once they have occurred, there is no point in trying to offset them through commercial policy. For example, subsidizing U.S. oil consumption to maintain the pre-1973 domestic price of oil did not eliminate the welfare cost to the United States of the 1973 oil price hike. (Of course it increased the cost.) Therefore, unless U.S. export credit subsidies are expected to change commercial policies abroad, the effect of these policies on U.S. welfare cannot be offset by a U.S. response.

This is not to say that foreign export credit subsidies benefit the United States, as has sometimes been argued (Schmidt 1981, Plaut 1980). This is only true when the subsidies lower the world prices of commodities that are net imports of the United States. Given the nature of most of the subsidies in existence, this is unlikely to be the case on average. Foreign subsidies are more likely to benefit the U.S. consumers of those commodities less than they harm the U.S. producers.

Achieving a Negotiated Reduction in Subsidies
The second strand of the argument that foreign subsidies justify U.S. subsidies has greater merit. The implication that foreign subsidies will evoke a U.S. response to maintain U.S. market shares removes the incentive for foreign governments to impose these subsidies in the first place. By providing Eximbank with a "war chest" to meet foreign subsidies where they affect U.S. exports adversely, the U.S. government has apparently contributed to the negotiated reduction in 1981 of the subsidy element in such credits (Baron 1983, Leland 1982).

As indicated previously, a reduction in foreign subsidies benefits the United States as a whole only if the subsidies reduce the world price of net exports of the United States. When the affected commodities are net imports, eliminating the foreign subsidy is harmful.

Offsetting the Effect of the U.S. Government's Commercial Policy

Although foreign governments' commercial policy is frequently cited as a justification for U.S. export subsidies, I could find no statement justifying Eximbank operations on the basis of U.S. commercial policy. From the perspective of trade theory, however, this is one of the strongest justifications.

The U.S. government has always pursued a number of policies that reduce U.S. imports below their laissez-faire level. Although GATT negotiations have reduced tariff rates significantly in the postwar era, the use of quotas and "buy American" restrictions on government procurement has been increasing. The view that U.S. protectionism (i.e., protection of U.S. firms from competing imports) will increase in the future seems to represent a consensus among trade policy experts.

Protecting U.S. firms from competing imports draws resources away from the production of exported items toward their use in producing commodities that compete with imports. The effect is to reduce U.S. national income below its potential under laissez faire. At the same time protection from imports raises the price that consumers pay for imports and their domestic competition and lowers the price of commodities that are exported (since lower U.S. imports lower purchases of U.S. exports by foreigners). Export subsidies have the opposite effect of drawing resources out of import-competing sectors toward export sectors and raising the domestic price of exports relative to imports and import substitutes. Export subsidies therefore offset the harmful effects of protection from imports. For any level of protection from imports (assuming the degree of protection is the same against all commodities imported) there exists a uniform level of subsidization of exports that leads to exactly the same allocation of resources that would emerge under laissez faire (administrative costs aside).

The degree of subsidization of U.S. exports achieved on average, through the operation of Eximbank and institutions such as the CCC and DISCs, probably does not approach the average level of protection provided imports. Hence an increase in the average amount of export subsidization is likely to raise welfare over some range. Neither import protection nor export promotion is provided uniformly for all product classes, however. Thus no exact prediction can be made in the absence of a disaggregated quantitative analysis, but there is a strong presumption that as long as import protection remains at its current level, some government export promotion raises national welfare.[4]

Although this argument in favor of a government export subsidy is powerful, it does not arise in policy discussions. Admitting that Exim-bank operations offset the effects of other government policies, however detrimental to U.S. welfare these policies may be, might not increase the support the bank has from national policymakers.

Strengthening the Strategic Position of U.S. Firms in Oligopolistic International Markets

A recent very sophisticated argument in favor of export subsidization has been given by Brander and Spencer (1983) and Spencer and Brander (1983). They demonstrate that the national income of a country with a firm competing with foreign firms in an oligopolistic foreign market can rise as a result of an export subsidy provided to that firm. The result requires that competition in the market be of a quantity-setting nature—that is, each firm sets its output taking the output of its rivals as given.

This is an important argument in favor of government subsidization that merits further investigation. Some limitations on the argument are that (1) if firms are price rather than quantity competitors, an export tax rather than a subsidy is called for (Eaton and Grossman 1983), and (2) if domestic firms compete for a common resource base, a subsidy may be detrimental (Dixit and Grossman 1984).

Finally, from a policy perspective, though the Brander-Spencer argument justifies an export subsidy from the viewpoint of a single country that takes other countries' export subsidies as given, export subsidization is a negative-sum game for all the exporters as a group. A negotiated agreement to desist from subsidizing exports, if universally honored, will yield higher welfare for all exporters than a situation in which each exporting country provides a subsidy. Importers of course gain from the subsidization.

Increasing Returns to Scale and Export Promotion

Until recently formal trade theory has left unexplored the implications of increasing returns to scale in production as a source of gains from trade. This omission is perhaps surprising since one of the first arguments in favor of free trade, the example of the pin factory in the *Wealth of Nations*, pointed to scale economies as the source of the gains from trade: increasing the scale of production leads to an increased division of labor that lowers the average cost of production. In Adam Smith's example the economies are external to the firm but not the national economy as a whole. Increasing the scale of production does not create rents for any single firm but lowers the cost of production, and the price charged, of all firms. Such external economies may emerge, for instance, when firms engage in on-the-job training. The human capital thereby created reduces costs to competing firms when the trained workers seek employment there. The presence of a pool of human capital created by the previous job experience of the local labor force may explain the emergence of regions with concentrated activity in certain high-technology products. Silicon Valley in California and Route 128 in Massachusetts are examples. These regions have a large number of small, competitive firms that seem to benefit from their proximity to their rivals. Presumably the larger scale of production reduces the average costs of all firms involved.

In the presence of economies of scale that are external to the firm but internal to the industry as a whole, the firm's marginal cost of production exceeds the industry marginal cost. In such a situation a perfectly competitive industry will produce less than the socially optimal level of output.

The implications of increasing returns to scale of this type for international trade have been examined by Kemp and Negishi (1969), Eaton and Panagariya (1979), and Panagariya (1980). A major implication of these papers is that countries can especially benefit from trade when such trade increases the output of industries in which economies of scale are most significant.

Explanations of the gains from trade based on an assumption of constant returns to scale imply that when competitive conditions prevail, gains from trade only accrue when trading parties are fundamentally different in terms of their endowments of factors of production, the technologies available to them, or the preferences of their consumers. In the presence of scale economies, however, gains from trade may emerge even when the two trading parties are identical in these respects. The benefits from trade may not be shared symmetrically, however, with the country exporting the commodities whose production involves greater scale economies typically benefiting more.

The presence of economies of scale that are external to the firm is therefore a reason to subsidize exports from industries with significant external economies of scale. Such subsidies are more likely to yield an outcome in which the home country specializes in the production of these commodities, thereby reaping greater benefits from trade. It is also true, however, that a direct production subsidy is a superior policy to an export subsidy to correct the distortion created by external scale economies.

Export Credits and the U.S. Gains from Trade

As discussed in the previous section, Eximbank lending activity has typically involved credits for the purchase abroad of capital goods produced in the United States. As a consequence the items financed are not consumed abroad but add to foreign production capacity, particularly in export sectors (Feinberg 1982, p. 79). To the extent that Eximbank activity results in a net addition to foreign capacity in any particular sector, it affects the world prices of the items produced by that sector. Through this channel Eximbank lending has additional consequences for U.S. welfare. For example, if an Eximbank loan leads to the eventual reduction in the world price of a commodity which the United States imports on net, the United States reaps a net benefit over and above the return on the loan itself—that is, the loan generates a positive externality to the United States through an improved terms of trade. Conversely, if the product is a net export of the United States, a negative externality is associated with the loan.

Affecting the terms of trade of the United States through changes in foreign production capacity has never been a major goal of Eximbank. Nevertheless, in some cases the consequences of Eximbank lending for U.S. terms of trade seem to have influenced decisions on particular loans. Feinberg (1982, p. 74) indicates that loans to Algeria in the early 1970s were targeted toward expanding that country's energy exports. Clearly such an expansion could benefit the United States by driving down the world price of energy products. In other cases Eximbank loans have been denied because of their terms-of-trade implications, not because the overall welfare consequences would be negative but because the loan would adversely affect production in a U.S. industry already competing with imports. Feinberg (1982, p. 72) cites the denial of a loan to Trinidad and Tobago for a steel plant as such a case, providing an example of "lack of export promotion as import protection."

Government Export Credits and Imperfect International Capital Markets

As suggested by the statement of Assistant Secretary of the Treasury Leland quoted earlier, international capital market imperfections, as well as the "predatory" export financing of foreign governments, are reasons for the current administration's support of Eximbank. Capital market imperfections can indeed provide a rationale for government participation in the international lending. To design the appropriate policy response, however, the nature of the imperfections must be identified. Unfortunately Assistant Secretary Leland's remarks provide no indication of administration thinking on this issue.

Perfect capital mobility between two countries is attained when their marginal product of capital, adjusted from risks that are exogenous to the actions of agents in the two countries, are equal. Baron's study of Eximbank suggests how the traditional insurance problems of moral hazard and adverse selection can lead to the underprovision of credit by private lenders in a country where the marginal product of capital is low to borrowers in a country where its marginal product is high. First, if lenders are themselves unwilling to take on the risk of nonrepayment, their purchase of insurance from other parties might increase the likelihood of default. Since foreign borrowers would presumably know that their creditors' losses would be covered by insurance, they would anticipate less severe retaliation from their creditors in the event of default and have less incentive to repay. Insurers of bank loans, in other words, reduce the incentive of banks to seek repayment of loans and to retaliate against borrowers.

This problem will lead to the underprovision of such insurance, forcing individual private lenders to assume more than the optimal risk of default, giving rise to a problem of moral hazard. The adverse selection problem arises because private lenders may have inadequate information about potential borrowers' characteristics that may be important determinants of their incentive to repay the loan. If banks cannot discriminate between foreign borrowers in low- and high-risk categories, a disproportionate share of bank customers will be in the high-risk category (i.e., those with a relatively low incentive to repay). Aware that offers of loans will draw from such a group disproportionately, lenders will not offer to make such loans to the extent that is optimal.

Baron argues that imperfections of these forms may justify government insurance and guarantees of private loans, but not direct credits. He does not suggest why government participation is justified on the basis of these imperfections. In the case of adverse selection, in particular, it is not clear why insurers would not extract the same penalty in the event of default as would the direct lender. The consequences of higher insurance fees in the future would worsen the terms on which a borrower could obtain credit later if he should default currently. At the same time the problems Baron points to arise, in principle, with equal frequency in domestic capital markets. They do not, by themselves, justify a separate government policy toward lending abroad.

Foreign Lending and the Risk of Default

If the penalty anticipated by a borrower in the event of his default on a loan were sufficiently high, the risk of default would never arise. Borrowers would only undertake financial transactions that would provide them the resources to make repayment with certainty and would always have the incentive to make such repayments. If such penalties were imposed universally and all information shared symmetrically, all contracts would be honored and, through the operation of insurance and loan markets free of default, perfect capital mobility would result.

If the penalty incumbent on default is not sufficiently great, however, capital mobility will be imperfect: some agents may not have any incentive to repay loans of the size necessary to equate their own marginal product of capital with the interest rate at which others would be willing to lend if repayment were assured. Such loans will not be forthcoming. Both potential lenders and borrowers will find themselves in a situation less desirable than one where lending could take place and repayment be assured. The absence of a sufficiently high penalty incumbent on default acts to everyone's detriment.

The cost of default is insufficient, both domestically and internationally, to eliminate default risk from financial markets. Nevertheless, differences in the consequences of default domestically and internationally imply significantly greater risks in lending to borrowers in some foreign countries, at least, than in lending to domestic borrowers.

When a lender finds a domestic borrower in default he has recourse to a local police authority to aid him in seeking repayment of the loan. If the loan is secured, the lender can use the police power of the state to seize control of the asset used as security. In the case of unsecured loans the creditor can force the borrower into bankruptcy. Most or all of the borrower's assets are then divided among the creditors.

Recourse to a government-enforced transfer of assets from the debtor to the creditor in the event of default increases the safety of domestic loans for two reasons. First, the debtor's assets, less the cost of the bankruptcy proceeding, set a lower bound on the value of debt. Second, the borrower's loss of his assets in the event of default constitutes a penalty that reduces the incentive to default in the first place.

The threat of bankruptcy proceedings has had important implications for the operation of domestic credit markets. A borrower whose tangible assets exceed the value of his debts is deemed "creditworthy." If the loan is secured (and if the loan is used for the purchase of a commodity, that commodity frequently is used as security), the term of the loan is usually matched to the expected lifetime of the product. In the event of default the value of the asset used as security will approximate the value of the debt at any period. Although the cost of the bankruptcy proceeding acts as an impediment to lending, there is usually a presumption that the creditor can draw on the police power of the state to transfer the debtor's assets to him if default should occur.

There is no difference involved in making loans to foreign borrowers when those borrowers have assets in the lender's country that provide appropriate security. For the case of foreign borrowers in developed countries this is typically the case. For many borrowers, however, especially those in developing countries where the marginal product of capital is high, nationally owned assets abroad may be insignificant.

If the foreign borrower cannot provide the lender with an asset located within the lender's borders as security, the lender must rely on the borrower's government to enforce repayment and to impose any penalty on the borrower. In the case of commercial loans (to private borrowers abroad) the borrower's government may not treat the lender as sympathetically as his own government would. In many cases the loans in question have the full faith in credit of the borrower's government itself (sovereign loans), in which case the borrower must rely on the government's incentive to repay. Anticipating the weakness of this incentive, private lenders are less likely to provide loans initially. Capital mobility becomes increasingly imperfect as the borrowing country's incentive to repay diminishes.

Since repayment of a loan reduces a borrowing country's current national income, it is perhaps surprising that foreign governments ever repay sovereign loans or enforce repayment of commercial loans. It is equally paradoxical that private lenders make loans to foreign borrowers in view of the incentive for foreign governments not to repay. In fact repayment of such loans frequently occurs, and lenders have profitably made foreign loans (although to some countries in amounts that are far less than what would be required to equate the marginal product of capital across borders). Clearly foreign governments have some incentive to repay loans from abroad. An assessment of the riskiness of foreign loans and the extent of international capital market imperfection requires an understanding of what these incentives are.

Incentives to Repay: The Self-Regulation of the System

Eaton and Gersovitz (1981a, 1983) discuss the incentive that a government has to repay its debts to foreigners. They identify the major consequence of a failure to honor debt-service obligations as the country's exclusion from participation in international capital markets in the future: the government's incentive to maintain the country's reputation as a borrower provides a reason to repay loans in the absence of a legal mechanism to enforce repayment or the transfer of assets.

The strength of this incentive depends on the benefit to the nation of maintaining access to capital markets, which may vary significantly from country to country. Eaton and Gersovitz (1981b) suggest four reasons why a government may wish to maintain its access to international capital markets. One is to smooth consumption: a country may have highly cyclical sources of income yet wish to spread its expenditures across periods. Borrowing in international capital markets provides a means of divorcing current income from current expenditure. Loss of creditworthiness may require a much more uneven expenditure pattern. Second, a country may anticipate future investment opportunities can best be exploited if the country has access to foreign capital. Loss of access to foreign loans may delay or prohibit exploitation of the investment opportunity. Third, a country may wish to maintain its creditworthiness to ease the adjustment to sudden, unanticipated drops in its income. Foreign borrowing may allow the country to complete investment projects that otherwise might have had to be abandoned. Fourth, a country may find that access to foreign capital significantly reduces transactions costs involved in international trade. After U.S. banks declared Iran to be in default in 1979, its exclusion from international capital markets seemed to increase the cost of international transactions considerably.

Maintaining access to international capital markets provides the governments of borrowing countries a strong incentive to avoid default on their own debt and to ensure that foreign lenders to nationals of the country receive satisfactory treatment in the country's legal system. The strength of these incentives in one case is described by Diaz-Alejandro (1984). When a number of Chilean private banks declared bankruptcy in 1982, many had large outstanding debts to U.S. banks. As part of its policy of promoting a laissez-faire financial system, the Chilean government explicitly had not guaranteed these debts. Nevertheless, when faced with the threat of an embargo on all lending to Chile, the government chose to assume these debt obligations.

Although loss of access to foreign sources of capital is a significant cost of defaulting, it does not outweigh the benefit of repudiating a debt of an arbitrarily large amount. At some point the cost of repaying exceeds the cost of the embargo. Lenders will provide loans only up to a point at which the borrower is reasonably likely to find it in his interest to repay. This amount may be less than the amount necessary to equate the marginal product of capital between the lender and borrower countries. The country will then find itself rationed in the market for loans.

For private sanctions against countries in default to provide an effective incentive to maintain their debt-service obligations requires that private lenders as a group be prepared to impose an embargo. An embargo imposed by a single lender or a group of lenders in a particular country would have little effect if the borrowing country could turn to another lender for funds. A coordinated embargo could be effected by explicit arrangement as it is when loans are arranged through consortia. A default against one borrower is treated as a default against other borrowers, and all are required to impose an embargo. The role of reputation in international capital markets may provide a more subtle and less explicit means of imposing an embargo. Lenders perceive borrowers who have defaulted in the past as more likely to default on subsequent loans. The exclusion of many less developed countries from international bond markets in the postwar era probably reflects the markets' memory of the substantial defaults by these borrowers in the 1930s.

Incentives to Repay: The Role of Public Policy

By imposing a credit embargo on foreign countries in default, private lenders have considerable leverage to ensure that their loans are repaid. Nevertheless, there is considerable scope for policies on the part of lender-country governments to affect the functioning of the system.

At one extreme governments can impose their police power in an extraterritorial manner to ensure that loan commitments are maintained. Strange (1979) documents cases of the armed forces of lender countries seizing customs houses in debtor countries to extract revenue to repay loans. If private lenders can depend on the extension of their government's police jurisdiction over the borrower's territory, foreign loans pose no greater likelihood of default than domestic loans.

Domestic political attitudes and foreign diplomatic constraints now make the use of government military force to extract repayment from foreign debtors unlikely. Nevertheless, a role remains for government policy in lender countries to maintain capital mobility. Eaton and Gersovitz (1981b) describe a set of U.S. laws that affect the conduct of U.S. policy toward countries that have expropriated property owned by U.S. nationals or repudiated contracts with U.S. nationals.[5]

Such legislation serves the purpose of increasing the penalty of default to a foreign borrower. Private lenders can thereby make larger loans with reduced probability of default, to the benefit of both borrowers and lenders. Legislating sanctions, rather than relying on discretionary policies to penalize default, reduce the likelihood that past unpaid debt will be viewed as a bygone in the formulation of policy. By committing itself to a set of rules, the government is less likely to find enforcement after the fact not worth the effort.

A particular role that Eximbank plays is as a U.S. government participant in the community of lenders to overseas borrowers. Because of the long-term commitment of Eximbank to foreign lending, loss of access to Eximbank credit may seem an especially stiff penalty for a borrower contemplating default. At the same time, in contrast with private banks with large domestic loan markets, Eximbank relies on the functioning of international capital markets with adequate incentives for borrowers to repay for its future livelihood. Its decisions may consequently reflect a greater concern for the long-term functioning of the system than those of private lenders who may regard their involvement in foreign lending as a "one-night stand." A danger, from the perspective of the functioning of the rules of the system, is that Eximbank decisions may become unduly influenced by foreign policy considerations of the U.S. government. This problem is discussed later.

From its inception Eximbank policy has played a role in penalizing countries in default on loans to private creditors. The consummation of its founding purpose, financing trade with the Soviet Union, was delayed more than forty years because of the outstanding unpaid debt of the Czarist government (Feinberg 1982, p. 66).

Although Eximbank is involved in the execution of U.S. government policies that affect the functioning of international capital markets, its role has been secondary to that of the International Monetary Fund. This role is appropriate for at least two reasons. The first is that the total resources of the IMF are significantly greater. The second is that borrowing as well as lending countries play a role in formulating IMF policy. Rules arrived at through joint negotiations of borrowers and lenders probably have greater credibility than those unilaterally imposed by lender country governments.

Delinking the Domestic Financial System from International Capital Markets

The decision of the Federal Deposit Insurance Corporation to assume control of the Continental Illinois Bank to rescue it from bankruptcy reveals a desire on the part of the U.S. government, even under an administration avowing laissez-faire policies, to avoid the failure of a large U.S. bank. Government intervention reflects a government perception that the social cost of bankruptcy exceeds the private cost. Two explanations for the external effect of a bankruptcy are (1) the public loss through FDIC insurance and (2) the public good nature of a relatively default-free deposit system. This paper does not attempt to evaluate these arguments but to discuss their implications for foreign lending.

International loans reportedly had nothing to do with Continental Illinois' troubles, but concern over the quality of the loans of other major banks to foreign borrowers has raised fears that the situation could repeat itself, this time with foreign loans the source of the problem. The government, through the Controller of the Currency, does in fact place limits on individual bank exposure to foreign borrowers, with the purpose of reducing the risk of bankruptcy. To the extent that foreign lending increases the fragility of the domestic banking system, a policy of limiting private bank lending abroad may constitute an appropriate policy response.

In this context a role could emerge for institutions whose liabilities are not directly tied to the U.S. financial system to make foreign loans or to guarantee such loans. The loans these institutions would make could be advantageous from both the borrower's and lender's perspective in terms of their risk and return, but the risk associated with the loans would not then impinge on the functioning of the U.S. banking system. Ideally such institutions would rely on equity finance. In their absence a government-backed institution could assume this role. Eximbank, with the full faith in credit of the U.S. government, would be an example.

The future role of the U.S. government in domestic banking activity is very uncertain. Furthermore, given the brief period in which U.S. banks have been heavily committed in overseas markets, little can be said about the implications of foreign lending for the long-term functioning of the system. Arguments in favor of alternative institutional arrangements for financing loans to foreign borrowers must be highly speculative.

Panics and the Lender of Last Resort

A recent paper by Cooper and Sachs (1984) provides an example in which lending by any single lender to a particular borrower can benefit other lenders by reducing the borrower's likelihood of default. In this context a role can emerge for a government institution to lend to foreign borrowers or to guarantee private lending to forestall their default.

Although this example does suggest a role for government participation in international lending, it suggests also the potential danger with such participation. The government could play the role of the final investor in a Ponzi scheme, buying up bad debts from private commercial banks.

The specific facilities set up in 1983 for lending to Brazil and Mexico, discussed in the following section, can be interpreted as part of a government program to avert a financial crisis. This apparently is not the first time that Eximbank has played such a role. Feinberg (1982, p. 113) reports:

In earlier times, Exim was willing to risk fresh funds to provide liquidity to a bankrupt country, permitting it to make hard-currency payments to foreign traders and investors. In frank statements in its annual reports, Exim admitted lending for this purpose to Argentina and Brazil in the early 1950s. "In May 1950, the Bank authorized a credit of $125 million to a consortium of Argentine banks to assist Argentina in the liquidation of past-due dollar obligations to United States commercial creditors both on private and governmental account" (Eximbank, *Semi-Annual Report for the Period January–June 1950*, 3). And again: "A credit of $300 million to Brazil was authorized in 1953 to assist that country in liquidating its past-due dollar accounts in order that Brazil might place its commercial transactions on a current basis" (Eximbank, *Semi-Annual Report for the Period January–June 1953*, 1). The Bank has since ceased extending large general lines of credit, however, and its individual loans are of insufficient magnitude, given today's levels of accumulated indebtedness, to save most countries in danger of going under.

Feinberg suggests that more recent Eximbank practice has been to follow the opinion of commercial lenders rather than to offset trends in commercial lending:

An example of the herd instinct is the denial of the Yugoslav loans, which noted that because private lenders were skeptical of the country's medium-term prospects, private loans might not be forthcoming and so balance-of-payments problems could develop. Exim's own restraint could help turn this opinion into a self-fulfilling prophecy (Feinberg 1982, p. 83).

Once again the Eximbank is involved in lending to avert a liquidity crisis in Latin America. The next section discusses its ability, as an official export credit agency, to perform in this role.

The Export-Import Bank and the Current Debt Crisis

In recent congressional testimony Assistant Secretary of the Treasury Marc Leland outlined the role that Eximbank is to play in the administration's general strategy to alleviate the debt repayment problems of two Latin American borrowers from U.S. private commercial banks.

The administration's overall plan has five components: (1) to provide short-term relief with funds from the Treasury and the Federal Reserve, (2) to provide more resources to developing countries on a multilateral longer-term basis through appropriations to the International Monetary Fund, (3) to encourage commercial banks to make new loans to the countries in question, (4) to provide more funds to agencies involved in bilateral lending (in particular, Eximbank) for export credits to these countries, and (5) to encourage reduced expenditures in the borrowing countries.

As Eximbank's part of the program, special facilities are being established to provide medium-term guarantees and short- and medium-term insurance on export credits to Brazil (for up to $1.5 billion) and Mexico (for up to $.5 billion). Availability of the facilities is contingent on the borrower's compliance with its IMF Extended Fund Facility, commercial banks having financed more loans for the recipient, and other creditor countries having extended further credit.

The administration's involvement of Eximbank in its overall debt-relief program represents a departure from the bank's previous role as an agency to advance U.S. exports. One explicit motivation for Eximbank's involvement is the importance of Brazil and Mexico for U.S. exports. Nevertheless, the primary reason for the special facilities is not to increase the value of U.S. exports to these countries but rather to ensure the overall stability of the world financial system. One indication that this is the overriding purpose is the larger size of the facility extended to Brazil, the larger debtor, even though Mexico is a more significant importer of U.S. products.

Eximbank had been involved in more general development lending in the early postwar era (McKitterick and Middleton 1972) but retreated from this role in deference to the World Bank, aiming its activity much more at the expansion of U.S. exports rather than the economic development of its borrowers. Despite Eximbank's traditional mandated role as a promoter of U.S. exports, the special facilities do increase the financial resources available to the countries in question and will reduce the exposure of the U.S. commercial banking system to the risk of default of these countries.

To a major degree the interests of the United States in general and U.S. exporters coincide, so the question of motivation is irrelevant. Nevertheless, there are several aspects of the export credits that Eximbank traditionally provides, guarantees, or insures that are not appropriate for the overall purpose of the special facilities—

stabilizing the situation in world financial markets and insulating the U.S. banking system from the disruption of a major international default. Other aspects of Eximbank lending, however, are ideally suited for these purposes.

Eximbank Activity and the Doctrine of Additionality

A major criterion for Eximbank involvement in direct lending has been the impact it would have on aggregate U.S. exports. According to this doctrine Eximbank should not be financing loans for exports that would have been purchased in the absence of Eximbank funding.

For the purpose of overall financial stabilization, a loan that increases the total imports of a borrower on a dollar-for-dollar basis does nothing to alleviate its current payments crisis.[6] Similarly Eximbank lending that simply leads to the substitution of a U.S. export for a foreign one by matching a foreign financial offer does not relieve the debt burden either. For the special facilities to provide relief from balance-of-payments difficulties requires that some net reduction in the country's demand for foreign exchange be achieved, which works against the additionality criterion. Since the special facilities involve guarantees and insurance rather than direct lending, the additionality criterion will not be applied. The principle should be remembered for future Eximbank activity however.

Eximbank Lending and the Term Structure of Debt

Besides achieving a reduction of the subsidy element in government-provided export credit, the new International Agreement on Export Credits, which went into effect in October 1983, also shortened the terms at which government export credit is available (U.S. Treasury 1982). Eximbank is the primary lending agency affected, since it had been engaged in supporting long-term export credits.

Although the reduction in the subsidy element is laudable, the reduction in term structure, for the purpose of international financial stability, is not. The lack of long-term borrowing options available to many LDCs is believed by many observers to constitute a source of the crisis. A major contribution of the United States at this point would be the provision of loans on a longer-term basis.

As discussed in the previous section, a frequent practice in lending to finance the purchase of a particular capital item is to match the terms of the loan with the flow of payments that the item is expected to generate. This practice is sensible when, in the event of default, the lender assumes control of the asset. The effect of the default on the lender's net worth is thereby minimized. In many cases a default on Eximbank's loans does lead to the transfer of the item financed to the bank. The loans to Laker Airlines to finance purchases of DC-10s are an example. A transfer requires, however, that the bank have access to a legal system that is likely to confiscate the item from the borrower. In the case of sovereign loans, or loans made with the full faith in credit of a foreign government, the transfer to the bank of the item financed in the event of default is unlikely. Tying the term of the export credit to the nature of the exported item in this case achieves no particular purpose. The likelihood of repayment of the loan depends on the foreign government's overall financial situation at the time of repayment, and its willingness to repay, which bear insignificant relation to a particular U.S. export item.

Aside from secured loans, commercial lenders perceive long-term lending to sovereign borrowers as riskier than short-term lending. Papers by Sachs and Cohen (1984) and Kletzer (1984) suggest how this view is justified by the inability to enforce seniority of claims in the case of sovereign lending. Long-term lenders may find their assets diluted by subsequent short-term borrowing on the part of the debtor. Some official export credit agencies have apparently adopted the same view. Feinberg (1982, p. 73) reports that in the mid-1970s Pakistan had been declared "off cover" (ineligible) for long-term loans by several members of the Berne Union.

The bias against long-term lending has been exacerbated by U.S. public policy. The Voluntary Foreign Credit Restraint (VFCR) Program in effect from 1965 to 1974 placed an "especially restrictive" ceiling on long-term loans other than export credits (Feinberg 1982, p. 45). It is interesting to speculate to what extent this program, introduced for U.S. balance-of-payments considerations, biased private commercial lending away from long-term lending.

Export Credits and Country Risk Analysis

Current Eximbank practice in assessing country risk and assigning exposure limits consciously mirrors that of private commercial banks. Clearly the special facilities, by their very nature, constitute a departure from this practice. Although the special facilities will play a role in alleviating the liquidity problems of Brazil and Mexico, it is worth examining the relevance of standard commercial practice for Eximbank's day-to-day lending.

In assessing the solvency of a sovereign borrower, notions of creditworthiness applicable in a domestic context may not be useful. For example, the value of the borrower's assets is of little relevance when the borrower is unwilling to repay the loan. Similarly, securing a loan with an export item is pointless if, in the event of default, the lender has no method of gaining access to the secured item.

The practice of securing loans with escrow accounts abroad provides some reduction in risk. The item being financed may be used in an activity that earns revenue in a country where the creditor has access to legal recourse in the event of default. The creditor can insist that a share of those earnings be directed into an escrow account to be transferred to the lender if default occurs. A decision to default on the loan will thereby reduce the value of the exported item by eliminating its use for production of exports to a particular market.[7]

An Eximbank loan decision that may have applied criteria relevant for domestic loans inappropriately to a sovereign loan concerns Pakistan in 1976. In April of that year a loan to a government corporation to purchase drilling equipment for gas and oil was denied because the project was speculative and the fuels used for import substitution (Feinberg 1982, p. 73). The next month a loan was approved for the purchase of a McDonnell-Douglas DC-10-30 for the national airline: "The airline was termed profitable and a foreign-exchange saver" (Feinberg 1982, p. 73). In lending to a sovereign borrower, the profitability of the particular project in question is irrelevant for the safety of the loan. All loans with the full faith in credit of the borrowing government are as safe as the government's willingness to repay the loan. The reason for the decision may not have been Eximbank's views on the profitability of the two projects but the mortgage they had obtained on the aircraft. In the event of a default Eximbank could seize the aircraft at many foreign airports. Default would significantly limit the value of the airplane to the Pakistani government.

Eximbank Activity and Fixed versus Floating Interest Rates

In three respects then current Eximbank procedures are not ideally suited to meet the borrowing needs of the large debtor countries. The doctrine of additionality, the short-term of the debt, and the general nature of Eximbank country risk analysis are inappropriate to the task of lending to avert a deterioration in the payments situation of the large borrowers. In other respects, however, Eximbank lending has been more suited to the situation of these countries than lending by commercial banks.

Eximbank's reliance on fixed interest loans has reduced the payment problems facing its borrowers. Most commercial bank lending to sovereign borrowers has been on a floating rate basis. Borrowers negotiate a markup above the London Interbank Offer Rate (LIBOR). Their debt service obligations therefore fluctuate with movements in this rate. The significant rise in the level of real interest rates generally in the last few years has consequently added substantially to the debt service obligations of large debtor countries even in the absence of additional borrowing.

The use of floating rate loans is well suited to periods in which the primary source of interest rate fluctuations is variation in inflationary expectations. When changes in nominal rates primarily reflect changes in inflationary expectations, short-term real interest rates (the difference between nominal rates and expected inflation) are relatively stable. Loan contracts specifying a fixed nominal rate over a long period of time subject both the borrower and lender to the risk that the inflation rate will rise (to the benefit of the borrower and detriment of the lender) or fall (with the reverse effect). Tying the interest rate to short-term interest rates, whose movement reflects changes in inflation, removes the risk for both parties. The real rate of interest on the loan is stabilized. Bankers' experience with unanticipated changes in inflation in the early 1970s probably contributed to the widespread use of floating rate loans in that period.

More recently, however, the real rate of interest itself has become more unpredictable. No contract can eliminate the risk of unanticipated changes in real rates to both borrowers and lenders. When the nominal rate is fixed, lenders absorb the risk, whereas with a floating rate loan, the risk is passed on to the borrower. By specifying loan contracts with a floating rate, commercial banks shed the risk that the interest rate on their liabilities (largely short term) would rise above the rate on their longer-term assets. In doing so, however, they exposed their borrowers to the risk of a substantially increased real interest rate on their loan. Term structure risk was traded in for default risk.

Eximbank lending has traditionally been on a fixed rate basis. The guarantees and insurance to be provided under the special facilities for Brazil and Mexico will have a greater stabilizing effect if they encourage fixed-rate lending. Ideally loan contracts would fix a real interest rate directly by tying the nominal interest rate to a price index rather than to a short-term rate. Such contracts have so far proved cumbersome and have met with little success, however.

Eximbank Activity and Direct Foreign Investment

In the 1970s bank lending far exceeded direct foreign investment (DFI) as the channel through which private transfers of capital to developing countries occurred. By financing development through debt rather than equity, developing countries absorbed the major risks associated with development. DFI would have transferred these risks abroad. Replacing direct loans with DFI will substantially reduce the risks facing developing countries in the future.

Eximbank plays two roles in furthering DFI. First, developed-country-based multinational corporations, as well as developing countries directly, have been major recipients of Eximbank loans. Consequently Eximbank has indirectly subsidized U.S. direct foreign investment abroad as well as U.S. exports (Feinberg 1982, ch. 8).

A second means by which Eximbank furthers DFI is in penalizing countries that have expropriated U.S. property. Peru, for example, was excluded from Eximbank lending during disputes over U.S. property in that country. The withholding of U.S. loans undoubtedly encouraged Peru ultimately to settle these disputes to the satisfaction of U.S. investors. Commercial bank lending, in contrast, remained available to Peru during the dispute. While protecting themselves against default through cross-default clauses, commercial banks do little to aid multinationals by imposing credit embargoes against expropriating countries.

By withholding its loans to countries that expropriate U.S. property, Eximbank encourages U.S. direct foreign investment. In this way a greater share of the risks of development investment can be redistributed to capital markets in developed countries.

The Export-Import Bank and U.S. Diplomatic Goals

An important role for Eximbank is furthering U.S. foreign policy objectives by providing financial incentives to support U.S. policies.

Withholding Eximbank loans can penalize foreign countries for pursuing policies that adversely affect U.S. interests or violate human rights. Feinberg (1982, p. 66) suggests that a loan to Algeria in 1974 was offered in part to bring that country closer to the U.S. sphere of influence. More recently the imposition of martial law in Poland provoked a U.S. embargo on Eximbank lending to that country. The embargo apparently had some success in alleviating the situation.

Eximbank does not always act to further overall U.S. objectives. In order to protect the solvency of a project it has financed, Eximbank has been known to impose conditions that are otherwise inconsistent with U.S. policy. An Eximbank loan to Iran for the construction of a synthetic fiber plant in 1976 was conditional, in part, on Iran's restriction of textile imports. Such a condition is inconsistent with the overall U.S. objective of encouraging free trade, especially among developing countries.

Conclusion

The activities of the Export-Import Bank subsidize U.S. exports, increase the flow of capital to developing countries, and provide the U.S. government with additional leverage to influence the policies of foreign governments. The most persuasive economic arguments for subsidizing exports are that (1) subsidies provide the U.S. government leverage in achieving a negotiated reduction in export subsidies worldwide and (2) export subsidies offset the distortions caused by U.S. protection from imports. The first justification would suggest as the appropriate response export subsidies for those products whose export is most subsidized abroad. The second would call for subsidization of those exports most adversely affected by import protection, or at least a uniform *ad valorem* subsidy on all exports. Eximbank practice satisfies the first criterion much more than the second.

Imperfections in international capital markets may justify the involvement of the U.S. government in foreign lending. The lack of a supranational agency to enforce contracts between parties in different countries is the primary source of market distortion. Arguments in favor of government involvement are not as straightforward and must be considered as much more tentative. The major arguments in favor of a government-sponsored agency to lend abroad are (1) the potential for a government lender to impose more severe sanctions on nations in default to U.S. lenders, (2) the danger that lending by commercial banks will expose the U.S. domestic banking system to an excessive risk of disruption due to overseas defaults, and (3) the role of a government agency as an international lender of last resort. None of these arguments justify U.S. government provision, insurance, or guarantees of export credits per se but U.S. government involvement in sovereign lending in general. Identifying the appropriate role for Eximbank in stabilizing domestic and international financial markets must await the outcome of the current restructuring of U.S. bank regulatory policy. It is important, however, that government policy be formulated with the objective of establishing and maintaining rules of behavior for the future operation of the international financial system. Policies designed with the sole objective of alleviating the current crisis invite another one.

Notes

1. Sachs and Cohen (1984) and Kletzer (1984) provide theoretical explanations for the unavailability of medium- and long-term loans to foreign borrowers.

2. The bias against consumer goods implicit in Eximbank's operation is offset, for the case of U.S. agricultural products, by the Commodity Credit Corporation (CCC), a U.S. agency that provides export credits to foreign purchasers of U.S. agricultural products.

3. Eaton and Gersovitz (1981a) provide some econometric evidence that private commercial banks rationed loans to developing countries in 1970 and 1974.

4. This argument is a consequence of what is known in trade theory as the Lerner symmetry theorem. Abba Lerner (1936) demonstrated that the general equilibrium effect of a uniform, across-the-board export tax is the same as that of a uniform, across-the-board tariff on imports. An export subsidy is therefore equivalent to an import subsidy, which offsets the effect of a tariff.

5. Such countries are prohibited from receiving foreign aid from the U.S. government and are ineligible for the application of the generalized system of preferences. U.S. representatives to the World Bank, Inter-American Development Bank, and Asian Development Bank are required to vote against loans to such countries. Since 1934 it has been a criminal offense for a U.S. national to lend to a country in default on a loan to the U.S. government. The Hickenlooper Amendment to the Foreign Assistance Act guarantees any claimant for property confiscated abroad the right to have his case considered on "principles of international law" rather than "state doctrine."

6. If such loans finance capital investment projects that add significantly to the country's future payments capacity, they may alleviate a future crisis, however.

7. Feinberg (1982, p. 74) reports that a bias exists in Eximbank loans toward investing in projects that earn export revenue, as opposed to serving the domestic market. This bias may be justified on the grounds that the bank has a greater chance to recoup the loss and to punish default by attaching the export revenue generated by these projects.

References

Baron, David P. 1983. *The Export-Import Bank.* New York: Academic Press.

Boyd, John H. 1982. "Eximbank Lending: A Federal Program That Costs Too Much." *Federal Reserve Bank of Minneapolis Quarterly Review* 6 (Winter):1–17.

Brander, James A., and Barbara J. Spencer. 1983. "Strategic Commitment with R&D: The Symmetric Case." *Bell Journal of Economics* 14 (Spring):225–235.

Cooper, Richard N., and Jeffrey D. Sachs. 1984. "Borrowing Abroad: The Debtor's Perspective." National Bureau of Economic Research Working Paper No. 1427 (August).

Cruse, Jim, and Sue Whitsitt. 1981. "Eximbank in the 1980's." Personal paper. Eximbank (April).

Diaz-Alejandro, Carlos F. 1984. "Good-Bye Financial Repression, Hello Financial Crash." *Journal of Development Economics,* forthcoming.

Dixit, Avinash, and Gene M. Grossman. 1984. "Targeted Export Promotion with Several Oligopolistic Industries." Woodrow Wilson School Discussion Papers in Economics No. 71. Princeton University.

Eaton, Jonathan, and Mark Gersovitz. 1981a. "Debt with Potential Repudiation: Theoretical and Empirical Analysis." *Review of Economic Studies* 48 (April):289–309.

Eaton, Jonathan, and Mark Gersovitz. 1981b. "Poor Country Borrowing in Private Financial Markets and the Repudiation Issue." *Princeton Studies in International Finance,* No. 47 (June).

Eaton, Jonathan, and Mark Gersovitz. 1983. "Country Risk: Economic Aspects." In Richard J. Herring, ed., *Managing International Risk.* Cambridge, England: Cambridge University Press.

Eaton, Jonathan, and Gene M. Grossman. 1983. "Optimal Trade and Industrial Policy under Oligopoly." National Bureau of Economic Research Working Paper No. 1236 (November).

Eaton, Jonathan, and Arvind Panagariya. 1979. "Gains from Trade under Variable Returns to Scale, Commodity Taxation, Tariffs and Factor Market Distortions." *Journal of International Economics* 9 (November):481–501.

Feinberg, Richard E. 1982. *Subsidizing Success: The Export-Import Bank in the U.S. Economy*. Cambridge, England: Cambridge University Press.

Hartman, David. 1981. "Tax Policy and Foreign Direct Investment." National Bureau of Economic Research Working Paper No. 689 (June).

Kemp, Murray C., and Takashi Negishi. 1970. "Variable Returns to Scale, Commodity Taxes, Factor Market Distortions and their Implications for Trade Gains." *Swedish Journal of Economics* 73 (1):1–11.

Kletzer, Kenneth M. 1984. "Asymmetries of Information and LDC Borrowing with Sovereign Risk." *Economic Journal* 94 (June):287–307.

Leland, Marc E. 1982. Statement before the Subcommittee on International Finance and Monetary Policy, Committee on Banking, Housing and Urban Affairs, United States Senate. September 16.

Lerner, Abba P. 1936. "The Symmetry between Import and Export Taxes." *Economica* 3 (August):306–313.

McKitterick, Nathaniel, and B. Jenkins Middleton. 1972. "The Bankers of the Rich and the Bankers of the Poor." *Overseas Development Council Monograph*, No. 6.

Panagariya, Arvind. 1980. "Variable Returns to Scale in General Equilibrium Theory Once Again." *Journal of International Economics* 10 (November):499–526.

Plaut, Stephen E. 1980. "Export-Import Follies." *Fortune* 102 (August 25):74–77.

Sachs, Jeffrey, and David Cohen. 1984. "LDC Borrowing with Default Risk." *Kredit und Kapital*, forthcoming.

Schmidt, Wilson E. 1981. Testimony Before the Subcommittee on International Trade, Investment and Monetary Policy, Committee on Banking, Finance and Urban Affairs, United States House of Representatives, March 12.

Spencer, Barbara J., and James A. Brander. 1983. "International R&D Rivalry and Industrial Strategy." *The Review of Economic Studies* 50 (October):707–722.

Strange, Susan. 1979. "Debt and Default in International Political Economy." In Jonathan D. Aronson, ed., *Debt and the Less Developed Countries*. Boulder, Colo.: Westview.

United States Congress, Congressional Budget Office. 1981. "The Benefits and Costs of the Export-Import Bank Loan Subsidy Program" (March).

United States Treasury. 1982. "International Export Credit Negotiations (1981–1982)" Report (September).

7

Industrial Policies for Emerging Industries

Geoffrey Carliner

Most of the recent debate over industrial policy has been about what government should do to promote high-technology industries. Supporters of government help for "emerging" industries claim that these industries are special. They provide important benefits to the rest of the economy. Because of various barriers to investment in new technologies, high-tech industries develop too slowly if left to private initiative. Without special help from government, industrial policy advocates say, new technologies will go undiscovered, downstream industries will not receive needed stimulus from the emerging industries, other countries may preempt the field, and economic growth will suffer.[1]

Critics of industrial policies respond that targeting high-tech industries is bad policy for several reasons.[2] First, market forces are better than politicians and bureaucrats at "picking winners." Developing a commercially successful technology requires a thorough knowledge of scientific possibilities, an appreciation of market demand for new or improved products, and a good sense of timing. Government targeting, claim industrial policy critics, may often fail to help emerging industries.

A second argument made against targeting emerging industries is that their spillovers are exaggerated. The products of high-tech firms may benefit other industries, but other industries pay for these benefits and generate profits for the high-tech firms. Although government support of basic R&D may be wise, adequate incentives already exist to encourage firms to invest in applied R&D.

Finally, industrial policy critics claim that targeting has little to contribute to a nation's overall economic strength and growth. Many targeted industries would have developed in any event. Even when such policies are successful in helping specific emerging industries, it is possible that alternative investments in other sectors might have been even more productive. Critics contend that high saving rates, skilled workers, smooth labor-management relations, and aggressive entrepreneurs are all more important for economic growth than targeted industrial policies.

The debate over industrial policy can be summarized in two basic questions: First, what types of government policies are most effective in developing high-tech industries?[3] And second, does support for such industries improve economic performance or does it merely real-locate activity from one sector to another? This paper will examine the experiences of Japan, the United States, and France to see what works and what doesn't work.

Japanese Industrial Policy

Japan's economic performance during the past thirty-five years has been very impressive. At the end of World War II its capital stock was in ruins, and starvation seemed a serious threat. After a quick period of rebuilding, however, output soon surpassed prewar levels, and economic growth averaged 10 percent annually for about twenty years. Real GNP rose eightfold between 1953 and 1973. Although growth has slowed significantly since the first oil shock, economic growth in Japan has continued higher on average than in any other OECD country.

During this period Japan has also become a technological leader. Although it qualified as a developed country before World War II and produced then-modern military equipment such as planes and ships, prewar Japan was significantly less advanced than Western Europe or the United States. In the early postwar period, textiles and other low-tech products were its main exports. By the 1960s and 1970s, how-ever, Japan's exports had shifted to capital-intensive goods like steel, cargo ships, and autos. Today, although such products are still im-portant, Japan now competes with the U.S. in high-tech areas includ-ing semiconductors and optical fibers. The Japanese are certainly doing something right.

Industrial policy proponents claim that government support for emerging industries is responsible for much of the growth and espe-cially for Japan's transformation from a low-tech economy to heavy industry and now to high tech. They believe that low interest loans, protection from imports, and R&D subsidies were instrumental in the development of many industries. In fact there was substantial government aid for steel and shipbuilding in the 1950s, encouragement of machine tools and to some extent autos in the 1960s, and help for various high-tech industries since the early 1970s. It is not clear, however, how much narrowly targeted industrial policies have contributed to Japan's economic growth and how much is due to other factors.

Japan's Rationale for Industrial Policy

The Japanese government officials responsible for industrial policy believe that Japan's comparative advantage in international trade has shifted since the early 1970s from capital-intensive heavy industries to knowledge-intensive industries.[4] The abundant factor in advanced countries is no longer physical capital but human capital, especially the human capital needed to develop new technologies and new industries. As Korea, Taiwan, Brazil, and other newly industrialized countries (NICs) accumulate capital and learn older technologies from more developed countries, their low wage rates will enable them to undersell rich countries like Japan in steel, shipbuilding, and other capital-intensive goods. The increasingly rapid transfer of technology will allow the NICs to follow ever more quickly in Japan's footsteps. Many Japanese feel that the only way to stay ahead of the NICs is to redirect Japan's output and exports into high-tech industries.

Proponents of industrial policies in Japan believe that market forces provide inadequate incentives to invest in emerging industries. The risks of creating a new technology may be too large for competitive firms to bear alone, perhaps especially in areas where they have little experience. Moreover the spillovers to other industries and other firms may be large, so that the social value of investing in emerging industries may far exceed the profits accruing to the private firm taking the risks. Because of these market imperfections, industrial policy advocates believe that government assistance is needed to stimulate the flow of resources into high-tech industries.

Japanese officials feel that capital and labor do not flow smoothly out of declining industries any more than they flow smoothly into emerging industries. Firms with large investments in physical capital and workers with skills specific to declining industries often resist adjusting to new market circumstances. Rather than abandon once profitable investments and leave well-paying jobs for uncertain investments and careers in new industries, firms and workers often avoid making adjustments. Because such adjustments are so difficult and costly, many Japanese feel that government should also assist declining industries adapt to structural changes in their economy. The rationale of Japanese industrial policy is thus to ease the flows of capital and labor for both emerging and declining industries.

In practice, this means that various ministries of the Japanese government review all sectors of the economy for signs of trouble and try to help whenever it is deemed advisable. The Ministry of International Trade and Industry (MITI) has primary responsibility for most manufacturing industries. The Ministry of Transportation (MOT) oversees the shipbuilding industry, and the Ministry of Posts and Telegraph (MPT) and the government-owned phone company (NTT) have been active in developing Japan's telecommunications sector.[5]

This responsibility for all sectors of the economy does not mean that the government closely supervises and directs Japanese industry. In discussing the government's role in encouraging emerging industries, it is easy to forget that the Japanese economy is very capitalist and very competitive. There is of course none of the central planning and tight control of the economy found in Eastern European countries. Although government corporations operate certain banks, most trains, and the telephone system, there is less government ownership in Japan than in the major Western European countries. And most industries, those that are considered to be doing well, receive only scant attention from government officials. Even in those industries with substantial government involvement, the key decisions concerning investment, research strategies, and product development are made by private firms trying to maximize long-run profits. Government subsidies are small, and protection from imports is similar to measures in some other developed countries.

Tools of Japanese Industrial Policy

The first step in helping the Japanese economy shift resources into high-tech industries is to choose specific industries for encouragement.[6] MITI tries to pick winners with the help of a council of experts from leading corporations, banks, universities, newspapers, and trade unions. The council's purpose is to gather information from the private as well as from the public sector and to form a consensus on the best policies to adopt.

The development of most industries proceeds without any formal plan. However, in some cases, for instance numerically controlled machine tools, a MITI council of experts issued a detailed "elevation plan" that specified types of machines to be developed along with investment and output targets. These targets are, however, voluntary. Private firms cannot be forced to follow elevation plans, and in fact the plans do not even commit the Japanese government to provide the financial aid specified in the plan.

Critics of targeted industrial policies claim that government councils and commissions often take their lead from government officials who know less about market prospects than private entrepreneurs. Critics also suggest that any centralized group, no matter how well informed, will tend to follow the conventional wisdom. Since new advances in technology are by their nature erratic, the conventional wisdom will often be wrong.

Japanese industrial policy has tried to avoid the first pitfall by genuinely seeking out the opinions of industry experts, including potential producers, potential purchasers, export trading firms, and banks. These experts try to figure out which development strategies suit the capabilities of Japanese producers. The experts also pay close attention to domestic and international markets.

Japanese councils have generally avoided grandiose schemes to produce the most sophisticated and perhaps most prestigious product within an industry. Instead, the typical strategy has been to start with a relatively simple high-tech product and then to learn to make it better and more efficiently than other countries. Only after mastering production for the relatively simple segments of a market have Japanese firms tried to move into more complicated areas. Perhaps because MITI's development strategies have relied on the opinions of businessmen as well as the views of government officials, Japanese industrial policy has generally not supported products that had no customers or that were too complicated for Japanese firms to master.

The Japanese council system also contributes to the successful development of emerging industries by creating a consensus between the private sector and the government. In other countries industrial policies have often been attempted by governments without active support from the private sector. Although private firms have been willing to accept government money for specific work, they have sometimes refused to invest their own money in projects they considered ill advised. Government efforts to redirect private activity have not always been successful. In Japan, there has generally been a consensus about which approaches to follow. With several notable exceptions, government attempts to develop new industries have generally been supported by the private sector.

Japanese industrial policies have also generally avoided the second pitfall of development by committee—picking the conventional solution over the innovative one that turns out to be right. Many observers suggest that choosing winners may be easier for follower countries than for technological leaders. The basic course of technological progress may be impossible to foresee, and for the leading technological country, picking winners by committee might not work. But follower countries may face different obstacles. Predicting where difficult, but nevertheless minor, improvements in product design or manufacturing processes can be made may be simpler than advancing the frontiers of technological developments. So far Japan's industrial policies have merely allowed her industries to catch up with the United States. Now that Japan is closer to the frontiers in many industries, it may be more difficult to pick winners by committee.

The second stage of Japanese industrial policy is to stimulate domestic R&D, investment, and production. MITI and other government agencies use a wide variety of tools to accomplish these goals. Until the late 1960s MITI and the Ministry of Finance (MOF) had very powerful tools for directing resources into targeted industries. Despite high tariff and nontariff barriers there was a chronic excess demand for imports of industrial raw materials and other products needed by Japanese manufacturers. MITI controlled the allocation of foreign exchange and used it to favor targeted industries. MITI also used foreign exchange allocations to persuade individual firms to follow its "administrative guidance" on specific actions such as mergers and new investments. MOF exercised similar control over the allocation of private bank lending and gave administrative guidance to banks on which industries and sometimes which firms to finance.

Since 1970 shortages of foreign exchange and bank credit have disappeared and with them has disappeared much of MITI's and MOF's power to direct the Japanese economy. Nevertheless, MITI still uses a wide variety of inducements to persuade private firms to go along with its development plans. These range from "administrative guidance" on specific merger and investment decisions to general assurances of help should the industry flounder.

Many industries have received R&D subsidies, sometimes in connection with joint research ventures organized by the government, such as those for semiconductors. Other industries have received loans at below-market interest rates, or loans that need only to be repaid if the firm's investment becomes profitable. For instance, when the domestic computer industry had trouble financing the leasing of its machines to potential customers, the government-owned Japan Development Bank (JDB) helped finance a fund to meet the industry's needs. Tax policy has also been used to favor certain emerging industries, for instance, to encourage purchases of numerically controlled machine tools and more recently of computer software.

Although these subsidies have been instrumental in developing Japan's emerging industries, they have not been large. By far the largest share of money, for R&D projects as well as production facilities, has come from private firms and commercial banks. Government subsidies in Japan have generally not financed investments in which the private sector was uninterested but have served as catalysts to stimulate private investments and vigorous domestic competition. Government seed money has encouraged private semiconductor firms to undertake—and pay most of the costs of—joint research ventures. JDB loans are also designed primarily to persuade commercial banks to lend to emerging industries and therefore are always made as a consortium with private banks.

Furthermore government subsidies to emerging industries are small compared to subsidies for other sectors of the economy. As in many other developed countries, the largest subsidies go to agriculture. Other subsidies go to the national rail system, to energy and environmental projects, and to investments in infrastructure, especially for regional development. Only a small share of government subsidies go to emerging industries and only a small share of the money for emerging industries comes from government.

Japan has also promoted high-tech industries by protecting them from imports. A decade ago tariffs or quotas and restrictions on foreign direct investment did the job. Most of these formal barriers have now been removed or reduced to low levels, but protection in other forms persists. For instance, NTT, the government-owned phone company, has worked closely with several private firms to develop an advanced telecommunications industry. Both R&D contracts and production contracts have generally been restricted to domestic firms within the "NTT family." Although NTT has begun to buy U.S. equipment, so far its purchases of imported high-tech products have been limited. The government is also considering whether to restrict procurement to domestic firms as a way of promoting Japanese production of space satellites with civilian uses. Health and safety standards are also used to protect domestic producers from imports. For instance, in the pharmaceutical industry, Japan has refused to accept evidence on the safety or effectiveness of new drugs from tests performed in other countries. This rule has made it more difficult for foreign firms to enter the Japanese market.

There are two dangers in sheltering domestic industries from import competition. First, downstream users of the protected items may themselves become uncompetitive in world markets. An industry that uses high-tech products may not be able to keep its costs down if the high-tech industry receives protection. The products of the downstream industry may then be priced above those of its international competitors. For instance, a consumer electronics industry that exports to the rest of the world cannot afford to pay substantially higher prices for semiconductors than its competitors in other countries.

However, if the output of downstream industries is not traded, for instance telephone service, then customers of protected high-tech industries can afford to bear the costs of expensive domestic goods. The downstream users will simply pass on the costs of protection to the ultimate consumer. Although consumers may be hurt by such protection, downstream industries that do not export or compete with imports will not be seriously harmed. Government officials seem to be aware of these considerations and have generally avoided imposing too much of the burden of import protection on downstream industries that export.

A second danger of protecting a domestic industry from imports is that it will never grow strong enough to face world competition. Protected emerging industries in other countries have often failed to develop into technological leaders. The Japanese have solved this problem by maintaining vigorous domestic competition. Domestic firms in emerging industries may be sheltered from competition from more advanced American or European producers, but they are not sheltered from each other. If they become complacent, other domestic firms will take their markets. Subsidized loans or government procurement contracts will not support them if they fail to keep in the race to develop new products, raise quality, and lower production costs.

The Japanese have not had to worry about inadequate domestic competition. In fact, once a consensus has been formed among government and business leaders that an industry will be targeted, there are often numerous firms that want to participate. On several occasions MITI has tried to limit the number of firms or otherwise to rationalize production in order to achieve economies of scale and to avoid what it viewed as unproductive competition. In at least some of these cases MITI has not been able to exclude firms or to persuade them to merge.

Once a Japanese industry becomes internationally competitive, government involvement decreases. Subsidized loans from the JDB, R&D subsidies from MITI, special tax treatment, and import protection are reduced or eliminated. The flow of public and especially private money into R&D and other investments in emerging industries, together with intense competition, leads to advances in technology, higher-quality products, and lower domestic costs. Once costs drop to world market levels, Japanese firms build capacity for export as well as for domestic markets.

Most Japanese exports do not receive special government aid. However, exports of capital goods are eligible for below-market financing by the Export-Import Bank of Japan (JEXIM). JEXIM has helped finance the development of overseas projects to provide imports of energy and other raw materials to Japan. Most JEXIM financing of exports has been for sales of ships and other large capital goods. Although some machine tools and robotics have been included in exported industrial plants financed by JEXIM loans, most high-tech industries in Japan have not benefited from this form of subsidy.

Many observers note that Japanese industrial policy seems larger than the sum of its parts. Each subsidy or trade barrier by itself may be small, in fact smaller than subsidies or trade barriers in other countries. But taken together, and offered judiciously by MITI or other ministries as solutions to specific problems, government aid has often been instrumental in reorganizing an industry, helping over a crisis, or stimulating new research or investment at a particularly opportune moment.

Such aid often forms part of an implicit promise to help targeted industries. This promise, rather than any specific guarantee of subsidy, is often a key part of MITI's contribution to forging the consensus among manufacturers, bankers, trading companies, and government officials to develop a high-tech industry. Because the firms understand that developing the industry has government support, they are more willing to take risks to undertake research or expand capacity than they would be without the implicit promise. This is so even though the promise is not with specific companies but only with the industry as a whole. In fact MITI's aid to emerging industries is usually designed to help the strongest firms. It thus encourages fierce competition as each firm attempts to achieve the fastest growth in efficient capacity and sales. As a result of these understandings between government and industry, and of MITI's skill in administering its programs, Japanese industrial policy has been more important than numerical measures of subsidy or protection might indicate.

Evaluating Japanese Industrial Policy

The Japanese have clearly discovered how to use government targeting to develop emerging industries. Without government guidance and assistance, it is unlikely that Japan would be as strong as it is in semiconductors, machine tools, telecommunications equipment, or fiber optics. Government policies, including the creation of a consensus with private firms, subsidies for R&D, special tax treatment, subsidized loans, government procurement, and import protection, have undoubtedly helped direct Japanese resources into targeted high-tech industries.

However, Japan's industrial policies have not always been successful. In some industries, for instance, computers in the early 1970s, MITI encouraged domestic production before upstream industries like semiconductors were advanced enough, and the effort was largely unsuccessful. Other favored industries like petrochemicals and aluminum were developed just in time for the increase in energy prices to ensure that Japan would always be a high-cost producer. Even industries in which Japan is internationally competitive, like steel and shipbuilding, have had long periods of excess capacity. Some critics claim that Japanese industrial policy may even have reduced overall economic growth and productivity by encouraging overinvestment in favored industries and presumably too little investment in industries that were not favored.

In any event industrial policy does not deserve most of the credit for Japan's postwar economic success. More important have been a very high domestic saving rate and a dramatic migration of labor from low-productivity sectors like agriculture to high-productivity manufacturing.[7] Rapid growth and structural change have also depended on entrepreneurs willing to take risks and on skilled and highly motivated workers. Even without an industrial policy, it is obvious that Japan would have grown rapidly and shifted from light, low-technology manufacturing to capital-intensive industries and then to higher tech.

Emerging Industries in the United States

At least since World War II the United States has been the undisputed leader in most knowledge-intensive industries. American firms have dominated international markets for computers, large civilian aircraft, and commercial satellites. We have led the development of semiconductors and sophisticated telecommunications equipment. And we are far ahead of other countries in such new industries as biotechnology and composite materials. Although our lead may be diminishing in some industries, our high-tech sector remains the envy of other countries.

The U.S. approach to developing knowledge-intensive industries has been quite different from Japan's. We have usually felt that government targeting of specific industries was not desirable. Commercial applications of new technology are best left to the private sector. The opportunity for a good rate of return on a new investment or for higher salaries and faster advancement in a high-tech firm would be sufficient to attract capital and labor to emerging industries. Although the risks might sometimes be high, the rewards would also be high.

Most Americans have felt that the appropriate role for government is to provide an environment that would stimulate private firms and workers to develop high-tech industries. This environment includes a well-educated labor force and a body of basic knowledge that could be used to develop specific commercial products and processes. Educating skilled technicians, engineers, and scientists may require government aid in part because young people may not be able to borrow to finance the costs of obtaining such skills. Financing basic research may be desirable because the spillovers are so large. Although investments in developing commercial applications in emerging industries may be adequately rewarded, the returns on basic research are not. Because the benefits are so widespread and the financial returns to basic research projects so low, such research requires government subsidies. But subsidies for commercial development of high-tech industries have generally not been considered appropriate.

The American attitude toward targeted industrial policies may reflect differences between our capital and labor markets and those in Japan or France. American markets for equity capital are very well developed. An inventor with a good idea can readily find private investors to put money into a new company in return for a share of the profits. Banks are also willing to take chances on small new firms in high-tech industries. Although new firms without past profits may not be able to take full advantage of various tax benefits, this will simply lower the aftertax return on investments and effectively raise the cost of capital to emerging industries. Capital will nevertheless flow into new industries without specific direction from the government.

American labor may also be more mobile than labor in other countries. Americans are more likely to move from one place to another. We are also more likely to change employers or to start new firms on our own. A scientist may start his or her career doing research at a university, move to an existing firm to develop commercial applications, and then quit to form a new firm.[8]

Critics of an industrial policy for the U.S. claim that we do not need targeting. They observe that American workers, especially highly skilled worker-entrepreneurs, are very mobile and that substantial capital is available for risky high-tech ventures. There are thus few barriers to prevent capital and labor from flowing into emerging industries, and ready channels exist to transmit the results of basic research from university research labs into commercial applications in the private sector. With such institutions, they claim, we do not need the government assistance to specific industries that may or may not be useful in other countries.

In the typical emerging industry, the government subsidizes technical training and basic research in university or government labs. When the field has advanced sufficiently, private firms invest in applied research to develop commercial products and sell their goods in the marketplace. Some of these firms may be large existing corporations with well-established sources of financing. Others may be new firms started by former employees of the existing firms or by former university researchers and financed by venture capital.

This model fits some of our emerging industries quite well, including biotechnology and parts of the computer industry. In many other high-tech industries, however, there is another very important factor—military and space spending. Military spending provided much of the early stimulus for computers, numerically controlled machine tools, large aircraft, satellites, and more recently composite materials and ceramics. Today's supercomputer project will also likely have important spillovers for civilian industries.

Pentagon and NASA spending have helped to develop our emerging industries in several ways. First, it has helped to finance much of the basic research needed to develop both the civilian and military sides of these industries. Much of this basic research has been done in universities and other institutions that publish their results. Even research that might originally have been classified eventually becomes part of the stock of knowledge of the scientists and technicians who work in an area.

Military procurement of final products also helped to develop our emerging industries. Military purchases of early computers paid for a substantial share of the development costs of a product that turned out to have numerous civilian as well as military applications. Some designs for military aircraft were modified slightly to become civilian planes. Even when military products were not directly useful in civilian markets, the firms and workers in emerging industries gained useful experience while working for the military. Designs for jet fighters may not have any direct civilian use, but learning to make such designs and manufacture such products gave American firms considerable skills that could be used to produce civilian products.

Some observers have argued that working for the Pentagon is poor training for competing in civilian markets. Defense contractors often have cost-plus contracts rather than competitors constantly threatening to undercut their price. Production runs for high-tech military goods are often very short. Learning to achieve economies of scale and efficient production techniques may be skills that military work discourages. And because there is only one customer, defense contractors may not be prepared to market their products to hundreds of firms or millions of individual consumers. In sum, military procurement may not encourage civilian high-tech industries.

The strength of so many high-tech industries that have benefited from military spending suggests that these effects are at best weak. Although some firms have had difficulty selling to both military and civilian customers, others have done so successfully. Remembering to keep production costs under control may be easier than learning to design computers and aircraft. If so, working for the Pentagon would improve the competitiveness of military contractors in civilian markets.

Other observers have argued that by using the services of such a large fraction of our scientists and engineers, defense spending may even inhibit the growth of civilian high-tech industries. Scientists who are working on military projects are not available to develop civilian goods. In the very short run it is true that the supply of scientists is fixed. In the longer run, however, more scientists can be trained. The long-run supply curve of scientific personnel is likely to be fairly flat.

Aside from government procurement, the United States has not generally used the targeting techniques employed by other governments. Except for restrictions on classified defense work, U.S. markets are open to imports of foreign high-tech goods or investments by foreign firms. There have been few attempts to subsidize loans to most high-tech industries, to help plan their development, or to provide incentives for investing in specific emerging industries.

There are, however, several exceptions to this general statement. A very expensive one has been subsidies for the energy sector. The U.S. government has subsidized the development of the nuclear power industry for many years, in part for the political purpose of turning swords into ploughshares. More recently subsidies have gone for extracting oil from shale and sand. Both industries have become very expensive failures. Although the reasons for these failures may be complicated, they should serve as a warning to advocates of more government influence over which industries and projects to favor.

Another exception is the wooing of high-tech firms by state and local governments. These governments offer tax breaks, subsidized financing, and other special aid to high-tech firms willing to locate in their jurisdictions. These efforts differ considerably from the targeting of specific emerging industries in Japan and elsewhere. The state and local governments are glad to attract any high-tech industry that will bring an educated workforce and lots of growth. As long as it is clean and promises to grow fast, they do not care if the industry produces optical fibers, semiconductors, satellites, or widgets. The state and local subsidies are more general support for any and all emerging industries than targeting for specific industries.

Finally, the U.S. tax system is far from neutral. We have had tax credits for R&D, for new investments in equipment, and for the preservation of historic buildings. Exports have received favorable treatment under DISC (and Export-Import Bank loans have tended to subsidize exports of commercial aircraft and electric generating equipment). Rules on accelerated depreciation favor certain types of investments over others. However, these tax measures have rarely been part of government targeting of specific civilian industries. Our subsidies, explicit and implicit, have generally encouraged a broad range of activity and have seldom been coordinated with other efforts to develop an individual high-tech industry.

French Industrial Policy

France has a long tradition of direct government involvement in the economy and specifically in the promotion of new industries.[9] The French feel that extensive government intervention is needed because their capital markets are too poorly developed to allow funds to flow readily into new industries, because French firms are too risk averse to take chances on investments in emerging industries, and because foreign competition from technological leaders is too powerful for less advanced French firms to overcome. In addition there has been support for the use of economic tools to achieve noneconomic goals, including the boosting of national security and national prestige.

The French government is in a powerful position to influence the development of the French economy. Since World War II the government has owned substantial portions of French industry and several large banks and insurance companies. In 1981 a considerable number of additional large industrial firms and banks were nationalized. Although these firms continue to operate in many ways like private corporations, they are nevertheless subject to general direction and sometimes very specific control by government ministries.

Another unusual feature of the French economy is indicative planning. Beginning in 1946, a series of five-year plans has spelled out growth targets by industry in considerable detail. Although these targets have not been binding on private firms, government-owned firms, or government ministries, they have served as publicly specified goals for economic development. The plans have been drawn up by the government-planning commission in consultation with industry and labor leaders. The plans attempted to provide an internally consistent set of investment and output goals for various French industries. The purpose of these goals was to decrease the uncertainty faced by firms in different industries in order to increase investment. For instance, investments in steel mills would be increased if the plan allowed the steel industry to know the future output of the shipbuilding industry.

By the early 1960s the immediate postwar reconstruction of France's heavy industries was complete, and the government began to put more emphasis in its plans and its budgets on developing high-tech industries. This emphasis was motivated by several factors. One was the desire for military independence from the United States. The French feared that relying on the United States for advanced weapons would reduce their ability to conduct an independent foreign policy. And without its own high-technology industries France would not be able to develop sophisticated weapons. These fears were strengthened in 1964 when the U.S. government prevented France from buying an advanced computer that could have been used to develop nuclear weapons.

A separate but related reason for favoring emerging industries was national prestige. Just as the United States decided to send a man to the moon partly to enhance national prestige, the French chose to build a supersonic passenger aircraft to show that they were technologically advanced. Decisions to favor other projects have also been influenced at least in part by considerations of prestige.

The last, but not necessarily least, important reason for favoring high-technology industries has been the belief that they are important for future economic growth. French officials, along with government officials in many other countries, have felt that high-tech industries will continue to grow rapidly and will provide stimulus for the growth of more traditional industries. Targeted industrial policies were necessary to channel resources into these emerging industries and to overcome the lead of more advanced foreign firms.

High-tech industries selected for favored treatment have included civilian aircraft, nuclear energy, computers, semiconductors, telecommunications equipment, machine tools, and biotechnology. Although development strategies have varied from inudstry to industry, the typical method has been to create a "national champion" by merging the strongest existing domestic firms. Without such mergers government officials felt that domestic firms in high-tech industries would be too small to compete with much larger American and Japanese firms. Only national champions that were large enough to dominate domestic markets and enjoy economies of scale in production and marketing would eventually be able to meet the international competition.

The French have used several tools to promote national champions and emerging industries. Government ministries have subsidized R&D projects and in some cases operating expenses directly from their budgets. Government-owned banks and other government financial institutions have been directed to make loans to targeted industries.

Tariffs have occasionally restricted imports of certain high-tech products, but since tariff rates are set by the EC and not independently by member countries, other trade barriers have also been used. These have included quotas, health and safety standards, and administrative customs barriers such as requiring documents in French or providing too few customs inspectors. Perhaps the most important barrier has been government procurement. Government agencies, and to a lesser extent government-owned firms, have avoided buying imported high-tech goods. Because government ownership of manufacturing firms is so widespread, this practice has ensured domestic firms in targeted industries of protected markets.

Despite substantial government aid and protection French industrial policy has generally been unsuccessful at developing internationally competitive high-tech industries. Unlike the Japanese, the French government has not yet found the appropriate set of policies for catching up with American technological leaders. French semiconductors and computers, for instance, are far behind their American and Japanese competitors.

Industrial policies for the French aircraft industry have also not succeeded. Although the Concorde and Airbus are technically accomplished, they have yet to make profits. The Concorde was produced for a market that never existed and was bought only by nationalized airlines that were instructed to do so by their governments. The French government and its British partners have paid subsidies for the Concorde's R&D production costs, and continue to pay operating subsidies to Air France and British Airways. The Airbus also is not a model that many would wish to imitate. It has sold well and is currently giving American firms stiff competition, but only with large government subsidies for R&D, production costs, and financing. It is possible that Airbus will eventually sell enough planes to become profitable, but so far the venture cannot be claimed as a commercial success.

Why has French industrial policy failed to develop targeted industries while the Japanese have done so well? One answer is the lack of market research. French officials have sometimes failed to consider whether demand for new products would be adequate. Of course predicting future demand can be difficult for a product that doesn't yet exist. But even before the sharp rise in energy prices in 1973, private experts predicted that the demand for supersonic civilian planes such as the Concorde would be too low to make such investments profitable.

French officials also seem to have ignored the supply side of high-technology markets. Most successful development strategies for follower countries have tried to find relatively unsophisticated niches in emerging industries and then to expand into more complicated areas. The French strategy for computers, however, was to try to build large mainframes to compete directly with IBM rather than to begin with smaller computers or peripheral equipment. Challenging the world leader in the most advanced segment of the market was too much for the relatively undeveloped French firms, and the effort failed.

Both types of mistakes might have been avoided if the government officials who made industrial policy had consulted more with private experts. These experts might have warned that demand would be inadequate or that the development goals were too ambitious. Private experts also make mistakes, but they are less likely to ignore market factors than government officials who may give undue emphasis to prestige or other noneconomic considerations.

The French seem to have learned from early mistakes. In developing plans for the Airbus, they not only tried to pick a segment of the market whose demand would be high. They also tried to line up their customers early by purchasing aircraft parts in exchange for orders.

Conclusions

The experience of the United States, and especially of Japan, indicates that government policies can indeed promote high-tech industries.

The essential ingredients are a work force with the necessary skills, private firms willing to invest their money in risky ventures, and vigorous competition among producers. Government subsidies for basic research or for applied R&D also help. Some guarantee of a market, either through government procurement or through formal or informal barriers to imports, may also be necessary to stimulate emerging domestic industries, at least in follower countries.

There are, however, numerous pitfalls in conducting an industrial policy. First, it is easy for government officials to choose politically powerful industries or projects that seem to boost national prestige but that have few potential customers or are too advanced for an undeveloped domestic industry. One solution is for private experts as well as government officials to help pick the winning industries and the winning strategies for developing them. Another approach may be to have the private experts choose with little or no help from the government officials. The best solution must depend on the economic, cultural, and political institutions of each country. What works in one situation might be a disaster in another one.

A second pitfall is that protecting an emerging industry may hurt a downstream industry that buys its products. The downstream industry may be naturally protected from imports because it produces goods or services that are not traded internationally, or it may also receive import protection. However, if the downstream industry exports its products or competes with imports, forcing it to pay more for its inputs is sure to hurt in the long run.

Protecting an emerging industry may also eliminate the competition that seems to be necessary to develop internationally successful firms. Without domestic competition firms in emerging industries often seem unable to develop sufficiently to survive without trade barriers. Small economies may not have large enough markets for several firms to produce at economically efficient levels. For emerging industries with large economies of scale, it may be difficult for smaller countries to have protection and domestic competition at the same time. However, the economies of the United States, Japan, and the EC are all likely to have markets large enough to support several firms except in a few industries like large passenger aircraft.

Another pitfall of industrial policy is to try to develop an emerging industry before the rest of the economy can support it. A successful domestic computer industry seems to require an advanced domestic semiconductor industry. A successful aircraft industry need suppliers who can produce technologically sophisticated metals. This suggests that industrial policies can make only a marginal contribution to economic development. Targeting specific industries will only succeed if related industries are also developing. If the goal of government policy is a broad technological advance, then spending on basic research, on technical education for workers, and general incentives for R&D may be more effective than narrow targeting of a few industries.

Even if industrial policies are successful in developing targeted industries, we have to remember that such policies are not free. Government subsidies are easy to measure, but import protection also costs something to downstream industries and individual consumers who must pay more for protected domestic goods. Furthermore the capital and labor that were attracted into the targeted industry might have been more productive elsewhere. Targeting may help the favored industry, but it imposes costs on the rest of the economy. It is easy for firms in targeted or subsidized industries to see the benefits of targeting, but the rest of us should realize that we must pay the costs.

Notes

1. See Thurow (1980), Magaziner and Reich (1982), Reich (1982), and Labor-Industry Coalition for International Trade (1983). Krugman (1983) summarizes many of these arguments. See also Brander and Spencer (1983, 1984) for mathematical treatments of some of these issues.

2. See Council of Economic Advisors (1984) and Schultze (1983), as well as Krugman (1983).

3. Nelson (1983) discusses numerous examples of different industries in different countries.

4. Japanese government officials expressed these beliefs at sessions of the U.S.-Japan Committee on Industry Related Policies and Their Effects on Trade, May 14–16, 1983, which the author attended as a member of the U.S. delegation.

5. Johnson (1982) offers a history of MITI from its precursor in 1925 until 1975.

6. See International Trade Commission (1983), Magaziner and Hout (1980), Semiconductor Industry Association (1983), Yamamura (1982), Wheeler, Janow, and Pepper (1982), and Ahearn (1981) for descriptions of Japanese targeting of specific high-tech industries, and general information on Japanese industrial policies.

7. See Denison (1976) for an analysis of the sources of Japanese growth.

8. Saxonhouse (1982) argues that much of Japanese industrial policy is merely a substitute for better-developed U.S. capital markets and more mobile labor.

9. See Ahearn (1981) and International Trade Commission (1984) for information on French industrial policies.

References

Ahearn, Raymond. 1981. *Industrial Policy: Background and Evaluation of Foreign Experience.* Congressional Research Service.

Brander, James, and Barbara Spencer. 1984. "Export Subsidies and International Market Share Rivalry." *Journal of International Economics.*

Council of Economic Advisors. 1984. *Economic Report to the President.* GPO, Washington, D.C., 3.

Denison, Edward, and W. K. Chung. 1976. *How Japan's Economy Grew So Fast.* Brookings.

International Trade Commission. 1983. *Foreign Industrial Targeting and its Effects on U.S. Industries, Phase I: Japan.*

International Trade Commission. 1984. *Foreign Industrial Targeting and its Effects on U.S. Industries, Phase II: The European Community and Member States.*

Johnson, Chalmers. 1982. *MITI and the Japanese Miracle.* Stanford University Press.

Krugman, Paul. 1983. "Targeted Industrial Policies: Theory and Evidence." In *Industrial Change and Public Policy.* Federal Reserve Bank of Kansas City.

Labor-Industry Coalition for International Trade. 1983. *International Trade, Industrial Policies, and the Future of American Industry.*

Magaziner, Ira, and Thomas Hout. 1980. *Japanese Industrial Policy.* Institute of International Relations.

Magaziner, Ira, and Robert Reich. 1982. *Minding America's Business.* Vintage Books.

Nelson, Richard. 1983. "Policies in Support of High Technology Industries." Mimeo.

Reich, Robert. 1982. "Making Industrial Policy." *Foreign Affairs* (Spring).

Saxonhouse, Gary. 1983. "Japanese High Technology, Government Policy, and Evolving Comparative Advantage in Goods and Services." Mimeo.

Schultz, Charles. 1983. "Industrial Policy: A Dissent." *Brookings Review* (Fall).

Semiconductor Industry Association. 1983. *The Effect of Government Targeting on World Semiconductor Competition.*

Spencer, Barbara, and James Brander. 1983. "International R&D Rivalry and Industrial Strategy." *Review of Economic Studies* (October).

Thurow, Lester. 1980. *The Zero-Sum Society*. Basic Books.

Wheeler, Jimmy, Merit Janow, and Thomas Pepper. 1982. *Japanese Industrial Development Policies in the 1980s*. Hudson Institute.

Yamamura, Kozo. 1982. *Policy and Trade Issues of the Japanese Economy*. University of Washington Press.

8

Caveat Emptor: The Industrial Policy of Japan

Kozo Yamamura

What follows is my best effort to answer—in a no-nonsense executive summary—a question many have asked of late: What is Japan's industrial policy, and how does it work? I shall not tarry to examine the myths, mirths, and malice injected into the discussion of the subject by foreigners and by the Japanese themselves for reasons of their own or, all too often, out of insufficient knowledge. Nor do I intend to commit gross economics on the subject using a neoclassical knife, known for both its sharpness and brittleness. What I hope to present is a full-bodied and well-balanced dissection of Japan's industrial policy.[1] The task can best begin by recognizing several essential, indisputable facts.

First, the Japanese had a strong, shared motivation—a national consensus—to recover as quickly as possible from the humiliation of defeat in World War II and to achieve rapid economic growth, which was regarded as the only means to regain national pride. This consensus made a progrowth policy (explicitly favoring growth over equity) politically possible and ensured the uninterrupted dominance of the conservative Liberal Democratic Party (LDP) over the next thirty years. Unlike in England (and elsewhere to a varying degree), there was little danger of debates on progrowth policies becoming ideological debates over distribution, which would have rendered the policies finally adopted totally ineffective, if not perverse.

As the rapid growth continued, this consensus grew weaker. By the late 1960s the LDP's political power began to erode. When the rapid growth period unmistakably ended in 1973—the first oil crisis—progrowth policies began to require more and more justification, and gradually substantive changes in the character of the policies became unavoidable. However, seen in a relative perspective vis-à-vis the industrial democracies of the West, no one can deny the fact that Japan is much less torn by distributional debates and that the promise of the better economic performance yet to be achieved through the growth of high-technology industries continues to help Japan retain political stability and a distinctively progrowth orientation in its policies. Politics do matter in discussing industrial policy.

Second, along with a national will to achieve economic growth, Japan had opportunity. Before the end of the 1960s Japan was a follower who could achieve rapid growth by "catching up" with the West, especially the United States. Japan readily borrowed technology and, by observing the patterns of growth in the West, could readily discern which industries would be the "winners" of tomorrow. Although not given sufficient emphasis, this fact should not be lost sight of by anyone discussing Japan's industrial policy. Another opportunity was the Pax Americana and what it implied in terms of the global trade regime and the growth of world trade. Opportunities have changed since the early 1970s and with it the character of Japan's industrial policy, as I shall discuss further. Only naivete of the worst sort would cause one to argue that other nations should adopt Japanese-style progrowth policies today to try to emulate Japan's performance in the rapid growth decades.

Third, Japan's institutions have been crucial in determining the type of policy adopted. Leaving a discussion of recent changes— some visible and others subtle—until later in this essay, few can quarrel with the observation that Japan's resilient LDP government, supported by rigorously selected elite bureaucrats in the ministries in Tokyo, commanded more power and a wider range of policy tools at its disposal than did, for example, the American or British counterparts. France comes closest to having an equally "strong" bureaucracy, but its political stability cannot be compared to that enjoyed by Japan.

Fourth, Japan's social and sociopsychological characteristics differ from those of the West. There is no mystery at all why economists invariably ignore this fact. Ignoring or belittling it is far easier than acquiring sufficient knowledge crucial in ascertaining the possible effects the difference might have on the character and effectiveness of economic policies. I have, however, absolutely no doubt that any discussion of the effectiveness of the ministerial administration guidance of industry—nonenforceable "suggestions" and "guidance"— based solely on economic motivations is woefully inadequate. The same applies to analysis of the permanent employment system, stockholder-management relationships, and interfirm relationships such as *keiretsu* ("industrial groups"). To be sure, as recent efforts by economists show, economic motivations explain these Japanese "social" characteristics much more that sociologists or anthropologists usually admit. But much more is not all. What remains can be ignored only by those brave souls who swear by the neoclassical economic theory that culture does not matter at all.[2]

Finally, Japan was lucky. During most of the rapid growth decades its labor supply was sufficient to ensure that real wages did not rise too rapidly ahead of productivity. Also oil prices were low and the supply dependable, defense did not drain resources away from industry, the Korean and Vietnam Wars boosted the Japanese economy and came at opportune times, and the strong American and other industrial economies readily absorbed Japanese products. As will be discussed, much of this luck has run out, profoundly affecting the character of Japan's industrial policy.

The Rapid Growth Period

Rapid growth occurred in a period of supply-side economics. The central goal of the progrowth policies adopted was to provide as much capital as possible at the lowest possible cost to the firms adopting new technology and increasing productive capacity. To realize this goal, an important element of the policies was to coordinate their expansion in order to reduce the risks of rapid investment while protecting firms from competing with imports until they had become internationally competitive, if not major exporters. The basic thinking behind the policy was that the fruit of such a strategy—increased productivity—would enable Japan to export more, generate rapid growth, and raise the Japanese living standard. An examination of policy pronouncements and views expressed during the rapid growth period by the LDP leaders, the bureaucracy, and academic and government economists leaves little doubt of the consensus on this policy goal.[3]

But what really was the policy of the rapid growth period, and how did it work? A case study will be presented in the next section, but let me here summarize only the fundamental characteristics of the policy and how it was administered by the Japanese bureaucracy. To do so, I shall focus my attention on the two ministries—the Ministry of Finance (MOF) and the Ministry of International Trade and Industry (MITI)—that played the most important roles in promoting the goal of supply-side economics, that is, promoting an "investment race" to adopt successively more efficient mass-production technologies and to reduce unit cost among the large export-oriented firms in the major industries that were to act as the engine of rapid economic growth.[4]

Sources of Bureaucratic Power

Japanese industrial policy was primarily designed and executed by the central bureaucracy which occupies a more important place in the national government than does its American counterpart. The ministries in Tokyo, led by career bureaucrats recruited from elite universities, draft most of the legislation that comes before the Diet, exert extensive control over the financial system, prepare the national budget, and use their substantial discretionary power to influence economic activity through administrative guidance. This flexible, quasi-legal "advice," backed by implicit threats and rewards, not explicit legal authorization, became the backbone of Japanese industrial policy.

An important, and some would argue, the most essential, pro-growth policy directly contributing to the investment race was pursued by MOF.[5] Simply put, on the strength of two "temporary" laws enacted in 1949 and 1950 and remaining in effect throughout the rapid growth decades, MOF made loan capital available to the largest banks (the thirteen "city" banks), which in turn were "guided" to make loans available to the largest innovating firms. What made the guidance effective was the fact that MOF was empowered to control the full range of the rate structure, enabling the ministry to set the subequilibrium rate for loans made to large firms. The chronic excess demand for loans created by the administered below-market rate allowed the MOF to engage in effective credit rationing to the point of guiding the largest banks to make loans to a specific industry or even to specific firms engaged in the investment race.

The Ministry of Finance and MITI maintained a standing committee to identify the industries to benefit from the former's "guidance." It goes without saying that such a policy providing capital to selected large firms (and depriving consumers and small firms of funds) was feasible because the Japanese capital market was insulated from international money markets. It is clear that MOF's policies of preferentially directing credit to large, efficient firms in each industry intensified the tendency toward the domination of each sector of the economy by a small number of large firms, for in addition to enjoying the cost reductions of mass scale, these firms had more secure and ready lines of credit than did smaller competitors.[6]

The Ministry of International Trade and Industry also played a vital role in formulation and implementation of Japanese industrial policy. During most of the rapid growth era the ministry had the power to allocate selectively foreign exchange for the purchase of imports; because nearly every Japanese industry relied heavily on imported raw materials, this discretionary power gave MITI a valuable "stick" for prodding business. This power also enabled MITI to restrict selectively the importation of goods that competed (or would compete) with those produced (or which would be produced) by certain Japanese industries, thereby providing the ministry with a "carrot" as well.

Another important source of MITI's power was its role as "doorman" to vital imports of Western technology which Japanese firms sought out and purchased in vast quantities during the rapid growth period. Because the prior approval by MITI of each contract for the purchase of foreign know-how was required, the ministry was able to influence the timing, composition, and allocation of a flow of knowledge that was essential to the competitive success of each rapidly innovating Japanese firm. As recently published "memoirs" of former MITI officers and leading businessmen make evident, this discretionary power was very important in threatening and enticing firms to adhere to MITI's ostensibly advisory "administrative guidance."[7]

The fact that most of MITI's interaction with private firms consisted of this "advice" rather than legally enforceable directives meant that the ministry had to compromise, cajole, and threaten companies into cooperation with MITI goals in cases where those goals differed from the desires of the large firms. However, during the fifties and sixties, there was seldom a major divergence between the basic aims of the largest firms and those of MITI.

Just as the ability of MOF to pressure Japanese financiers to divert funds into strategic industries was a result of structural and procedural features of the Japanese capital market, the power of MITI to influence the investment and marketing decisions of private companies was largely due to the ministry's control over essential conduits linking the Japanese economy to sources of raw materials and technology.

With these facts in mind, let us now examine the patterns of government intervention in the Japanese economy and the results of that intervention.

The Model

I shall argue here that the essentials of Japanese industrial policy during the rapid growth period consisted first of a widespread protection of domestic markets and of oligopolization of major industries which together allowed large firms in major industries to price their products sold in the domestic markets as would any oligopolist enjoying a protected market.

Despite the anticompetitive nature of this arrangement, major firms were encouraged to expand vigorously and were subjected to intense competition on the world market, as incentives generated by the intrinsic scale economies of the new mass production technologies drew Japanese firms into production for export. As the firms expanded, the protected markets, which had served as hothouses for the fledging industries, became export platforms, easing the risks of aggressive expansion into export markets. Of course, as the sixties drew to a close, the set of conditions that allowed this arrangement to operate gradually disappeared in one industry after another.

The protectionist stance taken by the Japanese government during the fifties and early sixties is evidenced by the high level of tariffs and the restrictive quotas that characterized Japan's imports. Until 1960 approximately 60 percent of Japan's imports were under quota; when international pressure forced the elimination of some of these restrictions, tariff rates increased on 253 newly liberated items.[8] Furthermore MITI could quietly restrict any given import shipment by withholding the allocation of foreign exchange. In the words of Edward Lincoln, a lobbyist for the Japanese government:

Commercial policy, which took the form of import barriers on goods and capital, was a major element of Japanese development strategy during the early postwar period. Protection—through the use of high tariffs and stringent quotas—was very heavy, but it also declined very rapidly from the mid-1960s . . . During the period when tariffs were high, the main impact was to favor raw material imports and all domestic manufacturing industries . . . all manufacturers had a protected home market.[9]

Despite the fact that protectionism is viewed by most Americans as tantamount to industrial stagnation, Lincoln along with many Japanese contends that "protection from foreign competition was probably the most important incentive to domestic development that the Japanese government provided."[10]

The coordination and export promotion policies of MITI were crucial in preventing the loss of competitive vitality which could result from the protectionist measures accompanied with progressive concentration and/or cartelization of markets that characterized many major Japanese industries during this era. Crucial to understanding the workings of this dynamic mix of collusion and competition is the fact that during the rapid growth period, Japanese firms faced what economists call a declining long-run average cost curve—if output expands, unit costs decline and production becomes more efficient. This was principally due to the availability of readily borrowable, successively more advanced foreign technology. Thus each firm in a typical industry could outcompete its rivals by investing more and producing more than others in the sector. The structure of such industries is inherently "unstable," again to use economists' jargon. In other words, competitive investment to increase productive capacity and outproduce one another could not but lead to the bankruptcy and exit of some of the firms, thus allowing the industry to regain its stability with fewer firms, each producing at a larger scale than before.

The costly dislocations and inherent risk of such an unstable situation, which would be detrimental to rapid economic growth could, however, be avoided if a power outside of the market could "coordinate" the pace of investment being made by the competing firms. In postwar Japan MITI acted as this power. In a nutshell, what MITI did was to "guide" the firms to invest in such a way that each large firm in a market expanded its productive capacity roughly in proportion to its current market share—no firm was to make an investment so large that it would destabilize the market. The policy was effective in encouraging competition for market share (i.e., preserving the essential competitiveness in the industrial markets) while reducing the risk of ill-timed or excessive investment. Thus it promoted the aggressive expansion of capacity necessary to increase productive efficiency and output.

However, this policy can be pursued only if market share competition does not result in profit-robbing open price war, especially in periods when demand declines or fails to keep pace with the rate of increase in productive capacity. MITI's solution for this problem, understandably welcomed by the firms, was cartels. As a result "administered prices" and de jure and de facto cartels among the oligopolistic firms engaged in the investment race proliferated in steel, chemical, and several other industries.

This is not to say that these industries fixed prices at all times and were not competitive but rather that cartels were frequently formed when the firms were adopting new "lumpy" technology (whose optimal scale usually exceeded that of the technology being replaced), when recessions occurred in the domestic and/or international market, or when inventories became too large for various reasons including a too-rapid increase in capacity. These were the reasons for the "administered pricing," the "rationalization" cartels, "recession" cartels, and cartels organized under MITI guidance. And these also were the reasons why in some instances the industry took initiative in forming cartels and at other times MITI did so. Both "rationalization" cartels (for the coordinated adoption of new technology) and the "recession" cartels (to prevent bankruptcies during periods of excess capacity or slack demand) were permitted under the Antimonopoly Act, as amended in 1953, and MITI's extralegal "guidance" cartels went unchallenged by the Japanese Fair Trade Commission (FTCJ), which remained only a minor irritant in the national effort to achieve rapid economic growth.

Finally, in examining MITI policy, it is important to be aware that the policy, although effective in achieving its goal of aiding the investment race, suffered from a vicious cycle of its own making: the more successful its policy was, the more MITI was put in the position of condoning or even promoting collusive activities among the increasingly oligopolistic firms. After all, the investment race could go on only because the policy was effectively minimizing the risks of the race.

The increasing exports that could be achieved by the investment race were crucial to the success of this policy of encouraging aggressive growth while allowing protectionism and cartelization to raise prices—and profits—on the domestic market. Thus Japan's export promotion policies to help its firms succeed in the wide-open and highly competitive world market was more than protecting its infant industries. In the words of a Japanese economist:

First, the lack of resources forced Japan to export fabricated goods in order to finance the importation of raw materials. This implied that protection of infant industries must go beyond the stage of import substitution and into export promotion. Granting its selfishness, Japan had to restrict imports of competing foreign goods and to erect tariff and nontariff barriers while key infant industries were being protected. And yet, once these industries grew up, they had to be able to sell their products in free overseas markets unencumbered by trade restrictions abroad.[11]

The actual mechanism by which this occurred is related to the fact that, for reasons we have already described, Japanese firms of the rapid growth era were under strong pressure to reduce per unit costs by increasing output. Because increased output meant reduced costs per unit, it translated into increased profits on the products sold at high fixed prices in the domestic market, even if the increased output had to be exported at no profit or even at a loss. Therefore, even if increased output yielded no profit (economic loss) on export markets, a rapidly expanding Japanese firm with a protected home market would actually invest, produce, and sell in order to achieve the efficiencies and cost savings associated with mass production.

An important fact to remember about this situation is that it was not a matter of manufacturers deciding to invest and expand in full knowledge that the resulting production would be sold at no profit or a loss on the world market, leaving them with only the reduction in cost on units sold domestically as a return on their investment. Rather, these manufacturers enjoyed a margin of error when making these major investment decisions. Essentially, even in the face of the high probability that the increase in output would have to be sold unprofitably on the international market, the expansion was still worth the risk. The stronger the "home market cushion"—or the more effective the cartels and protection on the domestic arena—the smaller the risk and the more likely the Japanese competitor was to increase capacity boldly in anticipation of demand growth. This can give the firm a strategic as well as a cost advantage over a foreign competitor operating in a different environment who must be more cautious.

The rapid penetration of foreign markets by high-quality, mass-produced Japanese merchandise, often initially accompanied by low-price marketing strategies, has created chronic trade friction between Japan and the countries that have absorbed large quantities of Japan's exports. Of course the most important foreign market is the United States.

In summary, we have argued here that Japanese industrial policy of the rapid growth era was essentially one of "protection and nurture" and that the anticompetitive impacts of the practices and attitudes of MITI and MOF with respect not only to import restriction but also to the promotion of oligopolization and cartelization in the major industries were offset to a large degree by the vigor of the "investment race" and the rigors of competition on the international market.

In an effort to make tangible the effects of the government policies and business practices of the rapid growth period, I will examine next in some detail the growth and market behavior of the consumer electronics industry, particularly in reference to the production and export of television sets.

The Rapid Increase in Export of Television Sets: A Case Study

A study of any one of the major industries, such as steel, chemicals, machinery, automobiles, and electric appliances, would provide insights into the character of Japanese industrial policy. Of course specifics differ by industry. The policy involvement in the form of guidance, subsidies, antitrust exemptions, and trade protection was more extensive in some than others. But an important common denominator was that the industries engaged in an investment race aided by government policy.

Here I discuss the case of the consumer electric appliance and electronics industry focusing on one of its most important products: television sets.[12] In comparison to others, this industry received much less guidance and fewer subsidies than did, for example, the shipbuilding, chemicals, or steel industries. But, as a case study of the effects of Japan's industrial policy of the rapid growth era, this industry is ideal for two very important reasons. One is that a study of this industry demonstrates, rather starkly, how the risks of the investment race were reduced by the policy and how the policy adopted directly affected the market conduct of the firms in their efforts to increase their market share in its largest foreign market: the United States. The other reason is that the firms that succeeded in achieving a rapid expansion of exports of television sets to their largest foreign markets—thereby becoming globally dominant firms—are the very same ones now participating in the MITI-led joint research efforts and today occupy important positions in the world market for high-technology products.

What the firms in this industry—Matsushita, Sony, Sanyo, Hitachi, Mitsubishi, Toshiba, and Sharp—accomplished in the rapid growth period is well known. They dominated the Japanese market—the aggregate share of the television set market of these firms and their subsidiaries was 100 percent (monochrome) and 99 percent (color) in 1980.[13] And their share in the American market rose rapidly during the 1960s and 1970s. The Japanese share of the monochrome set market rose from 0.8 percent in 1962 to 25 percent in 1977, and that of the color set increased from 3 to 37 percent between 1967 and 1977.[14]

This performance is generally credited to Japanese managerial and engineering superiority; most observers share the following assessment of the Japanese firms' competitive edge made by Robert Reich:

The reasons for the success of the Japanese producers relative to their American counterparts can be traced to their cost advantage, the better quality of their product, and their marketing and distribution strategies.[15]

However, there is abundant evidence that the policies of the Japanese government, particularly protection of domestic market and lax enforcement of antitrust statutes, profoundly affected the industrial structure and market behavior of these firms. The unique incentives created by these policies cannot be ignored when analyzing the reasons for the Japanese firms' success in the American market.

Essentially the seven major firms were allowed to cartelize and manipulate the consumer electronics and electric appliance market in Japan; import protection, effective nontariff barriers to the entry of new firms of any nationality, and long-term price-fixing allowed them to charge prices in Japan much higher than those charged for virtually identical goods on the world market.

Not only did this control of the Japanese market prevent world-preeminent American firms from expanding into Japan in the fifties and the early sixties, thereby denying them scale economies and a possibly permanent competitive advantage over embryonic Japanese television production, this control seems to have helped the Japanese firms to penetrate the American market. Their success in the American market at the cost of a near collapse of the U.S. television industry has enabled the Japanese industry to become the world-preeminent producer of this commodity.

How did it all come about? How correct is Reich? Looking first at investment and marketing patterns in the Japanese television industry, possibly the most outstanding characteristic has been the rapidity of growth of the firms. The industry is composed of production units and subsidiaries of seven very large, diversified firms, most of which produce complete lines of consumer electronics products and electric appliances—from washing machines to video cameras—as well as a host of related products, such as commercial electronics, industrial machinery, communications equipment, and, recently, semiconductors, computers, and other high-technology products.

The industry has been quite stable despite the rate of growth of each firm within it. The entire Japanese television industry has experienced no new entry since 1960 and the seven diversified majors have coexisted since 1947, when the youngest, Sanyo, began production.[16]

There are at least three reasons for the remarkable stability of the sector. One is the large scale necessary for efficient mass production, which preempts small would-be entrants. Another is that competition from imports has never been a factor in forcing industrial reorganization. Tariffs on televisions were between 20 and 30 percent until 1968, and imports were a mere 0.1 percent of Japanese consumption as late as 1980.[17]

However, probably the most important barrier to the entry of new firms has been industrywide vertical integration into marketing; each of the seven entrenched firms controls a complete marketing mechanism—a distribution *keiretsu*—composed of wholesalers and retailers who are discouraged from selling competitors' goods. This has enabled large manufacturers to close a large segment of the market to new entrants and has also enabled them to control retail prices and to set quantities. This vertical integration, which has combined to enhance greatly the producers' ability to fix prices collusively, was based on a variety of cooperative business practices. The most important were the ownership of distributor's stock, the advancement of loans to wholesalers and retailers (which were perpetually starved for capital because of discrimination against small firms in the capital market), and the extension of liberal trade credit in such a way as to reward "loyalty" and long-term service to one of the producers. The manufacturers also divided Japan into discrete territories and assigned one wholesaler to each region; many implemented the *itten itchoai* system, which specified the retailers to whom each wholesaler could sell and correspondingly restricted each retailer as to his source of supply.

Another important tool that fostered *keiretsu* ties was the industrywide rebate system. Under this arrangement retail prices were set by the manufacturer and the *keiretsu* outlets' observance of the price was ensured through capital provision and other mutually reinforcing tactics. The manufacturers also set the wholesale price in such a way that it differed little from the retail price, with the intent of providing the intermediate handlers of the good with barely enough profits to keep them in business; some goods had no margin at all. The *keiretsu* distributors were thus responsive to sporadic, arbitrary rebates that were manipulated to reward the sellers for manufacturer-preferred behavior. There are reportedly 500 names for different types of rebates; the most important were related to the proportion of an outlet's total sales which were of the affiliated brand and to adherence to the suggested retail price. Rebates were offered to distributors on a case-by-case, confidential basis and were often given for "loyalty," "cooperation," and "effort." The system was an excellent one with which quietly but effectively to reward and punish affiliates.

Another technique used was the underwriting of consumer installment purchase plans by the controlling manufacturer. Because of the MOF control of financial markets described earlier, credit for consumer purchases was virtually unavailable from banks in Japan and the extension of credit by large producers (enjoying preferential access to bank loans) to consumers via the marketing channels was a major booster of retail sales. Evidence exists showing that even more effective practices, such as refusals to deliver goods to retailers who shaved price, were used.[18]

Due to the efficient interweaving of business practices that both provided incentives to, and punished, distributors, the number of manufacturer-affiliated retail outlets doubled between 1956 and 1966 as each producer worked to create its own distribution system; by the mid-1960s each producer had built a chain of *keiretsu* retailers, and control of wholesalers was virtually complete. Matsushita, the largest producer, now has 25,000 affiliated retailers, and each of the other companies controls a *keiretsu* of size proportionate to its domestic consumer products sales.[19] Two-thirds of the appliance stores in Japan are clearly affiliated with a manufacturer, and 73 percent of the products sold in the nation were estimated to have moved through the *keiretsu* outlets as late as 1974.[20] Because important types of rebates were determined principally based on the degree of "loyalty" each retailer showed to his *keiretsu* producer, the typical *keiretsu* dealer came to derive about 70 percent of his revenue from sales of the products of his *keiretsu* producer, usually carrying one subordinate brand for customer appeal.[21]

These vertical channels are obviously ideal for the application of vertical restraints—that is, the restriction of the behavior of downstream agents. Though such restraints cannot be shown to invariably result in efficiency loss, as they have some beneficial effects, an industrywide system is a powerful tool in the hands of colluding upstream agents. The elimination of retail price competition and the immobility of intermediate agents greatly enhance the stability and profitability of horizontal agreements between oligopolistic manufacturers to restrict output and raise prices.

Considerable evidence has been found that the consumer electronics manufacturers organized to take advantage of this fact. The Japanese Fair Trade Commission (FTCJ) launched a series of investigations of the industry; first in 1956, then again in 1966, cases were filed against all the major producers except Sony (which was later implicated in a derivative case). The charges were essentially those of cartelizing the domestic market, enforcing industrywide retail price maintenance, collusively setting rebate rates and profit margins for distributors, and collectively boycotting unaffiliated wholesalers. These investigations ended, to borrow an American legal expression, with the industry in effect pleading nolo contendere. No fines were levied, no structural changes were ordered, and the manufacturers were allowed to continue meeting on a monthly basis.[22]

However, unequivocal evidence—the documents confiscated by the FTC—exists showing that the seven producers maintained from the late 1950s to as late as the early 1970s a multitiered system for coordinating production and prices; the decision-making structure consisted of monthly meetings on four levels of management—from mid-level supervisors in the television divisions up to the highest executives of each company. In addition each company submitted detailed information on a monthly basis concerning its production, sales, and inventory of each size and type of television set to the Electronic Industries Association of Japan (EIAJ), a legal trade association. The information was then distributed to all member firms.[23]

This cooperative behavior led to the charging of prices on the Japanese television market which were far higher than those charged in the United States for similar sets. In 1966 the *Yomiuri Shimbun*, a major daily, reported that while the average ex-factory domestic television price was 150,000 yen, the average FOB price on the U.S. market was only 64,800 yen. The discovery of these price differentials, which were large, persistent, and characteristic of the sales of every exporting company, led to a national public outcry. The Shufuren, a housewives' association, angrily staged a boycott of television sets. Japanese prices dropped marginally in 1967, but the mechanisms for maintaining high prices were largely undisturbed; by 1970 the differentials rose once again.[24]

Thus I have no hesitation in observing that a potent combination of early market protection and very lax antitrust enforcement, both progrowth policies of the Japanese government, allowed large firms to erect nontariff barriers around their market and to levy large sums of "taxes" for rapid economic growth on the Japanese public.

Meanwhile, the firms were expanding their production at an impressive rate. In the very midst of this collusive activity, MITI in 1966 organized a research project into solid state technology for use in color television which materially benefited these firms in their pursuit of international competitive edge. The output of color televisions increased twelve times between 1966 and 1970 (from 1.5 million sets to 6.7 million) while exports expanded rapidly.[25]

The main target of this growth in exports was the United States. The very low prices of many of the receivers created severe price competition on the U.S. market, and the entire American industry underwent reorganization. Though five U.S. companies survived and are now operating in the black once again, the restructuring resulted in the exit of twenty-one companies, in the internationalization of every remaining firm, and in the entry onto the American scene of a major Japanese presence, in both the form of direct imports and the production of Japanese-owned American subsidiaries.[26]

As imports from Japan increased and depressed prices causing American firms to move abroad, domestic employment in television receiver production fell 50 percent between 1966 and 1970, another 30 percent between 1971 and 1975, and by yet another 25 percent between 1977 and 1981.[27]

The International Trade Commission attributed much of the travail in the American industry to severe and sustained price competition; members of the industry attributed the price competition to dumping and collusive, predatory schemes on the part of the Japanese producers. Labor groups and manufacturers repeatedly appealed to the American government for antidumping relief and other forms of intervention. An Orderly Marketing Agreement was arranged for 1977–80. But the antidumping charges, under which the Japanese were found culpable in 1971, have since bogged down in legal maneuvering, and no duties have been collected. In the early 1970s the Japanese were hit with a billion-dollar civil antitrust suit, which also remains in litigation.[28]

Legal inquiry has turned up telling evidence that the Japanese orchestrated their export plans, allocated U.S. customers among themselves, and cooperatively concealed a web of illegal activity and kickback schemes. In essence, the motivations to expand export sales aggressively which arose from the "investment race" and simultaneous control of a protected domestic market seemed to have predisposed the Japanese to launch low-price "export drives." These were sudden surges in exports spearheaded by low prices as the firms' new facilities came on line—and the firms launched the "export drive" at nearly the same time due to MITI investment coordination. As the reductions in production cost associated with increased scale are invariably a source of profit for television sets (or any other products) sold on the protected, high-price domestic market, there is a tendency to market the "excess" on international markets at a low price, not earning normal profit in the short term.

To prevent the international political friction that results from this type of export behavior, MITI organized an export cartel, and the manufacturers agreed to observe minimum prices on all exports to the United States. However, every company, except possibly Sony, engaged in widespread, long-term undercutting of these minimum prices thereby suddenly capturing large parts of the U.S. market. (The largest jump occurred in 1976, when Japanese imports rose 156 percent.) The difference between the recorded, official export price and the actual price was then rebated to U.S. importers through checks drawn on Swiss and Hong Kong bank accounts and other covert methods. The majority of Japanese television sets exported to the United States in the sixties and early seventies seem to have been sold under this risky system of "double-invoicing," and several major cases of customs fraud eventually arose from the practice.[29]

Analysis of this anomalous behavior seems to reveal the impact of the protected home markets and government export promotion in encouraging expansion in anticipation of demand and in creating incentives to export at prices that may have been below the full cost of production. Once these infrastructural realities were set in motion, the firms found the temptation to subvert MITI's stop-gap cartel too strong to resist; the negative results of the government's twenty-year progrowth campaign were manifested in intense trade friction and internationally embarrassing legal battles.

The winners and losers in this series of events are fairly easy to identify. The Japanese public was forced to subsidize the expansion of their national electronics industry. American purchasers of Japanese television sets gained. The owners and employees of the competing American firms directly bore the costs of adjustment and unemployment; whether those costs are merely temporary dislocations or have compromised the future competitive strength of American firms in this sector remains to be seen. However, much has changed since the mid-1970s. The last ten years have brought changes to the Japanese economy and to Japanese industrial policy. These changes are the subject of the two following sections.

After the Oil Crisis

By the late 1960s businessmen in one industry after another were beginning to have a strong hunch that investment at the accustomed pace could lead more to excess capacity than to increased efficiency. Recessions were occurring a little too often and some seriously expressed suspicion that the rapid growth period might be ending. And in 1973, when the oil crisis came on the heels of the Smithsonian agreement which ended the export-enhancing exchange rate of 360 yen to a dollar, the suspicions turned, brutally and abruptly, into reality. The shocked Japanese government hastily dispatched an "oil-begging" mission to the Arab nations and MITI officials were thrown into frenzied all-night sessions to devise a means to survive the crisis. True to character, the Japanese mass media were frantic in warning the nation of the impending economic doom.

For several years pessimism had the upper hand. The worldwide recession and the increasing reluctance of foreign markets to absorb more Japanese products did not help matters. The rate of utilization of industrial capacity sagged, and it was as low as 55 percent for the steel industry in 1975. Real wages of industrial workers failed to rise and even declined 0.2 percent in 1975. Exports fared not much better until 1977.[30]

But, to the envy of other industrial nations and surprising to the Japanese themselves, the economy began to rebound in 1978 as it gradually succeeded in economizing the use of oil and in carrying out "the operation scale down" (slower capacity increases accompanied with increased efficiency). Rebounded is a little too strong a word here. What happened was that the economy returned to a growth course at a lower level, the level the Japanese have maintained ever since.

As will become evident later in this essay, the experience of the 1973 to 1978 period is crucial in understanding many of Japan's policy motivations. It impressed, anew and strongly, on the minds of the policymakers and the Japanese public as a whole that despite the rapid growth already achieved, the Japanese economy *au fond* is fragile and can be subjected to a severe dislocation and downturn whenever foreigners with resources and/or markets choose to withhold them from the Japanese. This "fragility obsession" of the Japanese is what causes policymakers to adopt policies that could help ease domestic worries—that is, policies that actively promote the performance of the Japanese economy. And this is the obsession that, if expressed with some depreciation, can be and is used as a tool to stave off foreigners' demands that Japanese policymakers internationalize capital markets, increase imports of manufactures, and adopt other "liberalizing" measures.

The fortunes of the Liberal Democratic Party (LDP) were similar to those of the economy. The party's political strength continued to wane, and in 1976 the party's leader barely managed to gain premiership by a one vote margin in the Diet. This was a reflection of the fact that the LDP, which had 296 members elected by 57.6 percent of voters in 1960, managed to win only 41.3 percent of the vote and to elect 279 members in 1976. The party fared even worse in the Upper House. Faced with such developments, the LDP had no choice but to adopt national budgets that would keep their loyal voters—largely in industry, agriculture, and professional ranks—and that could slow the desertion by wage-earners, old, disadvantaged, and others to the opposition parties.

The LDP had a problem on its hands. Though it was forced to fund increasingly expensive programs, revenues, unlike in the preceding decades, were not rising because of the prolonged recession. Tax increases were out of the question for both political and economic reasons. This meant that the problem could be solved only in one very familiar way: by deficit financing. Of the total expenditure of 1975, 25.3 percent was raised by selling national bonds. In 1976 and

1977 the percentages were 29.9 and 29.7, respectively—perilously close to the 30.0 percent line the LDP then vowed not to cross. But the Japanese soon found, as others before them, that deficit spending is both habit forming and vow breaking. The figures for 1978 and 1979 rose to 37.0 and 33.9 percent, respectively. The cumulative total national debt by the end of 1979 stood at 52.3 billion yen in comparison to only 10.5 billion yen accumulated between 1965 when the debt was legalized and 1974. The situation did not improve into the 1980s. At the end of 1983 the cumulative deficit stood at 108 trillion yen or 40 percent of GNP (in contrast to 30 percent in the U.S.).

The economic and political developments of the 1970s—the background essential in analyzing the industrial policy of the decade—would have occurred as an inevitable consequence of the ending of the "catching up" period begun in the 1880s. What happened in the 1970s appeared abrupt and brutal because Japan had been unusually successful in exploiting the advantages of being a follower. In the 1945 to 1973 period, when most industrial nations enjoyed prosperity, Japan achieved "miraculous" growth through its skill in mass production.

Japan in the 1970s was therefore experiencing a new and unfamiliar phase in its history. In many respects (not all), Japan now stood shoulder to shoulder with the United States, the industrial leader of this century. New status brought unaccustomed obligations and responsibilities that were difficult to accept willingly.

There was yet another dimension to the end of the catchup phase of Japanese economic history. After more or less catching up to the Americans, the Japanese discovered that the leader was no longer moving ahead and that both now share the same uncertain future, which can be called the "twenty-first-century system." As I have analyzed fully elsewhere, the twentieth-century system that had begun in the 1880s with the industrial uses of electricity and ended in the rapid growth in the 1945 to 1970 period of the Western industrial nations and Japan, was achieved on the strength in part of a steady increase in the consumption of consumer durables. But the new system now emerging—the twenty-first-century system—differs fundamentally and qualitatively from its predecessor. It is a system based on high technology, making use of, and depending crucially on a degree of precision measured in millionths of seconds and millimeters, on digital analytical constructs that have no visualizable analog and on multifaceted, complex scientific discoveries that are understood by only a very small number of specialists. The new technology also uses less energy but requires many novel skills.[31]

Though I shall not dwell on this point, I wish to stress that Japan's present industrial policy (or more narrowly, its trade policy) must be analyzed with the preceding perspective firmly in mind.

A new phase, if less dramatic, has begun also in the Japanese politics of the 1970s. The national consensus for rapid growth, like the catchup phase, began to end in the late 1960s and the loss of the consensus that once enabled progrowth policies to be carried out with a vengeance, became evident by the early 1970s. The LDP, as we have already seen, never managed to win more than 47 percent of the total votes cast in any election held in the decade. The party thus had no choice but to transform itself from a progrowth party betting on the "trickle-down" gains of rapid growth to ensure their retention of power to a "catchall party"—a party that adopts policies to win political support of as many as possible of the electorate. This is to say Japanese politics too have caught up with the West in its essential characteristics.

All of these economic and political developments could not but affect the character of Japan's industrial policy and reduce the range of tools available to carry out the policy. To illustrate these facts, let me offer glimpses of changes that occurred in the lives of the officials of the two ministries, MOF and MITI, most important in discussing Japan's industrial policy.[32]

The problem MOF officials faced in the 1970s is uncomplicated. They were losing both the power and the tools needed to engage in industrial policy because of the rapidly accumulating national debt and the foreign pressure to open the Japanese money markets. To sell large amounts of government bonds year after year, MOF was forced gradually but surely to pay the interest rate prevailing in the market. Then, when the rates on the ten-year bonds approached the market rates, and the same also began to occur for the shorter-term government bonds that began to be issued from the late 1970s, the MOF gradually lost its ability to maintain the once effectively administered rate structure across long-, medium-, and short-term loan markets. It was steadily losing its ability to price-discriminate, thus the ability to affect both the direction and amount of the flow of funds within the economy. The Ministry of Finance's power also declined due to the fact that many of the largest Japanese firms have become "world class" and are increasingly capable of self-financing to meet the needs of the distinctively slower pace of investment. Credit rationing, once a powerful tool, has become as potent as the threat of a strike in an economy suffering from high unemployment.

To make the situation even more difficult for MOF, the foreign, especially American, pressure to open the capital market chipped away its power to control the workings of the money market. By 1980 the three-decade-long "controlled in principle" policy had to be changed to "free in principle," and any policy or practice impeding free flow of capital had to be justified.

The foregoing does not mean that MOF has lost all its powers. It can still offer justifications, for example, to limit the amount of capital that Japanese firms can raise in the Euro-yen market and to restrict specific types of debt instruments or financial practices that could cause "undue instability" in the money market. But clearly these are the rear-guard actions of a once-mighty general in retreat. The extent of the changes that occurred in the lives of MOF officials is perhaps best indicated by the fact that differences in opinions have appeared within the usually tight-knit group of MOF officials with regard to the speed with which liberalization is to occur.

MITI did its level best, by means of "administrative guidance," to reduce existing capacities especially in such industries as aluminum, chemicals, and steel, industries with which MITI had become inextricably involved during the investment race of the preceding decade. However, MITI soon discovered, in its effort to reduce excess capacity, that "guidance" again had to be supplemented by laws promising subsidies and exemption from the Antimonopoly Act. Thus, at the strong urging of MITI, the Temporary Law to Stabilize Industries in Recession was enacted in 1978. However, given subsidies and allowed to form cartels, declining firms were none too anxious to reduce their capacities, and when this law expired in 1983, it was necessary to renew it for another five years under a new name: the Law to Promote Industrial Structure.[33]

Another difficulty MITI faced was increasingly vociferous foreign criticism of Japan's industrial policy, and especially its trade policy. Foreign complaints, often bitter, were no longer directed only at such targets as tariff rates and quotas (most of which Japan had quickly reduced) but struck at much more troublesome areas such as the "opacity" of the "administrative guidance," legal cartels, NTT purchasing practicing, the "outsider unfriendly" distribution system, inspection and certification procedures, and the like.

This steady onslaught of criticism, especially from Americans who now had more political and economic pressures of their own and who had become quite knowledgeable about the character and extent of Japanese industrial policy, could not but reduce the number and change the character of MITI's accustomed tools for carrying out its policy goals.

Such difficulties were symptoms of a fundamental fact which MITI was then encountering. In an important sense MITI in the early 1970s had become a ministry that had completed its goal of aiding the Japanese industries so they could catch up with their Western counterparts. MITI now had little it could do for the major industries that had made Japan's rapid growth possible. Thus the early seventies were extremely difficult for MITI officers; it was a sobering period during which they came to realize that there were no more proven "winners" of tomorrow, a direction identified by the American and European experience as the best path to economic success.

This realization is extremely important in understanding why MITI from the mid-1970s began to promote the high-technology industries with vigorous determination. These industries give MITI new goals that can be justified in the name of maintaining Japan's economic performance both at home and abroad and can enable MITI to retain and possibly increase its power and jurisdiction in the intensely competitive and jealous world of the Japanese bureaucracy. The prospect that it can help these industries achieve rapid increases in productive capacities is just the tonic MITI needs. In the next section I shall return to discuss MITI's active role in promoting these industries and the problems this role may be creating.

Though only briefly, two very important developments of the 1970s, which are also becoming even more evident in this decade, must be added. One is that because of such closely intertwined factors as the erosion of the progrowth consensus, the tight national budget, and the LDP's diminished political strength, the processes of both policymaking and execution have become increasingly politicized. In comparison to those of the rapid growth period, these processes today entail much more intense involvement of politicians, mostly those in the LDP but also including some from the opposition parties, who organize themselves into a *zoku*, literally a "tribe" but analogous to the caucus in the U.S. legislature. An active *zoku* now exists for virtually every industry and often for each part of a broadly defined industry such as high technology (i.e., there is a *zoku* for electronics communications, biotech, semiconductors, and the like).

What is noteworthy is that these *zoku* today are far more active than ever before in pressuring and cajoling the ministries (which in Japan draft almost 90 percent of the bills passed in the Diet). Their effectiveness of course resides in the fact that the bureaucracy needs the aid of these politicians in passing the bills they draft and obtaining funding out of the deficit-ridden budget.

As typified in the case of the new MITI policy to create "technopolises" (cities built around major cores of high-technology-related industries and government projects), an unescapable effect of the politicization is to reduce, if not rob, the policies of their coherence and efficiency. In this case MITI initially hoped to create half a dozen technopolises, but the politicians, who have their own constituencies to please, have now increased the number to eleven. Few would be surprised if the number rises even further before the policy can be implemented.

The other development, which is no less troublesome in pursuing a coherent and coordinated industrial policy, is the recent visible increase in the intensity and frequency of interministerial rivalry. The best known of the most recent interministerial squabbles and confrontations include *MITI* v. *Ministry of Telecommunications and Postal Services* on the so-called VAN (value-added network, which is made up of various forms of electronic communications) issue, MITI and the Ministry of Education on the legal changes involving copyrights of computer software, MOF and MITI on the degree and types of capital market liberalization, MITI and the Ministry of Agriculture on the liberalization of imports of beef, oranges, and other agricultural products still subject to import quotas, and MITI and the Fair Trade Commission on the nature and effects of MITI's "administrative guidance" that might violate the Antimonopoly Act.

In examining these and other recent interministerial conflicts, several facts become evident. One is that they often involve MITI, especially the "new" MITI which is more "liberal" than other ministries, chiefly because many of the industries under its jurisdiction are export oriented and the ministry as a result is more anxious to reduce international trade conflict. Another is that many of the confrontations are "jurisdictional" in that as new "industries" are created (because of technological changes as in the cases of the VAN and computer software), both MITI and the opposing ministry attempt to exert their power over these industries and jurisdictional clashes result. Yet another is that most of these confrontations become intense and "open" (to outsiders like the mass media) principally because they are significantly more politicized than those of the past; that is, they tend to actively involve politicians speaking on behalf of the industries affected.

Though much more can be said of these interministerial conflicts (e.g., the organizational characteristics of Japanese ministries), suffice it to observe here that these conflicts too are developments of the post–oil crisis years characterized by the new problems and issues the Japanese economy and these ministries must now face. The bureaucracy now must cope with more of these conflicts, and as it does so, the collective institutional capability of the Japanese bureaucracy to carry out a coordinated and coherent industrial policy will be reduced from that of the rapid growth era.

In making the preceding observations, I am not suggesting that the institutional capability of the Japanese government has been lost. What I assert is simply that the institutional ability of the Japanese government to formulate and administer its industrial policy has declined in comparison to that it possessed during the 1950s and 1960s. The extent of this decline will determine the extent of diminution of whatever effectiveness Japan's industrial policy had before the first oil crisis.

The Semiconductor Industry

In the changing environment described in the preceding section, MITI is doing its utmost to assist Japan's high-technology industries. As already noted, MITI's motivations are not difficult to see. The ministry is convinced of the importance of these "industries of the next generation," a conviction made unwavering because MITI's increased role in promoting these industries can boost its power and prestige.

This section examines MITI's roles in R&D activities of the semiconductor industry in order to provide insights into the character of the policy being adopted in the changed economic conditions of the post–oil crisis. I shall also offer a broad comparative assessment of Japanese and American perceptions of the role public policy is to play in promoting innovative activities.[34]

However, before proceeding, two caveats are in order. Though this case study clearly demonstrates the essential policy approach of MITI in aiding Japan's high-technology industries, it does not represent many of the specific methods adopted in other high-technology industries. The needs of each high-technology industry differ because of their respective market structure, relative technological capability (especially vis-à-vis that of the American firms), and other reasons.

A second caveat is that the large firms in both the computer and semiconductor industries engage in a substantial and increasing amount of their own R&D activities unrelated to those involving MITI. Today these firms are competing against American and European firms much more directly and vigorously in the Japanese markets than did the large firms of the major industries in the rapid growth decades.

What we observe, however, amply demonstrates that Japanese policy toward high-technology industries, especially the semiconductor industry, differs substantively from that in the United States. A salient fact of MITI policy is that the ministry takes vigorous initiative in organizing and administering joint research projects among large oligopolistic firms; this joint research frequently involves applied (production for market) research, although of late more and more research activities are in basic research. Table 8.1 summarizes recently completed and ongoing MITI-related projects which give some indication of its scope and type of joint research activities.

As the table shows, MITI (and its research arms) in virtually all projects invites a varying but relatively small number of selected large, typically oligopolistic firms to join its joint research projects. (The only major exception is the "software automation" project shown in the table.) To select the firms to participate in the joint research projects, MITI consults trade associations (existing or created for specific projects), top managerial and research representatives from large firms in the relevant industry, as well as leading scientists. However, the final judgment as to which firms have adequate research capabilities and are large enough (to be able to "match" research support given by MITI and to make "effective" use of the fruits of the joint research) is made by MITI officials. All of this is done quietly.

This method of final selection of participating firms must necessarily result in the exclusion of some large firms. A result is that the competitiveness of exluded firms against "chosen" firms can be re-

Table 8.1
Major MITI projects in semiconductors (and computers), 1966 to 1980

Project area	Time schedule	Funding[a]	Companies involved
3rd, 5th generation computers	1972–1976	8,700 ($29.4)	Fujitsu, Hitachi, Mitsubishi Electric, NEC, Oki, Toshiba
Very large-scale project (VLSI), 4th generation	1976–1981	30,000 ($132.3)	Fujitsu, Hitachi, Mitsubishi Electric, NEC, Toshiba
Development of basic software and related periphery, 4th generation	1979–1983	47,000 ($102.3)	Fujitsu, Hitachi, Matsushita Electric, Mitsubishi Electric, NEC, Oki, Sharp, Toshiba
Pattern information processing system (PIPS)	1971–1980	22,073 ($82.7)	Hitachi, Fujitsu, Matsushita, Mitsubishi, NEC, Oki, Sanyo, Toshiba, Koya Glass
High-speed scientific computer	1981–1989	22,073	Fujitsu, Toshiba, NEC, Mitsubishi Electric, Sanyo, Matsushita, Konishiroku, Hoya Glass
Flexible manufacturing system using lasers	1977–present	13,000	na
Software automation	1976–1981	6,600 ($30)	Over 100 software firms
Development of 5th generation computers	1979–1991	11,375 ($45.5)	Fujitsu, Hitachi, Mitsubishi, NEC, Oki, Toshiba
Supergrid components (ICs)	1981–1990	8,000 ($36.4)	Fujitsu, Hitachi, Sumitomo Denko
Three-dimensional components (ICs)	1981–1990	9,000 ($40.9)	NEC, Oki, Toshiba, Mitsubishi Electric, Sanyo Electric, Matsushita Electric, Sharp
Elements with increased resistance to the environment (ICs)	1981–1988	8,000 ($36.4)	Toshiba, Hitachi, Mitsubishi Electric

Source: Data compiled from, U.S. International Trade Commission, *Foreign Industrial Targeting and Its Effects on U.S. Industries Phase I: Japan*, USITC Publication 1437 (October 1983), Appendix G, Table G-2.
[a] Million yen (million dollars).

duced or even eliminated. At the same time, in some major projects with research efforts more immediately applicable in marketable product development, firms demonstrating technological superiority and already conducting research (analogous to that contemplated by the joint project) did not participate in the MITI-initiated projects. Though reliable information is difficult to obtain, this occurred because either the firm declined to participate or MITI saw no need of assisting the firm.

However, in the past few years, and especially in the major projects now being carried out, fewer private firms appear to have declined MITI's invitation to participate in joint research projects. More recently a clear tendency has been that even the technological leaders seek inclusion in MITI's projects. This apparently is because they believe that the joint basic research, on which MITI is placing increasing emphasis, is less likely to compromise the technological superiority they are currently enjoying (in some product lines within a market) and because nonparticipation in MITI projects can be detrimental to a firm's future competitive position.

Extremely significant also in these MITI-initiated joint research projects is that the MITI officials, usually senior officials with close knowledge of the affected industry and even of necessary technological expertise, often exert leadership quite openly. This clearly reflects MITI's desire to ensure that effective and full research cooperation will take place among the scientific personnel sent to the joint research project by the participating firms. When they consult extensively with scientists and industry representatives, the MITI officials also are exerting strong leadership in the selection of specific research agendas for the joint programs. In other words, it is not an overstatement to observe that the MITI officials are exhibiting a strong sense of "mission" and unusual zeal in promoting joint R&D activities and are playing a much more visible, as well as important, role in determining the research agendas than they ever did in promoting the technological capabilities of the major industries during the rapid growth period.

To support these observations of MITI's leadership in joint research projects, let me present the following two quotations. They offer readers a closer feeling and an understanding of the modus operandi of these projects and MITI's roles in them, as well as the reasons for the projects. Despite their length the observations contained in these quotes are precisely what are missing in the descriptions and analyses made by Americans discussing the MITI-initiated projects in relation to the desirability of adopting an "industrial policy" à la Japanese. On the 1976–81 VLSI project, a reporter of *Asahi* (a major daily) observed that:

To challenge IBM, the VLSI research and development was begun, uniting government and the private sector. To carry out the research, the VLSI Technology Research Association was formed in April, 1976. Its membership consisted of five firms in two groups of domestic computer producers: Fujitsu-Hitachi-Mitsubishi and NEC-Toshiba . . . Approximately 100 researchers from the member firms and MITI's Electronics Research Institute gathered at the [newly established] joint research institute. During the following four years, about 70 billion yen, including a government subsidy of 30 billion yen, was spent. The technology necessary to develop VLSI was developed and the Association disbanded . . .

Initially, given the differing ideas concerning VLSI development among the member firms, decisions on the extent and nature of the joint research and which firm was to be responsible for which aspects of development, were extremely difficult to make. Interests of the member firms conflicted. And, even after the research topics were settled, there were the numerous problems to be expected in such a joint venture. Thus, six research rooms were created, each headed by a leader from one of the five member firms and one headed by a person from the Electronics Research Institute. During the first year, the walls between these rooms were thick. Participants tried to prevent others from finding out the progress being made in each room. "In extreme cases, the entrance was barricaded to prevent other researchers from coming in," recalls Nebashi [of MITI, who headed the joint research institute].

Nebashi did his best to eliminate the egoism of the member firms and to create the harmony among researchers necessary for joint research. In the evenings he went to the rooms and listened to the researchers' opinions and any dissatisfactions they had. At times, he drank *sake* with the researchers. . . . The monthly meetings, attended by senior officers of the member firms, were intentionally held at the joint research institute . . . The purpose was to let these officers become familiar with the projects and boost the morale of the researchers. In time, tennis and golf clubs were organized among the researchers . . . and the walls of secrecy dividing the research rooms were gradually removed.[35]

On the same project, "a techno-science" team of reporters from *Chūō Kōrōn* (a major monthly) wrote:

An executive of an IC producer in Kansai complains that "not having been able to join the VLSI project was a severe blow. Our company asked to be allowed to participate, but we were denied on the grounds that VLSI was for computers. We are doing our utmost, but we have not caught up with those who were selected to participate in the joint program." Oki Electric, which also expressed a strong desire to participate but was rejected, must also be extremely resentful of not having been selected. All the firms in the industry know full well the merits of participating in the government-private joint research projects.[36]

Although these observations constitute only a very small fraction of existing descriptions of MITI projects relating to the semiconductor and other high-technology industries, they nevertheless can tell us the following. Above all, MITI evidently has no doubt of the social desirability of joint research activities among selected oligopolist firms. MITI officials, in their public pronouncements and interviews, stress the necessity of pooling R&D efforts in order to make the most efficient use of scarce scientific manpower and research funds. MITI clearly believes its joint research projects serve the national interest. Many of its officers argue that these projects are helping Japan become a provider of advanced technology and also serve the interests of the world. On the basis of this policy rationale, MITI feels fully justified in taking aggressive leadership in joint research projects.

Indeed, without this rationale, MITI could not have selected a small number of large firms to join in these projects, provided partial funding, and assumed the role of an effective coordinator capable of guiding profit-motivated firms to cooperate. Had such projects been privately organized, they too would have most likely faced the difficulties that the Microelectronics and Computer Technology Cooperation (MCC, a privately organized American joint research corporation based in Austin) is now encountering:

While the consortium is beginning to make progress, most of its participants say that in its first 18 months, it has yet to usher in the new age of cooperation needed to match Japan's Government-sponsored efforts to dominate these markets . . . "Many of the shareholders have dived in and established that in America you can truly create a workable research consortium . . . But others are sitting back and sipping with a long straw."[37]

The difference between the MITI-led joint research projects and the MCC reflects even more basic differences between Japanese and American perceptions of the appropriate role government is to play in promoting technological progress and the national economic interest. In both economic and theoretical literature and in the minds of policymakers, Americans are far from reaching a consensus as to the desirability of encouraging, as a matter of public policy, joint research ventures among firms, especially among large oligopolistic firms.

In contrast, however, MITI and Japanese political leaders are little troubled by questions that continue to be debated in the United States: Is it not possible that joint research ventures could reduce "the center of innovative activities," thus reduce the total innovative activities within a society? Will not the "savings" of "wasteful" duplicative research accrue to a few large firms and not to society? Will not the joint research ventures in effect make it difficult, if not impossible, for new entrants to enter markets? Will not joint basic research ventures in time "spill over" into the market and thus indirectly induce anti-competitive market conduct among the firms involved in the joint basic research? If MCC becomes successful, can it be certain that it will not face antitrust problems under a different administration and in a changed political climate?

In not being asked these questions, it appears that MITI and the political leaders supporting the MITI-led joint research projects are neglecting the lessons of the policy they adopted during the rapid growth decades. In aiding the research efforts of large firms, and in effect totally ignoring all potential antitrust issues, the MITI-led joint research projects (and the trade associations organized for joint research) are again reducing the risks involved in the R&D activities of selected large firms and in the rapid expansion of their productive capacities. In short, MITI is actively and even aggressively involved in the growth of high-technology industries as it was with major industries during the rapid growth period.

The problems such involvement creates do not surface when the MITI-involved industries are in a rapid expansion phase, as they were during the 1950s and 1960s. But what can MITI do when temporary or chronic excess capacity develops for reasons of recession or overinvestment in many of the major industries promoted by MITI during the rapid growth years? Given its involvement in the growth phase of industry, MITI could hardly ignore industry's plight. Is not MITI again encouraging the firms, no less directly than it did during the rapid growth period, to engage in "export drives"? In other words, in having presided over the successful VSLI projects and in taking initiative in and providing subsidies for other ongoing projects relating to the semiconductor and other industries, is not MITI, to a significant extent, responsible for such a development as described below?

As was seen in the electronics industry, the pattern of massive investment by Japan's major companies in cost-reducing mass output facilities followed by intense price competition in world markets is being repeated in the semiconductor industry. As a result, industry sources anticipate intense trade friction involving such products as the 64K DRAM to be developed by 1985.[38]

Let me conclude this section with a restatement of the preceeding discussion in broader terms. I believe the fundamental difference in the American and Japanese attitudes toward public policy regarding promotion of innovative activities in the high-technology industries can be summarized as follows: Though specific expressions may vary, it is reasonable to observe that the majority of Americans, in principle, continue to hold that the market power possessed by large firms can, and does tend to, exceed socially desirable limits. The social costs of having such large firms, manifested in varying ways, is sufficiently high to require an antitrust structure capable of limiting, or preventing the exercise of, their market power. Thus as a matter of principle a more competitive market structure, essential for competitive market behavior, needs to be preserved, and no public policy should be adopted if its direct or potential consequence is to bring about a market structure conducive to restricting competition.

Given these circumstances, in matters relating to technological progress, Americans are not inclined to support a public policy intended primarily to promote the technological capabilities of large firms. The large majority of Americans, specialists analyzing such issues and laymen alike, justify this policy inclination based on their belief that the competitive and unconstrained market is better able to predict and "pick" future technological "winners" than the government officials who administer a public policy intended to achieve the same goal.

A necessary corollary of this view is that no one wishing to engage in innovative activities should be deterred in any manner from doing so as a direct or indirect result of public policy, even if it results in duplicative innovative efforts. The principal reason for this American view is that in the past, and likely in the future as well, even seemingly "wasteful" duplicative research has been a source of major research breakthroughs. Thus both large and small firms should pursue research goals independently, and no public policy should be adopted if its effect is to limit the innovative activity of small firms or to give preference to groups of large firms.

In contrast, most Japanese implicitly accept the view that the contributions large productive firms make to society are evident in the performance of the Japanese economy, so these contributions more than compensate for social costs the large firms might impose, for example, as a result of their anticompetitive practices at home or even of trade conflicts they create. Thus, for most Japanese, the oligopolistic market structure and even various indications of collusive conduct and "export drives" are not viewed with concern, as they might be in the United States. Rather, the existing market structure is seen basically as a necessary consequence of scale economies to be realized, and the indication of collusive conduct is accepted as an inevitable side effect of achieving rapid economic growth.

Because of this view, held with little variation for over a century of Japanese industrialization, the various forms of government involvement in aiding the efforts of the large firms to increase their productive efficiency are widely accepted as socially necessary and not regarded as an undesirable intrusion in market activities. The favored status that is accorded to the large firms by the public policy therefore has not, as a rule, been challenged to date on the grounds of economic efficiency or public welfare, as it would be in the United States.

Thus the Japanese are inclined to support a public policy whose goals and effective results are to promote virtually exclusively the technological capabilities of the large firms. Questions are rarely raised regarding the potential risks involved in nonmarket, but MITI-led, selection of future "winners"—the socially undesirable consequences of, in effect, restricting the chance of technological breakthrough occurring in seemingly "wasteful" duplicative innovative activities. In short, the Japanese have few doubts about the relative advantage of MITI-led joint research accompanied by other forms of government involvement over the American-style, "market-determined" innovative activity with the government basically standing aside.

Concluding Reflections

Industrial policy has much in common with religion. Avowed supporters of industrial policy include true believers and those who confuse their own greed with national interest. The market-trusting critics of industrial policy, on the other hand, call it a hocus-pocus having no "rational" basis and often accuse if of being detrimental to economic efficiency. As in the debate on the existence of God, neither side really has infallible means to prove their case. The supporters rely heavily on faith, on observed "correlations" (Japan grew rapidly and has industrial policy) and on their critics' inability to refute convincingly the claimed efficacy of industrial policy. Like atheists unable to explain how the universe really works, the academic critics of industrial policy—the neoclassical economists—are forced to admit that their analytical tool kit does not contain all the tools needed to discredit the belief cherished by supporters of industrial policy. All too often the best these economists can do is to tackle only those analytically congenial parts of the large and complex reality we call the political economy of industrial societies. Because of this fact and because the economists' analysis is "static" or at best "comparatively static" (i.e., does not deal with dynamic changes over time) and seems to work well only when aided by assumptions (which the believers are unwilling to grant), their efforts remain substantially less effective than they wish them to be in dissuading the supporters of industrial policy from their faith.

The foregoing is merely to warn readers that this concluding note assessing the effectiveness of Japan's industrial policy contains my view, much of which is based not on unequivocable evidence but on a conviction I have come to have after twenty-odd years of studying Japanese industrial policy.

My view on Japanese industrial policy is that it has been more effective than many economists would admit but substantially less so than maintained by the Americans urging adoption of industrial policy à la Japanese. I am also persuaded that the effectiveness of Japanese industrial policy was achieved at the cost of economic efficiency and political "fairness" which was not readily visible while the policy was being pursued. As in the preceding sections, let me offer my assessment separately for the rapid growth and the post-1973 periods.

As Krugman's and other economists' telling analyses have shown, the Japanese economy in the rapid growth period would have achieved much of what it accomplished even without industrial policy.[39] Japan's rapid growth was principally a result of the availability of readily borrowable technology (the "catchup process"), a large saving enabling firms to increase per-worker capital investment, and several other important reasons I have already described. There, indeed, is much truth in an observation an economist-friend of mine once half-jokingly made: "Even had all MITI officers been graduates of third-rate universities, the economy would have grown very rapidly."

But what is crucial is the fact that even the economists would not argue that Japan's industrial policy was totally without salutary effects. A careful reading of their analysis shows that they invariably include several qualifiers in their analysis. Even so, my view simply is that economists still tend to acknowledge too grudgingly the contribution industrial policy made to Japan's economic performance.

I am pursuaded that, in Japan's catchup growth, the multifaceted MOF-MITI strategy to encourage the "investment race" played not a negligible role in increasing the productivity and exports of the major Japanese industries during the 1950s and the 1960s. That increasing exports was essential for the economic growth of Japan in these decades can hardly be overemphasized. Neither should we forget that throughout the rapid growth period, the high saving rate also was due, not to a minor degree, to the many pro-saving policies adopted, and the neglect of social welfare programs by the government intent on increasing capital investment.

Although I did not stress it sufficiently in the preceding sections, we should also note the fact that Japanese industrial policy was basically "market conforming." The policy prompted firms to adopt successively newer technology and invest rapidly while inducing firms to compete fiercely for market share in improving product quality and services, and in the terms of credit they advanced. Though cartels prevented price competition when the major industries were suffering from recession or overinvestment, price competition was in most industries also fierce when the economy was in an upswing and demand was strong. In the rapidly growing economy, boom years enjoying buoyant demand were many.

Put differently, I believe that Japanese industrial policy was more effective than many economists seem to concede because it intervened to affect resource allocations and the pace of investment in advanced technology without attempting to counter the dictates of market forces. I contend that this assessment differs crucially from a simplistic deduction often made of this observation: that Japan's industrial policy did no more than to validate the market dictates, thus it was merely a placebo handed out with fanfare.

The crux of the matter is that it was possible in Japan in the rapid growth period to intervene effectively in basically market-conforming ways (with several glaring exceptions of course) and to do more than validate what the market dictates. As I have described, Japan had this possibility because of the pro-growth consensus, the fact that Japan was catching up, the prevailing Pax Americana, and other reasons which in turn made "administrative guidance" workable and the continuing LDP dominance possible. I find the view, expressed by some, stating in effect that Japanese industrial policy was no more than bureaucratic breast-beating exceedingly naive.

But exploiting this possibility was far from costless. And the social costs of the MOF-MITI pro-growth strategy gradually rose as the rapid growth continued. By the mid-1960s the Japanese were beginning to weigh carefully the trickle-down gains being realized from the policies against their costs. To the costs I described in the earlier sections, I should add those imposed by pollution of air and water and the fact that Japan came to be viewed by its trading partners as being unfair or even selfish.

But these remarks should not be construed to mean that I am suggesting emulation by the United States of the Japanese industrial policy of the rapid growth decades. As I emphasized earlier in this essay, to suggest such a course would be worse than naive. Industry-specific subsidies, cartels, fixed interest rates, and many other policies of Japan of the rapid growth years should have no place in the U.S. economy of today. The United States in the 1980s and Japan in the rapid growth period differ in so many ways that such a suggestion is hardly credible.

On the Japanese industrial policy of the post-1973 period (and what the U.S. policy must be today and in the coming decades), I offer the following reflections. I am persuaded that Japan's industrial policy will be decreasingly effective and can even be perverse in its effects. As the number and efficacy of the policy tools declined because of trade liberalization, and the internationalization of capital markets, and as the politicization of the policy formulation and administration continues to increase because of the rising distributional conflicts, much of the essential policy flexibility and the effectiveness of the all-important administrative guidance has been lost. Given the loss, Japan cannot hope that its policies will be as effective as before. The conditions required to maintain a delicate balance between the market-conforming virtues and market-intervening efficacy of its policies no longer exist in Japan which ceased to be a follower and is now entering the twenty-first-century system characterized by all of its economic and political uncertainties.

To be more specific, Japan's efforts, for example, to promote its high-technology industries, employing policies similar in intent to those adopted in the 1960s to increase international competitiveness of the major industries of the decade, is fraught with the problems I described in the preceding secion. One of the most important problems is that Japan, in pursuing the policy, is demonstrating its reluctance to give due consideration to the fact that it is no longer a small economy in the process of catching up—it is now the second largest economy in the world and is capable of seriously challenging the technological leadership of the United States. Clearly, if Japan continues to maintain its current policy orientation, it will pose an extremely difficult problem to the United States. Indeed, the performance of the American high-technology industries in international markets could be further threatened. Thus the choice Americans face today is either to adopt policies that could counter the Japanese policies or to adopt no major policy, trusting in the market to provide correct signals and sufficient vitality to ensure the competitiveness of the American industries.

Although expressing my views on this choice is not a task assigned to me, let me conclude by reminding readers that the American choice must be made keeping in mind the following facts and observation:

First, it is not likely that Japanese policy vis-à-vis its high-technology industries will change in the near future. Instead, there is a distinct possibility of it becoming even more activist. Attesting to this possibility, MITI announced on August 27, 1984, two new proposals. One is legislation (to be submitted to the Diet) to request increased funding to add four more major MITI-led "next-generation" research projects to the ten currently under way. One of the important functions of this proposed agency will include provision of funding for up to 90 percent of the costs of joint private research ventures between two or more firms. If the MITI proposal is enacted, funds provided by the agency need not be repaid if a venture fails, and successful ventures repay the fund paying interest of only 7.1 percent.[40]

Second, in debating the American policy, we must not lose the sight of the fact that the competitiveness, if not the leadership, of Japanese high-technology industries in the international market is regarded as essential to the future of Japan by the policymakers and most Japanese. Despite the recent "high-tech fever" seen in the United States, its temperature can hardly match that which one senses in Toyko.

Of course this difference reflects, among other factors, the Japanese "fragility obsession" and the fact that welfare losses suffered by Japanese consumers (or, more broadly, the distributional issues) still affect the policy course less than they do in the United States. In other words, Japan's political economy is still demonstrating, and is likely to continue to do so in the coming decades as well, a strong pro-export orientation despite the recent developments in both Japanese domestic politics and its relations with trading partners. This is the reason why Matsushita, Hitachi, Toshiba, and others, are today the principal members in many of the MITI-led semiconductor-related and other joint research projects.

Third, in taking time to decide on policies, Americans may be affording themselves a chance to observe negative results of current Japanese policies. However, delaying adoption of policies could cause irreversible disadvantages to the American high-technology firms that must compete against the increasingly formidable Japanese rivals. In the twenty-first-century system there is no guarantee that the patterns observed in the twentieth-century system will be repeated in a similar way. Technological changes in the coming decades can be much more "cumulative" and/or can take far more unexpected forms of "branching out" than we have seen to date. Those currently counseling that the United States adopt no policy to aid high-technology industries must be prepared to accept the possibility of placing American firms at a serious competitive disadvantage to Japanese firms.

The Japanese are challenging us to rethink how and what policies we must adopt in order to maintain the competitive abilities of the American economy and its firms.

Notes

1. Unless stated otherwise, I mean by "industrial policy" all types of "creative tinkering" with familiar policy tools such as the antitrust, trade, tax, labor, and other laws as well as establishing new institutions for the purpose of influencing resource allocations and the rate of technological innovation within an economy so that its performance will be improved. My definition of "industrial policy" will exclude macroeconomic policy, which is capable of changing the rates of saving and investment as well as influencing aggregate demand.

2. Japan's leading business leaders are known to speak publicly for the virtues of cooperation among the major firms in an industry on matters relating to investment, exports, and even prices. Their American friends do so only privately. The relative laxity of the antitrust enforcement in Japan explains only a part of this difference.

3. Three scholars at the University of Tokyo succinctly summarized this consensus in an article they coauthored. They found that in the rapid growth period, "there was no politics in the sense of the competitive advocacy of the

fundamental goal of society" because rapid economic growth was "a war to be won, the first total war in Japanese history for which all of the nation's resources were mobilized voluntarily." Seizaburo Satō, Shumpei Kumon, and Yasusuke Murakami, "Datsu-hokaku jidai no tōrai" (The Arrival of the Post-Conservative versus Progressive Period), *Chūō Kōron*, (February, 1977), p. 82. Also see Takafusa Nakamura, *The Postwar Japanese Economy* (Tokyo: University of Tokyo Press, 1981), pp. 80–91.

4. Those interested in further elaborations of observations and analyses presented in this section are referred to Kozo Yamamura, "Success that Soured: Administrative Guidance and Cartels in Japan"; Yasusuke Murakami, "Toward a Socioinstitutional Explanation of Japan's Economic Performance"; and Y. Murakami and K. Yamamura, "A Technical Note on Japanese Firm Behavior and Economic Policy," in K. Yamamura, ed., *Policy and Trade Issues of the Japanese Economy* (Seattle: University of Washington Press, 1982), pp. 3–46 and pp. 77–122.

5. John Zysman, *Governments, Markets and Growth* (Ithaca: Cornell University Press, 1983).

6. For a concise treatment of the Japanese capital market of the period, see Ryoichi Mikitani, "Monetary Policy in Japan," in Karel Holbik, ed., *Monetary Policy in Twelve Industrial Countries* (Boston: The Federal Reserve Bank of Boston, 1973), pp. 246–281; and for a more extended discussion of fiscal policy and capital market, see Henry C. Wallich and Mable I. Wallich, "Banking and Finance," in Hugh Patrick and Henry Rosovky, eds., *Asia's New Giant* (Washington D.C.: The Brookings Institution, 1976), pp. 246–315. Over the past few years several authors have offered a revisionist view of the role of MOF in the rapid growth period, arguing that the MOF policy had little effect on market forces, namely that MOF's "subequilibrium interest rate policy" was ineffective. In English, this revisionist view is available in Eisuke Sakakibara et al., "The Japanese Financial System in Comparative Perspective," a study prepared for the Joint Economic Committee, U.S. Congress, 1982, and Akiyoshi Horiuchi, "Economic Growth and Financial Allocation in Postwar Japan," Brookings Discussion Paper, No. 18, 1984. However, their view, which may appeal to those interested in a theoretical analysis, is seriously flawed because they typically assume away important institutional and behavioral characteristics of Japanese monetary policy, capital market, and the participants in the market. Space does not permit me in this paper to enter into specific criticisms, both theoretical and empirical, of the revisionist view; let me only add that I remain convinced by a more widely accepted view of the character and effectiveness of the MOF policy as Murakami, after assessing the revisionist view (or the market school as he called it), has summarized: "if all relevant facts are considered in a comprehensive way, it may be a sound judgment that the interest rate was regulated at an artificially low level in the following sense. The effective interest rates in most financial markets would have been significantly higher, and never lower, if the network of financial regulations had been removed," Murakami, "Toward a Socioinstitutional Explanation," p. 14.

7. The *Mainichi* newspaper published a book (in two volumes) entitled *Shogen: Kodo seichoki no Nihon* (Testimonies: Japan in the Rapid Growth Period) (Tokyo: The Mainichi Shimbun, 1984). The book contains eighty-three interviews conducted with the former government officials, leading politicians, businessmen, union leaders, scholars, and others who played key roles in formulating and administering the policies or in affecting in various capacities Japanese economy and society during the rapid growth period. Anyone arguing that the economic policies of this period merely validated the dictates of market forces, thus having little effect on the performance of the Japanese economy, is suggested to read in the first volume pp. 296–319 and 333–337, and in the second, pp. 233–242, 281–285, and 343–388. The interviews in these pages contain remarkably candid responses to the questions asked regarding how policies were formulated and implemented, and how they affected various aspects of the domestic economy and Japan's trade during the rapid growth years.

8. Edward J. Lincoln, *Japan's Industrial Policies* (Washington, D.C.: Japan Economic Institute of America, 1984), p. 14.

9. Ibid., pp. 14–15.

10. Ibid, p. 15.

11. Hiroya Ueno, "The Conception and Evaluation of Japanese Industrial Policy," in Kazuo Sato, ed., *Industry and Business in Japan* (White Plains, N.Y.: M.E. Sharpe, Inc.), p. 381.

12. The discussions and analyses of this section are adapted from Kozo Yamamura and Jeannette VanDenBerg, "The Rapid Growth Policy on trial: The Television Case" (manuscript completed in summer 1984).

13. Akira, Senō, *Gendai Nihon no Sangyō Shūchū* (Industrial Concentration in Modern Japan) (Tokyo: Nihon Keizai Shimbunsha, 1983), p. 288, and *Japan Electronics Almanac, 1981* (Tokyo: Dempa Publications, Inc., 1981), pp. 221–305.

14. These figures were computed using U.S. market totals from the *TV FACT Book, 1980,* Vol. 49, as published annually by TV Digest, Inc., Washington, D.C., and from U.S. International Trade Commission, *Television Receivers, Color and Monochrome, Assembled or not Assembled, Finished or not Finished and Subassemblies Thereof,* Report to the President on Investigation No. TA-201-19, USITC Pub. 808 (Washington, D.C.: GPO, 1977). Japanese import figures are from the U.S. Bureau of the Census, U.S. Imports for Consumption and General Imports, Rpt. FT246, Annual Issues. The 1977 Japanese share of the color market is from Robert Reich and Ira Magaziner, *Minding America's Business: The Decline and Rise of the American Economy* (New York: Vintage Books, 1983), p. 170. The other figures do not include the production of the Japanese company's third-country and American subsidiaries.

15. Reich and Magaziner, *Minding America's Business,* p. 171.

16. The entire Japanese electronics industry experienced only one entry during the period 1960 to 1980, that of Kensonic into audio component production. *Japan Electronics Almanac*, pp. 221–305.

17. Takeshi Kanasaki, *Kadengyōkai* (The Home Electronics Industry) (Tokyo: Kyōikusha, 1982), p. 172.

18. For more information on distribution *keiretsu*, see M. Y. Yoshino, *The Japanese Marketing System* (Cambridge, Mass.: The MIT Press, 1971), esp. pp. 91–124; Mistuaki Shimaguchi, *Marketing Channels in Japan* (Umi Research Press, 1978); Misonou Hitoshi et al., *Kokumin no dokusen hakusho: kigyō shūdan* (People's White Paper on Monopoly: Manufacturer-Headed Business Groups) (Tokyo: Ochanomizu Shobo, 1978); Fair Trade Commission of Japan, "Ryūtsū keiretsu-ka ni kansuru dokusenkinshihōjō no toriatsukai" (The Treatment of Vertically Integrated Distribution under the Antimonopoly Act); this is a report issued by an internal FTCJ studies group in March 1980 and is discussed in English in J. Amanda Covey, "Vertical Restraints under Japanese Law: The Antimonopoly Study Group Report," Law in Japan, Vol. 14 (1981), pp. 49–81; Ishida Hideto, "Anticompetitive Practices in the Distribution of Goods and Services in Japan: The Problem of Distribution *Keiretsu*," *Journal of Japanese Studies* (Summer 1983), pp. 319–334.

19. Kanasaki, *Kadengyōkai*, p. 106.

20. Ibid., p. 110.

21. Yoshino, *Japanese Marketing*, p. 116, Kanasaki, *Kadengyōkai*, p. 169.

22. For further information on the FTCJ proceedings, see FTCJ, *Kōsei torihiki iinkai shinketsu-shū* (Collection of Judicial Decisions of the Fair Trade Commission) (Tokyo: FTCJ, 1971), No. 17, pp. 187–208; and FTCJ, *Kosei torihiki iinkai hōkoku* (The Annual Report of the Fair Trade Commission) (Tokyo: FTCJ, 1979).

23. This information originates in documents siezed by the FTCJ and is now available in English in *Appellants' Brief*, in RE: Japanese Electronic Products Antitrust Litigation, 723 F. 2d 238 (3rd Cir. 1983), pp. 37–38.

24. Yomiuri Shimbun, November 10, 1966; Van Zandt, "Learning to do Business with Japan, Inc." *Harvard Business Review* 50 (July–August 1972), p. 90.

25. James E. Millstein, "Decline in an Expanding Industry: Japanese Competition in Color Television," in John Zysman and Laura Tyson, eds., *American Industry in International Competition* (Ithaca: Cornell University Press, 1983), p. 122; and *Japan Economic Yearbook*, 1971 (Tokyo: The Oriental Economist, 1971), p. 208.

26. See Reich and Magaziner, *Minding America's Business*, pp. 160–180.

27. Changes in employment were computed using figures from USITC Pub. 808, cited in footnote 12; Bart S. Fisher, "The Antidumping Law of the United States: A Legal and Economic Analysis," *Law and Policy in International Business* 5 (1973), p. 120; and U.S. International Trade Commission, *Summary of*

Trade and Tariff Information on TSUS Items 685.11-685.19, USITC Pub. 841, Control No. 6-5-33 (Washington, D.C.: GPO, 1982), pp. 11–12.

28. The most concise source on American reactions is USITC Pub. 841, Control No. 6-5-33. See also Phillips B. Keller, "Zenith Radio Corp. v Matsushita Electrical Industrial Co.: Interpreting the Antidumping Act of 1916," *Hastings International and Comparative Law Review* 6 (1982), pp. 133–159; Japanese sources include Yoshio Ohara, *"Nichi-bei-ō kankei no sōgōteki kōsastsu"* (A Comprehensive Analysis of Japan-U.S.-European Relations), Japan-EC Studies Association Annual Report, No. 3 (1983).

29. A concise summary of these practices is found *Appellants' Brief* and *Appellants' Reply Brief,* in RE: Japanese Electronic Products Antitrust Litigation, 723 F. 2d 238 (3d Cir. 1983).

30. See *Keizai Yōran* (Essential Economic Facts), compiled by the Research Division, Economic Planning Agency (Tokyo: Economic Planning Agency, 1982).

31. Yasusuke Murakami and Kozo Yamamura, "Technology in Transition: Two Perspectives on Industrial Policy," a paper presented at the Conference on Japanese Industrial Policy in Comparative Perspective, New York, March 17–19, 1984.

32. For further discussions of the recent changes in the character of Japanese industrial policy, see George Eads and Kozo Yamamura, "The Future of Japanese Industrial Policy," presented at the Conference on the Japanese Political Economy, August 19–25, 1984. Tokyo, Japan.

33. See Gary Saxonhouse, "Industrial Restructuring in Japan," *Journal of Japanese Studies* (Summer 1979), pp. 273–320.

34. For a further treatment of the problems and issues discussed in this section, see Kozo Yamamura, "Joint Research and Antitrust: Japanese vs. American Strategies," paper prepared for the Conference on Japanese Industrial Policy in Comparative Perspective, New York City, March 17–19, 1984.

35. *Asahi Shimbun,* June 22, 1981, p. 9.

36. *Chūō Kōrōn,* Fall 1981, p. 120.

37. *The New York Times,* September 5, 1984, p. 27.

38. See Tetsuro Wada, "Trilateral Friction in Microchip Business Seen among Japan, U.S. and Korea," *The Japan Economic Journal,* July 24, 1984, p. 20.

39. Paul R. Krugman, "Targeted Industrial Policies: Theory and Evidence, in Federal Reserve Bank of Kansas City, *Industrial Change and Public Policy* (Kansas City: Federal Reserve Bank of Kansas City, 1983), pp. 123–156; and Paul R. Krugman, "The U.S. Response to Foreign Industrial Targeting," *Brookings Papers on Economic Activity,* 1 (1984), pp. 77–121. Also see Hugh T. Patrick and Henry Rosovsky, "Introduction" and "Prospects for the Future and Some Other Implications," in Patrick and Rosovsky, eds., *Asia's New Giant,* pp. 1–61 and 897–923.

40. *Asahi Shimbun,* August 28, 1984, p. 9.

9

U.S. Trade and Industrial Policy: The Experience of Textiles, Steel, and Automobiles

William R. Cline

The Nature of U.S. Policy

This paper considers U.S. trade and industrial policy in declining industries, primarily in textiles, steel, and automobiles because these three sectors alone constitute the bulk of the problem of sectoral protection in manufactures in the United States today. All three have experienced decline or stagnation. Production in 1983–84 was 35 percent below the 1973 peak in steel and 22 percent below in automobiles. Ironically the sector with the longest history of protection, textiles and apparel, has shown less decline: in 1984 textiles output stood at the same level as its previous 1973 peak, while apparel production was only 7 percent below its previous peak (1979). (See table 9.1.)

In principle, U.S. industrial and trade policy is premised on market determination and free trade. The nation has specifically rejected the idea that the government should favor specific sectors and discourage others. The only significant areas of positive stimulus to specific industries have been in defense and agriculture.

The principal form of industrial policy in the United States has been the limited granting of exceptions to open trade for individual product sectors. In practice, these exceptions have not been the consequence of any grand design for infant-industry development or, in the terms of other papers in this volume, for strategic trade purposes. Instead, they have been reluctant departures from the general free-trade principle where political pressures have been irresistible, or where more technical criteria of "import injury" (under section 201 of U.S. trade law) have been met.

The political dominance of the protection process in the United

Table 9.1
Production and employment in steel, automobiles, textiles, and apparel, 1960–84 (thousand employees)

	U.S. manufacturing		Steel		Autos		Textiles		Apparel	
	Q	N	Q	N	Q	N	Q	N	Q	N
1960	171.80	16,796.00	71.15	574.20	6.67	724.10	69.300	924.400	81.700	1,233.200
1961	172.00	16,326.00	66.13	524.90	5.50	632.30	71.400	893.400	82.200	1,214.500
1962	186.70	16,853.00	70.55	522.50	6.90	691.70	76.200	902.300	85.500	1,263.700
1963	202.20	16,995.00	75.55	520.00	7.60	741.30	78.900	885.400	89.100	1,282.800
1964	216.70	17,274.00	84.94	554.00	7.80	752.90	85.200	892.000	92.200	1,302.500
1965	236.70	18,062.00	92.67	584.00	9.30	842.70	92.800	925.600	97.400	1,354.200
1966	254.90	19,214.00	90.00	576.00	8.60	861.60	98.400	963.500	99.900	1,401.900
1967	254.30	19,447.00	83.90	555.00	7.40	815.80	100.000	958.500	100.000	1,397.500
1968	268.20	19,781.00	91.86	552.00	8.80	873.70	107.900	993.900	102.900	1,405.800
1969	277.20	20,167.00	93.89	544.00	8.20	911.40	112.600	1,002.500	106.700	1,409.100
1970	261.20	19,367.00	90.80	531.00	6.60	799.00	111.800	974.800	101.400	1,363.800
1971	266.80	18,623.00	87.04	487.00	8.60	848.50	116.500	954.700	104.700	1,342.600
1972	292.50	19,151.00	91.81	478.00	8.80	874.80	132.700	985.700	109.400	1,382.700
1973	325.30	20,154.00	111.43	509.00	9.70	976.50	142.900	1,009.800	117.300	1,438.100
1974	311.70	20,077.00	109.47	512.00	7.30	907.70	132.800	965.000	114.300	1,362.600
1975	289.60	18,323.00	79.96	457.00	6.70	792.40	122.300	867.900	107.600	1,243.300

Year										
1976	317.40	18,997.00	89.45	454.00	8.50	881.00	134.600	918.800	125.700	1,318.100
1977	339.20	19,682.00	91.15	452.00	9.20	947.30	134.400	910.200	134.200	1,316.300
1978	357.20	20,505.00	97.94	449.00	9.20	1,004.90	137.500	899.100	134.200	1,332.300
1979	367.00	21,040.00	100.26	453.00	8.40	990.40	145.000	885.100	134.400	1,304.300
1980	351.00	20,285.00	83.85	399.00	6.40	788.80	138.600	847.700	127.000	1,263.500
1981	361.10	20,170.00	88.45	391.00	6.30	788.70	135.700	823.000	120.400	1,244.400
1982	336.10	18,853.00	61.57	289.00	5.10	704.80	124.500	749.400	116.100	1,161.100
1983	357.90	18,678.00	67.58	243.00	6.80	772.70	140.800	743.500	126.900	1,164.100
1984	377.30	19,736.00	77.99	242.00	7.70	864.00	142.900	762.200	125.000	1,209.700

Sources: *Economic Report of the President* (Washington, D.C.: GPO, February 1984), pp. 223, 263–264; American Iron and Steel Institute, *Annual Statistical Report: 1983* (Washington, D.C.: 1984), pp. 8, 20; *The US Auto Industry: US Factory Sales, Retail Sales, Imports, Exports, Apparent Consumption, Suggested Retail Prices, and Trade Balances with Selected Countries for Motor Vehicles, 1964–82*, USITC Publication #1419, August 1983; *The US Automobile Industry: Monthly Report on Selected Economic Indicators*, USITC Publication #1551, July 1984; *Motor Vehicles Manufacturers Association, Facts and Figures, '84*, MVMA, 1984, p. 67; *Employment and Earnings, United States, 1909–1978*, U.S. Department of Labor, July 1979, pp. 505, 547; *Supplement to Employment and Earnings*, U.S. Department of Commerce, October 1980, p. 13; *Survey of Current Business*, various monthly issues; *Survey of Current Business: 1979*, U.S. Department of Labor, July 1984, pp. 174, 188; *Business Statistics: The Biennial Supplement to the Survey of Current Business: 1979*, U.S. Department of Commerce, October 1980, p. 13; *Survey of Current Business*, various monthly issues; 1980–84, U.S. Department of Commerce; U.S. Department of Labor, Bureau of Labor Statistics, Office of Productivity and Technology. April 1984, Unpublished data on auto wages.

Note: For U.S. Manufacturing, Q = GNP in manufacturing, billions of 1972 dollars; N = total employment. For steel, Q = total net shipments of steel mill products, thousands of tons; N = average total number of iron and steel employees. For autos, Q = U.S. factory sales of new passenger automobiles, millions of vehicles; N = total employment in motor vehicles and equipment manufacturing (SIC371). For textiles and apparel, Q = Fed's index of production for textile mill and apparel products; N = total employment.

States is apparent in a recent empirical analysis. I have estimated a statistical (logit) model, explaining the presence or absence of major nontariff barrier protection across 80 manufacturing sectors (at the four-digit level of the International Standard Industrial Classification) for the late 1970s through early 1980s.[1] The model treats trade barriers that result from the interaction between an industry's demand for protection and the government's willingness to supply protection. Influences affecting the demand side involve the return to industry and labor from protection campaigns. Higher import penetration means higher potential industry benefits from protection, higher firm concentration means greater lobbying efforts (because there are fewer small "free-rider" firms that may benefit without contributing their share), and various indicators of underlying comparative advantage also enter on the demand side (more competitive industries stand to gain less from protection and may even suffer from foreign retaliation). On the supply side the government may be more likely to grant protection if the industry has a large labor force (because of the number of votes at stake), if wages are lower (because of greater public sympathy), and if sectoral growth is low and the rate of increase in import penetration is high (two measures of the cost of adjustment in the absence of protection).

The results of this model indicate that two influences are dominant in U.S. protection: the size of the sector's labor force, and the level (not rate of change) in import penetration. The first is an indicator of the political clout of the industry. The second reflects the degree of economic interest of the industry in restricting imports. Thus political influence and the relative size of the interest group's potential gains from protection appear to determine U.S. protection. Other factors more relevant for national economic costs and benefits (in particular, adjustment costs) prove not to be statistically significant.

The role of the industry's labor force is evident when one considers the sectors that enjoy protection today. Textiles and apparel number two million workers; automobiles, nearly one million; and steel, as high as half a million until the mid-1970s. All three of these giant sectors are protected. The weight of the number of workers involved was illustrated again recently by the decision on copper, in which the president rejected protection for a sector that has few workers (though there are considerably more workers in the fabricating industries that use copper as an input, a factor explicitly cited in the decision).[2]

In the last three years pressures for increased protection in the United States have been severe, initially because of the worst recession since the 1930s and more recently because of an overvaluation of the dollar by perhaps 30 percent.[3] Overvaluation acts like a 30 percent subsidy to imports and a comparable tax on exports. These protectionist pressures have taken their toll. An administration philosophically committed to free trade has adopted several major protectionist actions, including sugar quotas, successive tightening of textile protection, voluntary restraints on Japanese automobiles, and a new regime of steel quotas (including the most recent measure, extension of the network of voluntary restraints to important developing country suppliers).

Abstracting from the pressures of the business and exchange rate cycles, there are fundamental difficulties with an active industrial policy. Although it might seem superficially attractive to replace the negative industrial policy of protectionism by a positive policy of stimulus to individual sectors, there are strong reasons for suspicion about this strategy. There is the obvious difficulty of picking winners and losers: it is difficult to judge in advance which industries will develop future comparative advantage. In addition favoring certain sectors would mean bidding up the cost of resources diverted away from the general economy. And active industrial policy would almost inevitably fall prey to the same political/interest-group forces that have shaped trade protection, and the United States could end up with government stimulus to the industries of the past rather than those of the future. Experience in Europe would tend to support this diagnosis; there industrial policy has tended to prolong the agony of the losing industrial sectors rather than to promote transition to new sectors, suggesting that policymakers give greater weight to political than economic considerations.

Even if the policy process could look toward the future, it would be dubious that the argument of providing government support to "infant industries" could be justifiably invoked in the context of an advanced industrial country. To cite just one reason, the classic infant-industry argument assumes that capital markets are poorly developed and are unavailable to provide the financing private firms would need to weather the initial years of learning-by-doing at losses (to be followed by subsequent years of high profits as the infant industry matures). Yet U.S. capital markets are the most advanced in the world.

Concepts of Adjustment

An integral part of the concept of permissible trade protection in postwar U.S. trade policy has been that any such protection is temporary for the purpose of softening injury from imports, and that the industry in question is expected to adjust over time rather than receive permanent protection. This underlying concept of "protection for adjustment" has inherent appeal, even though most empirical studies demonstrate that the total economic costs of even unsheltered adjustment to imports are considerably smaller than the costs of protection to the economy as a whole. Yet even this principle has been increasingly honored in the breach. Textiles and apparel have enjoyed ever-tightening protection since the early 1960s. The steel sector increasingly has the appearance of a similar sphere of permanent protection. And, if automobile protection is renewed for 1985 on the heels of record profits and a rebound in employment, it will be difficult to see the end of protection there as well.

A fundamental difficulty with the concept of adjustment is that it has never been clear whether the term is supposed to mean upward or downward adjustment. An industrial sector conceivably could sharply improve its competitiveness during a temporary phase of protection and then confront imports successfully after a new liberalization. This type of adjustment is "revitalization." Alternatively, for a sector in which the country lacks comparative advantage, for example, because unskilled labor is the crucial input and the country has a scarcity of this factor relative to human and physical capital, the proper concept for adjustment is the "phase down" of production at a pace that permits reduction of employment through attrition and an acceptable rate of out-migration from the industry. In this alternative approach the role of temporary protection is merely to soften the inevitable process of job loss and to reduce the concentration of the burden of costs of international specialization on the existing work force in the industry losing comparative advantage.

A serious political difficulty is that industries themselves, and their labor groups, rarely accept that there can be any kind of adjustment other than revitalization. They do not accept down-phasing as an option. This viewpoint is understandable, but it is too narrow for purposes of public policy. For the economy as a whole, both concepts of adjustment must be recognized as policy options.

Protection of a selected industry is costly for the rest of the economy. For example, protection of steel raises steel prices and adversely affects the competitiveness of automobiles using steel. Protection ultimately raises prices to the consumer. It redistributes income from the consumer to domestic producers and workers in the protected industry. Worse, under voluntary export quotas, protection transfers income from domestic consumers to foreign producers by increasing the monopoly power of all producers—domestic and foreign— relative to consumers. At least the old form of protection, the tariff, transferred the income from consumers to the government in the form of tariff revenue.

Because protection is costly, the public has a right to expect that protected industries set clear timetables for adjustment and elimination of protection. The public has a right to expect concrete performance in the direction of adjustment.

Conceptually the two types of adjustment may be illustrated using figure 9.1. The vertical axis in this figure shows the industry's rate of productivity growth, normalized by subtracting the average rate of productivity growth for U.S. manufacturing. Ideally, total factor productivity would be used (including output per unit of capital as well as output per worker), but in practice, data availability limits the analysis here to productivity as measured by output per worker. In addition productivity ideally should be measured in real values at world (not protected domestic) prices. On the horizontal axis appears the rate of change of employment in the industry. Once again this rate is normalized by subtracting the rate of employment growth in the U.S. manufacturing industry as a whole for the same period.

Adjustment through revitalization is represented in the figure in quadrants I and IV. In this half of the figure the industry's productivity growth exceeds that for U.S. industry as a whole. The industry is making progress in improving its competitiveness, at least judged relative to other U.S. industries. It is still possible that even faster productivity gains abroad leave the industry in a worse relative position internationally. In quadrant IV revitalization is accompanied by lower employment. Whether production actually declines as well depends on whether productivity growth is greater than employment decline. (Thus, if output per worker grows at 5 percent while employment declines at 3 percent, output is still rising, though with an adjustment for industrywide normalization.) In quadrant I revitalization is so successful that not only is productivity growing rapidly but in addition total employment is growing.

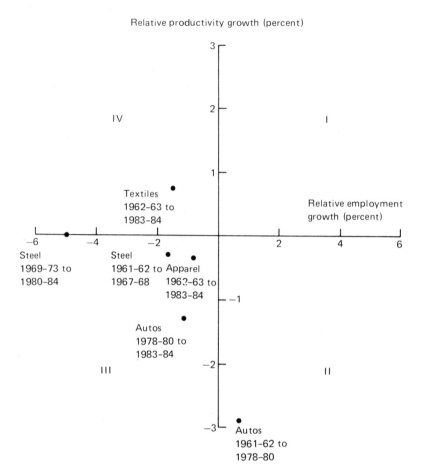

Figure 9.1

The other type of adjustment is represented by quadrants III and IV. Here employment is unambiguously declining. In quadrant III relative productivity is also declining, so there is evidence of further enervation instead of revitalization. In quadrant IV the zone relatively close to the horizontal axis will be one of actually declining production, and the entire quadrant represents a phase down in terms of employment (at least relative to overall manufacturing employment growth).

In short, the public should expect protected industries either to revitalize or phase-down. Such industries should be in quadrants I, III, or IV. If they are in quadrant II, they are failing to revitalize or to phase-down. Even the right-hand portion of quadrant III represents failure to adjust in a sense, because the smaller the rate of reduction of employment (the closer to the vertical axis), the slower the industry's rate of phase down and the longer the public is being asked to foot the bill.

The observations in figure 9.1 show the experience of the three industries considered here. These observations are calculated from the data on production and employment in table 9.1. Productivity is expressed in terms of output per worker (manufacturing GNP at constant prices, steel mill products in tons per worker, number of passenger cars per worker, and for textiles and apparel the Federal Reserve's index of industrial production, divided by employment).

Figure 9.1 indicates surprisingly poor performance of automobiles in the 1960s through 1978–80. Productivity declined at 0.6 percent annually, placing it nearly 3 percent below the U.S. average. Employment actually grew somewhat more rapidly than the U.S. average. In the period 1978–80 to 1983–84, the sector began to show some adjustment in the sense of phasing down, and its relative productivity performance was not as poor as before (although the sector continued to lag behind manufacturing as a whole). This pattern suggests that the sector has responded to protection (1981–84) with some adjustment, but so far only mild and in the phase-down mode rather than revitalization. It is possible that the large investments made in the sector will begin to bear fruit in terms of revitalization in the future.[4]

The sector of apparel is shown in the figure for the entire period 1962–84, during which it has enjoyed protection. The sector is in the quadrant of "phase-down" adjustment. There has been lagging productivity growth, presumably in large part because it is difficult to mechanise many of the operations and the industry remains labor intensive. The observation is so close to the vertical axis—so close to zero relative employment reduction—that it is even questionable whether the sector meets the test of phase-down adjustment. Essentially the sector's timetable for phase down has been extremely slow.

Steel in the period 1961–68 was also in the third quadrant, showing somewhat faster phase down and somewhat better relative productivity performance than apparel. The pattern for steel moved toward more rapid adjustment in the period 1969–73 to 1980–84. (The use of just recession years 1969–70 and expansion years 1983–84 would overstate relative productivity growth for steel which is highly cyclical.) In this second, protected period productivity growth was virtually identical to that for manufacturing on average, while down-phasing in terms of reduced employment was rapid—averaging 5 percent annually while manufacturing employment stayed virtually constant.

The contrast between adjustment in steel and that in apparel is striking. From 1969 to 1984 employment in steel has declined by 56 percent while apparel employment has fallen by only 14 percent, a rate of less than 1 percent annually (and a pace surely smaller than quit rates alone). It is little recognized that in terms of phasing down, steel has indeed achieved far more adjustment than apparel.

Textiles has also shown considerably more adjustment than apparel. As shown in figure 9.1, this sector lies in quadrant IV, showing both revitalization and down phasing in employment. Its output, as shown in table 9.1, has achieved relatively steady, if slow, advances. The basic difference between textiles and apparel, both of which have enjoyed the same regime of protection, is that it has proved easier to adapt the textiles sector to capital-intensive technological change to save on labor.[5]

In sum, the analytical framework proposed here suggests that there has been considerable adjustments in steel and textiles. Both sectors, accordingly, might be candidates for trade liberalization soon. Both sectors have shown the joint presence of revitalization and phasing down of employment. Autos and especially apparel have shown less adjustment (although future output gains in autos as the result of heavy recent investment could change this pattern). For apparel, in particular, the pace of adjustment has been glacial. It must be asked whether the public should accept such a pace indefinitely or whether instead an acceleration of adjustment should be the price of continued protection.

Transfers and Costs of Protection

The costs of protection are potentially high. The bulk of these costs amount to a transfer from consumers to producers (home and foreign). The remainder of the cost is a "deadweight loss" of economic efficiency, caused by allocating resources to the production of goods that can be more cheaply obtained abroad and by the fact that the scope for consumer choice is restricted (loss of "consumer surplus" of benefit over market price).

Crandall has suggested, on the basis of analysis by Wharton

Econometrics and his own statistical tests, that automobile quotas in 1981–83 raised the prices of Japanese cars in the U.S. market by $920 to $960 per car and increased the prices of domestic automobiles by $370 per car. On this basis the automobile restraints have cost American consumers approximately $4.5 billion annually.[6]

The Congressional Budget Office has analyzed the costs of proposed protection in steel. Pending legislation, which would limit imports to 15 percent of the market, would cause income transfers from steel consumers to domestic producers in the amount of $1.5 billion in 1985 and $3.4 billion by 1989; in addition consumers would transfer $2.1 billion to foreign producers in 1985 and $1.7 billion by 1989 (all figures in constant 1983 dollars). The total cost would amount to $178,000 for each job created.[7] In textiles and apparel one expert has estimated that tariffs cost U.S. consumers $9 billion annually and quotas add further costs of $2 billion to $4 billion.[8]

There is a need for more empirical analysis quantifying the costs of protection. But equally important, there is a need for greater public awareness of the costs. It is unlikely that the political process has decided on protection on the basis of a fully informed judgment by the public at large that it is prepared to bear these costs so that workers and firms in particular sectors may suffer smaller dislocations from imports. Instead, consumer opposition to protection is generally unorganized, and as a result the policy outcome represents a tilt in the direction of producers and directly affected workers. It is important to redress this imbalance by wider publicization of consumer costs of protection. Indeed, it would be a healthy development if U.S. trade law incorporated a "sunshine law" provision that required the calculation of costs to consumers in addition to the other various economic analyses required when a protection decision is to be examined in the International Trade Commission.

Textiles and Apparel

Nontariff protection goes back the farthest in textiles and apparel. In 1961 the United States organized the multilateral Short-Term Arrangement on cotton textiles, followed in 1962 by the Long-Term Arrangement. In 1974 the Multifiber arrangement (MFA) incorporated man-made fibers into international protection. The renewal of the MFA in 1977 increased protection in Europe, which had experienced rapidly rising imports after tighter U.S. implementation of the 1974 arrangement.

Successive renewals have tightened the regime of quotas further. Thus in the 1970s the MFA provided in principle for 6 percent annual growth in imports. But the renewal of 1981 effectively facilitated restricting import growth to minimal or even negative rates (e.g., by including language relating import growth to the growth in per capita consumption and by obliging "dominant suppliers" to reach mutually acceptable solutions).[9] In December 1983 the United States tightened restrictions further by formulating more automatic rules, triggering temporary holds on imports and calls for bilateral negotiations.[10] (Earlier in the year the threat of Chinese retaliation against grain imports averted a tightening of quotas against that country.) And most recently, in August 1984, the administration tightened rules of orgin for apparel made up in one country with materials from another, more tightly restricted country, such as China.[11]

Nor are the quotas on textiles and apparel ineffective, as is sometimes argued. Although the real value of apparel imports did grow at a relatively rapid rate of 8 percent annually in 1971–77, after the tightening of the MFA in 1977 the real value of imports actually declined by 1.8 percent annually in 1978–81. And the real value of imports of textile fabrics declined steadily from 1971 through 1981.[12]

In sum, the tourniquet on imports of textiles and apparel has been successively tightened over more than two decades. Far from being a temporary and digressive arrangement for adjustment, the MFA has proved to be a permanent mechanism for restrictions of continually increasing severity.

As noted earlier, the performance of productivity growth in the subsector of textiles fabric is the one encouraging sign in this industrial sphere. Indeed, the United States has moved to a position of modest net exporter in textiles (by value).[13] And although this outcome would be likely to experience some reversal under the elimination of quotas, it is nevertheless evident that at least in the textiles subsector it is time for a thorough reassessment of the need for protection.

Steel

Protection also has a long history in the steel sector. From 1969 through 1974 voluntary export restraints limited imports from Europe and Japan. Strong domestic demand and high inflation in 1973–74 brought an end to the first round of steel restraints. But by 1976 deep recession in the U.S. industry brought renewed pressure for protection. U.S. firms flooded the government with antidumping petitions.

In 1978 the Carter administration responded with a "trigger price mechanism" (TPM) that provided for fast-track antidumping investigations of steel imports entering at less than a "fair-value" reference price estimated on the basis of Japanese production costs. The mechanism was designed to be an alternative to massive litigation by the steel companies against foreign dumping.

In principle, enforcement of antidumping laws is "fair trade," not protection. But, in practice, the TPM appears to have been relatively protective.[14] Moreover since 1978 Japanese firms appear to have exercised a tacit export restraint themselves (presumably under the perceived threat of more aggressive U.S. restriction). Their exports to the United States in 1978–83 remained virtually frozen at 6 million tons annually, a phenomenon that would have a very low probability of occurrence on the basis of market forces alone.

The TPM did act as an umbrella to permit European sales at Japanese prices, even though European suppliers tended to be subsidized or dumped (making up for their higher production costs than those in Japan). From early 1980 through the autumn of 1982 there ensued a series of industry assaults on European imports using the antidumping and antisubsidy laws, parried by administration retaliation through suspension of the TPM, subsequent reinstatement at higher reference prices (October 1980), renewed industry suits against subsidized imports from Europe and some other countries. The Reagan administration itself initiated some suits (fearing collapse of the TPM) and encouraged foreign cutbacks and price increases.[15]

By mid-1982 the U.S. International Trade Commisson had issued a number of findings of significant subsidy on imports from Europe. However, steel from the more efficient producers in Germany and the Netherlands was found to have minimal subsidization, though preliminary findings placed subsidies in the range of 20 percent and higher for imports from France, Italy, Belgium, and the United Kingdom.

At this point the trade regime in steel faced a crucial turning point. The Europeans argued that the assessment of subsidies had been miscalculated, in considerable part because those government payments associated with phasing down European steel (including worker severance compensation) should be omitted. The United States and the EC might at this point have reexamined the levels of subsidies and addressed the steel problem through application of the normal fair-trade remedies (countervailing and antidumping duties). But intra-EC politics complicated this process. This outcome would have meant minimal penalties for the efficient European suppliers but substantial new duties against more heavily subsidized suppliers. Within the EC the voices of the less efficient, more heavily subsidized nations prevailed, and the EC made it clear that a solution had to be reached that had a more proportionate effect on the various European suppliers. The result was a new regime of voluntary quotas negotiated in the autumn of 1982. This new regime paved the way for what is rapidly becoming a rigid worldwide regime of quotas not unlike the Multifiber Arrangement—surely a far more protective outcome than might have occurred if the EC had been able to accept outright countervailing duties and abide by the more serious consequences for those European countries more heavily subsidizing their production.

The next major step in this process of cartelization of world steel has now arrived. In September 1984 the Reagan administration announced its rejection of an affirmative ITC recommendation supporting an industry petition for protection from injury by imports. But the administration's alternative appears approximately as protective as the ITC recommendation. The administration's plan is to tighten coverage of existing voluntary restraints on Europe, and in addition to negotiate new voluntary restraints on a long list of other suppliers (including Brazil, Mexico, Korea, South Africa, and Argentina). By the administration's estimate its solution will result in an import market share of 20.5 percent, compared with 19.8 percent under the ITC solution.

The administration argues that its remedy is more free trade because it will be based on pursuit of fair-trade principles. But that concept will be severely stretched. In particular, the administration appears to intend to act against imports from a country not subsidizing itself (e.g., Korea) on grounds that unfair practices in third markets (Japan) diverted exports from the country to the U.S. market.[16]

As if this response were not protective enough, in its trade bill of October 1984 the legislators expressed a "sense of Congress" that steel imports should be limited somewhere between 17 percent (the target voiced by presidential candidate Mondale) and 20.5 percent (the administration's figure).[17] Although Congress did not pass pending legislation that would have set a ceiling at 15 percent market share, this expression of congressional intent came closer to setting a rigid ceiling on imports as a fraction of consumption than has ever been done before.

Viewed as a whole the path of ever-tightening protection of steel since 1978 is sobering indeed. The United States has come close to establishing a rigid regime of quotas at highly restrictive levels. It has done so despite the free-trade philosophy of two successive administrations. The decision to protect has been taken even under the awareness that there could be dangerous repercussions in other areas. In particular, the new network of voluntary export restraints will restrict imports from (among other countries) Brazil, Mexico, and Argentina, three nations whose large and precarious external debt threatens the world banking system.

That this outcome could have occurred reflects the severity of steel's plight. As shown in table 9.1, in 1982 steel output fell 45 percent below its 1973 peak level. In 1982 steel production was operating at only 43 percent of capacity (compared with 77 percent in 1981).[18] Clearly the domestic recession and the overvalued dollar played major roles in this situation. But the protective regime that has now been assembled (and whose specific components are in process of negotiation) almost surely will long outlast the more temporary, cyclical phenomena of recession (already past) and dollar overvaluation.

More basic economic forces lie behind the difficulties of steel in the United States, however. Walter and others have suggested the basic dynamics of growing competitive problems in steel. The industry has an oligopoly structure among producers and faces a monopoly supply of unionized labor. In the 1960s and early 1970s the industry acquiesced in large wage increases demanded in labor negotiations. The firms did so in considerable part because they could rely on their oligopoly power to pass along to steel users the costs of high wage agreements.[19]

Table 9.2 reports the trend of steel wages relative to those in U.S. manufacturing as a whole, for the last two decades. The ratio between the two rose over this period from a range of 150 to 160 percent in the 1960s to 180 percent in 1974–78 and nearly 200 percent in 1980–82. The first sign of an arrest in this trend was the significant reduction to approximately 175 percent of the U.S. average in 1983.

Rising relative labor costs were not substantially offset by rising relative productivity. Thus, in the decade 1969–73 to 1979–83, output

Table 9.2
Relative wages in automobiles and steel, 1963–83

Year	Average wage U.S. manufacturing[a]	Automobiles[b]	Steel[c]	Ratio to U.S. manufacturing (percent) Automobiles	Steel
	A	B	C	D	E
1963	2.45	3.85	3.93	157.1	160.4
1964	2.53	4.01	4.01	158.5	158.5
1965	2.61	4.24	4.14	162.5	158.6
1966	2.71	4.46	4.25	164.6	156.8
1967	2.82	4.58	4.32	162.4	153.2
1968	3.01	5.02	4.58	166.8	143.6
1969	3.19	5.37	4.85	168.3	152.0
1970	3.35	5.65	5.08	168.7	151.6
1971	3.57	6.45	5.56	180.7	155.7
1972	3.82	7.03	6.22	184.0	162.8
1973	4.09	7.51	6.66	183.6	162.8
1974	4.42	8.34	7.80	188.7	176.5
1975	4.83	9.44	8.71	195.4	180.3
1976	5.22	10.27	9.50	196.7	182.0
1977	5.68	11.45	10.55	201.6	185.7
1978	6.17	12.67	11.57	205.3	187.5
1979	6.70	13.68	12.84	204.2	191.6
1980	7.27	16.29	14.43	224.1	198.5
1981	7.99	17.28	15.80	216.3	197.7
1982	8.50	18.66	16.81	219.5	197.8
1983	8.84	19.07	15.55	215.7	175.9

Sources: See table 9.1 for sources.
a. Average gross hourly earnings, in current dollars, for production workers in all manufacturing industries.
b. Average total compensation payment, including wages and benefits, for production workers in motor vehicles and equipment manufacturing.
c. Average payroll cost, per hour worked, for all workers.

per worker in U.S. manufacturing rose by 22.9 percent while that in steel rose by 23.1 percent, giving no relative rise in productivity. In the same period the ratio of steel wages to U.S. manufacturing wages rose by 22 percent.

The logical result of relative wage increases exceeding relative productivity gains was an upward trend in the relative price of steel. During 1960 through 1973 the ratio of U.S. steel prices to the domestic producer price index was relatively constant. But considering this period as a base of 100 (the level for both indexes in 1967), by 1974–76 the ratio of steel to general producer prices had risen to an index of 133, and by 1978–82 it had risen to 142.

A 42 percent rise in the relative price of steel was certain to have adverse consequences for the quantity of steel demanded. Steel was literally pricing itself out of the market. As a result the use of steel in the economy declined in absolute and relative terms. Thus in 1964 the U.S. economy used 100,000 tons of steel per billion dollars of GNP (at 1972 prices). By 1975–77 the ratio was down to 75,000 tons, and in the recession year of 1982 it touched as low as 51,000 tons. Undoubtedly the trend toward smaller cars played a role in this reduction of steel use. But it is difficult to avoid the conclusion that rising relative steel prices, driven in considerable part by rising relative wages, caused a major portion of the relative decline in steel use.[20]

The final step in this causal chain was a rise in imports. In the face of rising relative costs of domestic steel, U.S. purchasers turned increasingly to imports. Their share in total U.S. supply rose from a negligible fraction in the early 1960s to approximately 25 percent today. It is not surprising that the domestic industry has sought protection to remove this one obstacle to the otherwise successful arrangement whereby oligopoly firms have passed on to consumers the higher costs from negotiated wages.

Many other factors affect the steel industry, including management strategy, the rise of the mini-mills (which are efficient producers using scrap metal input) at the expense of the integrated mills, technological considerations, changes in transportation cost, and developments in foreign production. However, the diagnosis that emerges from the preceding analysis is that the industry has suffered from excessive wage growth and has sought protection to compensate. From the trade policy standpoint the one encouraging pattern is that the industry has at least adjusted considerably in the sense of down-phasing employment. The alternative of adjusting by returning to more normal relative wages is explored later. It should also be noted that with its labor force having declined from nearly 600,000 workers to only 242,000 (table 9.1), the steel sector stands in jeopardy of losing the political clout it has enjoyed in the past. The footwear sector has almost two-thirds as many employees as steel today, and yet decisions on footwear in the last four years have reflected that sector's lack of political influence.

Automobiles

The case of automobiles is a vivid illustration of the dominance of politics in U.S. trade policy. The normal channel for decisions on

protection is the International Trade Commission's review of petitions for safeguard protection against injury from imports, under
section 201 of U.S. trade law. In 1980 this process yielded a rejection
of automobile protection, on grounds that the ITC considered the
difficulties of the sector to be caused primarily by domestic recession
and not imports. Within months the new administration negotiated
voluntary export restraints on Japanese automobiles, under the threat
of congressionally approved U.S. quotas if Japan did not cooperate.

The move to auto protection was a major shift for the industry,
which had long been considered unlikely to seek protection because
of its own international orientation and long-term strategy of global
sourcing. That the industry succumbed to protection is again an indication of the severity of employment and import pressures in the
early 1980s in the face of recession and dollar overvaluation.

The discussion here will not seek to present a broad analysis of
the automobile sector. However, certain considerations warrant
highlighting.

The same process of relative wage inflation has occurred in automobiles as in steel. As table 9.2 indicates, auto wages (including
fringe benefits) have risen from approximately 160 percent of average
U.S. manufacturing wages in the early 1960s to over 200 percent in
recent years. Much the same dynamics may be identified as in the
case of steel: an oligopoly production structure passing on wage
increases negotiated by monopoly labor. As in the case of steel
other structural factors have been important (in this case the shift to
small cars in response to higher oil prices, combined with the dominance of foreign supply of small cars), but as in steel, wage pressure
must be recognized as a significant factor explaining declining
competitiveness.

An important question is whether the sector has used the period of
protection to revitalize. As suggested by the analysis of figure 9.1,
there has been some modest move in the direction of revitalization as
compared with the period before protection, but productivity growth
still lags behind the U.S. average.

The case of automobiles is more complicated than that of steel,
because of the emerging phenomenon of coproduction between U.S.
and Japanese producers as well as the strategy of responding to Japanese competition through production in such countries as Mexico and
Brazil. Likewise the emerging production of Japanese and European
firms within the United States has led to additional dimensions of

protection, especially the effort toward domestic content legislation that would force the largest Japanese producers to establish production facilities in the United States.

One pattern that does appear to be clear is that protection in automobiles has heightened the oligopoly power of the industry as a whole including the major foreign producers. Profits at the three largest Japanese firms are much higher than before, the result of a large new transfer of income from U.S. consumers to these producers (as they collect the higher profits made possible by sharp increases in their prices). The rise in oligopoly profits is also evident in soaring profits of domestic producers.

Adjustment through Wage and Exchange Rate Correction

As an illustrative calculation of the potential for U.S. industrial adjustment from the reversal of past trends toward wage excess and correction of the overvalued dollar, the appendix sets forth a simple model of the impact of a roll-back in both wages and the dollar. The wage calculation is primarily relevant for steel and automobiles, considering that wages in textiles and apparel are already below the national average.

The calculations in the appendix first determine a plausible magnitude for reduced wages. For this purpose the past ratios of steel and auto wages to the average for manufacturing are examined. The lowest one-fourth of yearly observations may represent a useful basis for analysis. On this basis steel wages could return to 151 percent of the U.S. average, and auto wages to 161 percent. These levels would mean a reduction of 21 percent in steel wages in comparison with the levels reached in 1980–83 and a 26 percent reduction for automobile wages for the same period.

Considering that wage costs amount to approximately 41 percent of total costs in automobiles and 32 percent in steel, these wage reductions would reduce product price by 10.7 percent in autos and 6.7 percent in steel (see the appendix). Taking account of the responsiveness (elasticity) of total demand to price, and of the relative demand for domestic production compared to imports as the domestic price becomes relatively lower, the result of wage reductions on this scale would be a total increase in domestic production by 17.3 percent in autos and 10.2 percent in steel. The increase in autos would be composed of 10.7 percent from the increased quantity of domestic demand and 6.6 percent from substitution of auto imports by domestic output. The corresponding estimates for steel are 6.0 percent and 4.2 percent.

Incorporating the impact of dollar depreciation approximately doubles the scope for domestic production increase. In this case the effect works solely on substitution of imported supply. Assuming that the dollar were to depreciate by 20 percent, and taking into account the market share of imports as well as the degree of substitutability between domestic and imported supply, the result would be an increase of domestic production by 12.4 percent for automobiles and by the same amount for steel.

Although the model in the appendix is extremely simple, it is highly suggestive that the plight of automobiles and steel could be addressed to a considerable degree by the correction of two important disequilibria—one microeconomic (excessive sectoral wages) and the other macroeconomic (an excessively strong dollar). Together these improvements in market signals would appear capable of raising domestic output (and employment) on the order of 32 percent in automobiles and 24 percent in steel.

Strategic Trade?

The theory of strategic trade relies on the idea that there are oligopoly profits to be made in certain industries. If a government can intervene in the industry equilibrium among oligopoly producers to shift a greater share of these global oligopoly profits to its own producers, the nation may benefit by trade intervention for this purpose.

The assumptions of this line of modeling would appear somewhat at variance with policy reality. Thus in one of the main formulations, the analysis assumes that the government applies an export subsidy as its means of shifting the oligopoly equilibrium in favor of the home country. But the existing mechanisms of countervailing duties provide ample means for thwarting this stratagem (as should by now be clear from the experience of steel). Although there may remain a problem in third markets (and in one model formulation the analysis is limited solely to such cases), the subset of third-market trade problems is surely too limited to serve as a basis for a broad strategy.

At a more abstract level the new approach resembles the "optimum tariff" literature. In that analysis it may be desirable for a country to impose protection in order to reduce demand for imports, driving down their price and improving the country's terms of trade (export price relative to import price). In the emerging strategic trade literature, the country does essentially the same thing, but at the micro level and on the other side of the trade flow: it subsidizes exports (instead of taxing imports). But just as in the case of the optimal tariff, application of the approach is likely to founder on foreign retaliation. Only under extreme conditions will an optimum tariff benefit the home country if the foreign country responds with its own retaliatory tariff. Similarly it is hard to believe that the United States could adopt a new strategy of subsidizing exports of oligopoly-profit goods without provoking retaliatory measures of the same sort from foreign competitors.

Strategic trade has little relevance to textiles and apparel, sectors of relatively perfect competition in terms of large numbers of small producers. Some would argue, however, that in steel and automobiles foreign producers have achieved unfair advantage over U.S. producers through government intervention. Strategic trade might be adduced as an argument for responding with U.S. subsidies or other government intervention in these sectors.

The fact is that the U.S. response already appears to have exceeded what might be justified by responding to foreign subsidization in these sectors. Thus Japanese and Korean supplies of steel are not subsidized like European production, yet these Asian sources of steel are to come under the emerging net of voluntary export restraints. And as argued before, the protective effect of application of the antidumping and antisubsidy mechanism has probably exceeded the amount warranted by the unfair trade involved, especially after the metamorphosis of countervailing duties on European steel into outright voluntary quotas.

To the policy-oriented observer the basic thrust of the message of the strategic trade literature must be that nations would do well to revert to the negotiating table before pursuing aggressive unilateral strategies. The alternative approach would be a sad and ultimately counterproductive reversal of U.S. postwar leadership of an open trading system.

Implications for U.S. Trade and Industrial Policy

The principal policy implications of this paper are as follows:

First, it is essential to get the macroeconomic price signals correct.

The overvaluation of the dollar has had a serious corrosive effect on U.S. competitiveness and U.S. open-trade policy.

Second, it is equally important to get the microeconomic prices right. Excessive wage increases have contributed importantly to the competitive difficulties of automobiles and steel in particular.

Third, it is time to get serious about adjustment as an essential part of U.S. trade policy. Industries that enjoy protection should be expected to demonstrate adjustment progress through either rapid increases in productivity (revitalization) or reductions over time in production and employment (down-phasing). Protection is costly to the public at large, and the public has a right to expect concrete measures by protected industries to hasten the day when protection may be removed.

Fourth, the policymaking process should begin to pay more attention to the costs of protection to the economy as a whole and to consumers in particular. A healthful measure for transparency in trade policy would be to require that in any decision to protect there be a comprehensive and well-publicized estimation of the costs involved for consumers.

Finally, the principles of U.S. trade and industrial policy are sound. Past policy has been well advised to follow the principle of free trade and to avoid active industrial policy that seeks to favor some sectors (at the explicit or implicit cost of others). The need today is for a return to the basic principles of open trade. It will be difficult to reverse the clear trend away from these principles that has prevailed since the late 1970s. Appropriate economic policies to sustain recovery and correct the exchange rate could help achieve this reversal. In addition, however, it is likely that a stronger mobilization of countervailing forces (e.g., consumers and retailers) will be necessary if the political influence of sectoral interest groups is to be more appropriately balanced by the interests of the public at large in the process of trade policy determination.

Appendix: A Model of Wage and Exchange Rate Effects

This appendix examines the impact of possible wage reduction and exchange rate correction on production in U.S. automobiles and steel.

Let δ be the proportionate reduction in wages being considered. Let γ be the share of wages in production costs. Then the proportionate reduction in product price (assuming proportionality of retailing markups) is $\delta\gamma$.

Let β be the price elasticity of domestic demand. Let α be the elasticity of substitution of imports and domestic production, defined as the percentage change in the ratio of import quantity to domestic output quantity demanded per unit percentage change in the price ratio for imports relative to domestic output.

The impact on domestic production of a reduction in wages is composed of two parts. The first is the increase in total quantity demanded by consumers holding imports constant. This amount equals the percent change in price multiplied by the price elasticity of demand, times the original level of demand for domestic output. (Note that this approach treats the domestic product as an imperfect substitute for the imported good and considers—for this first effect— a demand elasticity relevant for the domestic product only. If the demand elasticity instead were interpreted to be for total quantity demanded, summing imports and domestic production, the proportionate increase of domestic output alone would be greater, considering that the entire increase in quantity supplied is to come from domestic production since only the domestic good's cost, and price, is declining.) Thus

$$\Delta D_1 = \delta\gamma\beta Q_0, \tag{A.1}$$

where ΔD_1 is the increase in total demand as well as the first component of increased domestic output, and Q_0 is initial domestic output.

The second part of the effect of lower wages on domestic output is from the resulting partial replacement of imported goods by domestic output. From the definition of the elasticity of substitution,

$$\frac{\dot{m} - \dot{q}}{\dot{p}_m - \dot{p}_d} = \alpha, \tag{A.2}$$

where $\dot{m}$ is the percent change in import quantity (which in turn is designated by M), $\dot{q}$ is the percent change in domestic output, $\dot{p}_m$ is the percent change in import price, and $\dot{p}_d$ is the percent change in domestic output price. (This relationship follows from the fact that the percent change in a ratio—imports to domestic output, or import price to domestic product price—also equals the difference between the percent change in the numerator and the denominator.)[21]

Import price is unchanged, so $\dot{p}_m = 0$. The percent change in price of the domestic product is $\delta\gamma$. Thus from equation (A.2),

$$\dot{m} - \dot{q} = \alpha(\dot{p}_m - \dot{p}_d) = \alpha(-\delta\gamma). \tag{A.3}$$

Considering that the change in import quantity must equal in magnitude the change in domestic output attributable to substitution for imports, $\dot{m}$ must equal $-\Delta Q^\delta/M$, where ΔQ^δ is the change in domestic output attributable to substitution (also defined as ΔD_2). By definition, $\dot{q} = \Delta Q^\delta/Q$. Setting $h = M/Q$, $\dot{m}$ may be written as $\dot{m} = -\Delta Q^\delta/hQ$. Thus

$$\dot{m} - \dot{q} = \frac{-\Delta Q^\delta}{hQ} - \frac{\Delta Q^\delta}{Q} = -\frac{\Delta Q^\delta}{Q}\left(\frac{1}{h} + 1\right)$$

$$= \frac{-\Delta Q^\delta}{Q}\left(\frac{1 + h}{h}\right).$$

(A.4)

From equations (A.3) and (A.4),

$$\frac{\Delta Q^\delta}{Q} = -\alpha(-\delta\gamma)\left(\frac{h}{1 + h}\right).$$

(A.5)

From equation (A.5) the increased domestic output attributable to replacement of imports is

$$\Delta D_2 \equiv \Delta Q^\delta = -\alpha(-\delta\gamma)\left(\frac{h}{1 + h}\right)Q_0.$$

(A.6)

In summary, equations (A.1) and (A.6) state the two component parts of increased domestic output: the rise to meet the increase in the quantity demanded as the price of domestic output declines and the rise to replace a portion of imports as the domestic price becomes more attractive compared to the import price.

The elasticity of substitution α is by definition negative. In the case of a wage cut the term $\delta\gamma$ is also negative. The size of increased domestic output to replace imports (equation A.6) will therefore be larger as the ratio of imports to domestic output (h) is higher, the size of the wage cut (δ) is larger (in absolute terms), the share of wages in output cost (γ) is higher, and the size of the elasticity of substitution is higher in absolute terms ($|\alpha|$).

The total increase in domestic output is the sum of the two components ΔD_1 and ΔD_2. In percentage terms this increase is (from equations A.1 and A.6)

$$\frac{\Delta Q^*}{Q_0} = \delta\gamma\beta - \alpha(-\delta\gamma)\left(\frac{h}{1 + h}\right)$$

(A.7)

Table A9.1 sets forth the various concepts used in this model and corresponding estimates for the automobile and steel sectors. The

Table A9.1
A model of domestic output response to reduction in wages

Concept	Symbol	Automobiles	Steel
Percent change in wage	δ	-26.0	-21.0
Labor share in cost	γ	0.41	0.32
Percent price reduction	$\delta\gamma$	-10.7	-6.7
Price elasticity of demand	β	-1.0	-0.9
Elasticity of substitution between domestic and imported goods	α	-2.5	-2.5
Ratio of imports to domestic output	h	0.33	0.33
Percent increase in output for extra consumption	$\Delta D_1/Q_0$	10.7	6.0
Percent increase in output to replace imports	$\Delta D_2/Q_0$	6.6	4.2
Total increase in output (%)	$\Delta Q^*/Q_0$	17.3	10.2

percentage cut in wages is based on a return to wages relative to the average for U.S. manufacturing as a whole in the lowest one-fourth of all yearly observations for the last twenty years (approximately a return to relative levels of the early 1960s). The reduction in wages is specified as occurring from the average (relative to manufacturing) in the period 1980 to 1983. For automobiles the five years with lowest relative wage showed wages at 161.0 percent of the manufacturing average. For steel the ratio was 151.2 percent. The corresponding reductions from 1980–83 average ratios to manufacturing as a whole are 26.4 percent for automobiles and 21.4 percent for steel. Note, however, that if the 1983 relative wage levels were continued, a portion of these declines will already have been achieved (compared with the 1980–83 average, the 1983 relative wages had declined by 1.5 percent in automobiles and by 8.6 percent in steel; see table 9.2).

The share of labor costs in total cost (γ) is estimated as 41 percent for automobiles and 32 percent for steel.[22] The price elasticity of demand for domestic output is estimated as -1.0 for automobiles and -0.9 for steel.[23]

For steel Crandall estimates the elasticity of the import value share in the market to be in the range of -1.4 to -7.4. The corresponding quantity concept of the elasticity of substitution would be larger by unity (in absolute value), giving a central estimate of -5.4. However, Crandall also notes that although steel imports are sensitive to price in a certain range of products, there also seems to be a duality to the overall market, and a considerable portion of the market remains committed to domestic suppliers because of longer-run considerations of supply certainty.[24] Accordingly the calculation here reduces the substitution elasticity by half, to -2.5.

The calculation for automobiles applies the same substitution elasticity as that for steel, -2.5. Although direct estimates on the elasticity are not available, this value is approximately consistent with empirical estimates of the short-run elasticity of demand for automobile imports.[25]

The final parameter for the model is the ratio of imports to domestic output. For both automobiles and steel the current ratio of imports to domestic consumption is approximately 25 percent. Thus, for both, the ratio of imports to domestic production is approximately one-third $(0.25/0.75)$.

The results of the model are shown in table 9A.1. A cut of wages by 26 percent in automobiles and by 21 percent in steel reduces product price by 10.7 percent and 6.7 percent, respectively. The resulting increase in demand for domestic output in automobiles is 17.3 percent (10.7 percent from increased consumption and 6.6 percent from replacement of imports). In steel, demand for domestic output rises by 10.2 percent (6 percent for increased consumption and 4.2 percent for replacement of imports).

These changes are substantial and suggest that major adjustment in both sectors could be accomplished through the return to a more normal wage structure relative to average U.S. manufacturing wages.[26] Note that employment would be expected to rise by at least the same percentage as output and might rise relatively more as the consequence of substitution of more labor for capital as the relative price of labor declines.

Finally, the model may also be used to identify the potential impact of correction of the overvalued dollar. In the model this effect is equivalent to increasing the term $\dot{p}_m$ in equation (A.3). The effect is only on increased domestic output to replace imports. In equations (A.3) and (A.6) the percentage price change becomes $\dot{p}_m$ rather than $(-\delta\gamma)$.

Assuming that the dollar would depreciate by 20 percent, and applying equation (A.6) to an increase in import price by 20 percent, the result would be an increase in domestic production by 12.4 percent in both automobiles and steel. (Because the same elasticity of substitution is used for both, and both have the same ratio of imports to domestic production and face the same import price increase from a given devaluation, the impact is the same for the two sectors.) Again the favorable effects for adjustment could be substantial.

The combined impact of a return to more normal relative wages and a correction in the overvalued dollar would appear to be large indeed. For automobiles domestic output would rise by 31.8 percent (1.17×1.12); for steel the increase would be 23.9 percent. These magnitudes would imply a cutback by approximately one-half in the quantity of imports in both automobiles and steel. Such a large reduction would be likely to induce price cuts by foreign suppliers, moderating the domestic gains. Nevertheless, the qualitative implication of the estimates is that a large contribution to the prospects for increased domestic output and employment could be achieved in both automobiles and steel through two policies alone: return to earlier wage rates (relative to the manufacturing average) and depreciation of the dollar to more normal and sustainable levels.

Notes

I am indebted to Ronald Friedman for research assistance.

1. William R. Cline, *Exports of Manufactures from Developing Countries: Performance and Prospects for Market Access* (Washington, D.C.: Brookings Institution, 1984), ch. 2.

2. *Washington Post*, September 7, 1984.

3. Williamson estimated dollar overvaluation at 24 percent in the first quarter of 1983, and the dollar has continued to rise since then. John Williamson, "The Exchange Rate System," *Policy Analyses in International Economics*, No. 5 (Washington, D.C.: Institute for International Economics, 1983).

4. Note that the base year affects the calculation. The period 1978–80 is chosen as the base because it includes both a peak and a recession year. Use of 1981 as the base would show sharply rising productivity through 1984, but this trend would be misleading because it would merely reflect the shift from recession to expansion, and because employment does not vary as rapidly as output over the cycle, productivity per worker declines during recession and rises during expansion.

5. Peter Isard, "Employment Impacts of Textile Imports and Investment: A Vintage-Capital Model," *American Economic Review* 63, June 1973, pp. 402–416.

6. Robert W. Crandall, "Import Quotas and the Automobile Industry: The Costs of Protectionism," *The Brookings Review*, Summer 1984. Note however that Feenstra concludes prices of Japanese imports rose by only 3.1 percent

after accounting for changes in quality (an important consequence of protection has been to induce Japanese producers to upgrade the mix of their exports to the United States). On this basis the increased price per car would be only $150. Feenstra omits any calculation of the induced increase in prices of U.S. automobiles. Robert C. Feenstra, "Voluntary Export Restraint in U.S. Autos, 1980–81: Quality, Employment, and Welfare Effects," forthcoming in Robert Baldwin and Anne Krueger, eds., *The Structure and Evolution of Recent U.S. Trade Policy*, University of Chicago Press.

7. Congressional Budget Office, *The Effects of Import Quotas on the Steel Industry* (Washington, D.C.: CBO, July 1984).

8. Martin Wolf, "Textile Pact: The Outlook," *New York Times*, January 12, 1982.

9. Martin Wolf, "Managed Trade in Practice: Implications of the Textile Arrangements," in William R. Cline, ed., *Trade Policy in the 1980s* (Washington, D.C.: Institute for International Economics, 1984), pp. 455–482.

10. *Wall Street Journal*, January 6, 1984.

11. *New York Times*, September 8, 1984.

12. Cline, *Exports of Manufactures from Developing Countries*, p. 64.

13. In 1980–82 the United States averaged a trade surplus of approximately $500 million in textiles, compared with a deficit of approximately $7 billion in apparel (GATT, *International Trade 1982/83*, table A10). Note that higher unit value of exports than imports permitted this performance for textiles, considering that the physical volume of exports was only two-thirds as large as imports. U.S. International Trade Commission, "U.S. Imports of Textile and Apparel Products under the Multifiber Arrangement, 1976–1982," USITC publication 1392, June 1983, p. A-6.

14. Walter notes that "the dubious nature of the fair-value estimates and the impact of the trigger device itself through increased risk faced by shippers and importers deterred steel imports in general. Especially the Japanese import share dropped dramatically from 1977 to 1978." Ingo Walter, "Structural Adjustment and Trade Policy in the International Steel Industry," in Cline, ed., *Trade Policy in the 1980s*, p. 492. Crandall reaches a similar judgment; see Robert W. Crandall, *The U.S. Steel Industry in Recurrent Crisis* (Washington, D.C.: Brookings Institution, 1981).

15. Ibid., pp. 492–497.

16. Office of the U.S. Trade Representative, "Brock Announces President's Steel Decision," Press Release, September 18, 1984, pp. 1–3.

17. *Washington Post*, October 6, 1984.

18. Walter, "Structural Adjustment and Trade Policy in the International Steel Industry," p. 494.

19. Ibid., pp. 484–485.

20. If the price elasticity of demand for steel is − 1, the 40 percent rise in the relative price of steel would provoke a comparable percentage decline in its relative use.

21. R. G. D. Allen, *Mathematical Analysis for Economists* (London: Macmillan, 1964), p. 331.

22. Altschuler et al. (1984) estimate the average revenue per vehicle for General Motors at $9,077 in 1982, average man-hours per vehicle at 210 hours, and average labor cost at $17.55 per hour, giving labor costs at 40.6 percent of revenue per vehicle. Alan Altschuler, Martin Anderson, Daniel Jones, Daniel Roos, and James Womack, *The Future of the Automobile* (Cambridge, Mass.: MIT Press, 1984), pp. 157, 160, 208. The American Iron and Steel Institute reports that in 1982 total steel revenue was $52.37 billion and total employment costs were $16.71 billion, or 31.9 percent of total revenue. American Iron and Steel Institute, *1982 Annual Statistical Report* (Washington, D.C.: AISI, 1983), p. 12. Note that these ratios may understate the term by using the ratio of labor cost to revenue rather than total cost.

23. Crandall estimates the demand elasticity for steel in a range of − 0.5 to − 1.5. Robert W. Crandall, *The U.S. Steel Industry in Recurrent Crisis* (Washington, D.C.: Brookings Institution, 1981), p. 69. For automobiles, the price elasticity of demand may also be approximately − 1; see Feenstra, "Voluntary Export Restraint in U.S. Autos, 1980–81," p. 27.

24. Crandall, *The U.S. Steel Industry*, p. 69.

25. Feenstra reports this range at 1 to 2, as estimated by Toder and others; see Feenstra, "Voluntary Export Restraint in U.S. Autos, 1980–81," p. 27. As shown in table 9A.1, the results of the calculations in the present study indicate that a reduction in the price of automobiles by 10.7 percent causes a decline of imports equal to 6.6 percent of domestic output or, accordingly, 19.8 percent of imports, consistent with an import elasticity of demand of approximately 2.

26. Grossman has used statistical regressions of steel employment to conclude that if steel wages had grown at the same rate as average U.S. manufacturing wages between January 1976 and October 1983, there would have been only 5,047 more jobs in steel (an increase of only 2 percent). This finding is not surprising, because the relative wage in steel had already started to decline in 1983 and was far above its early 1960s level by 1976. (In fact comparison of just 1976 and 1983 alone shows a decline in the relative steel wage; see table 9.2.) If Grossman's underlying model is applied to the wage assumption here, a very different picture emerges. Grossman's elasticity of employment with respect to wage is − 0.596. Applied to the 21 percent cut in wages assumed here, this estimate implies a rise in employment by 12.6 percent— modestly larger than the estimate here. Gene M. Grossman, "Imports as a Cause of Injury: The Case of the US Steel Industry," (Princeton, N.J.: Princeton University, mimeograph, July 1984), pp. 11, 20.

10

Strategic Behavior and Trade Policy

William H. Branson
and
Alvin K. Klevorick

Experimental economics is in vogue these days. A new and exciting development, it has provided added income for numerous undergraduate economics majors and economics graduate students as they have been brought to "laboratories" to test various economics hypotheses—for example, to explore the effects of different auction mechanisms on the behavior of market participants. After several academic conferences on strategic behavior and trade policy we decided that this area was ripe for an experiment of its own, though one rather different from the laboratory tests of market behavior—and one in which the participants would not be paid by the experimenters! At the academic conferences, with the standard format of papers presented by authors and critiqued by discussants, a dialogue developed between members of the trade policy community and academic analysts of trade and industrial policy. The policymakers were in command of the detailed facts concerning policy problems, while the academics were able to see that particular models, in the existing or developing literature, could be matched up with the facts to yield useful insights. It seemed clear that combining the capabilities of members of the academic and policy communities would provide the potential for improved analysis of the policy problems, as well as additional information and data for research and the stimulation for analyzing new theoretical models.

Recognizing this potential gain, we agreed with David MacDonald, then Deputy U.S. Trade Representative (USTR), to arrange the first of a series of meetings in which USTR staff and academic analysts of trade and industrial policy would participate. The USTR staff would prepare and distribute in advance case materials on current policy problems. At the meeting itself, the USTR people would present and discuss the materials, and the academics would, we hoped, bring the relevant analytical frameworks to bear on the issues. Several meetings have been held. The sectors discussed were semiconductors, large civilian jet aircraft, telecommunications equipment, automobiles, and steel. Naturally, in addition to the presentation and analysis of the characteristics of particular sectors, there was, at each meeting, a running discussion of the trade policy process. Furthermore, as we jointly examined the high-technology areas, it became apparent that research and development policy was central to any discussion of the international trade position of the United States in these industries. Hence we also devoted time at one meeting to the role of research joint ventures in the U.S. and American antitrust policy toward them—a focus of current concern in R&D policy circles. Finally, we held a more standard conference in which members of both the policy and academic communities discussed papers that had been stimulated by our earlier discussions.

In this paper we will present the "data" gathered in our experiment in the form of a summary of the discussions of each of the sectors. We are not by any means attempting to present a full case study of each of the sectors. That would be impossible in such a short space, for each of these sectors has been the subject of several monographs and numerous articles. Rather, we will describe the discussion that was generated by the background materials prepared by USTR and Department of Commerce staff, and we will note the implications of the discussion for trade policy in that area. In each case we will also draw on arguments and results presented in the academic papers that were stimulated by the sectoral discussion. Then we will interpret our data by drawing together their lessons for formulation of trade policy in general.

Sectoral Problems and Issues

In this section we describe the data from our experiment (as of October 1984, since the experiment is ongoing), and note some of the important implications for thinking about trade policy. These generally involve the particular technology or industrial organization of a sector or industry, and the process by which the sectors arrive on the trade policy agenda. The discussion will proceed sector by sector—semiconductors, large jet transports, telecommunications, steel, and autos—and end with an analysis of research joint ventures.

Semiconductors

The structures of the U.S. and Japanese semiconductor industries are significantly different, as indicated by the case materials developed by USTR. In the United States there are a few large vertically integrated manufacturers, such as IBM and Western Electric, but also many small producers. In Japan the industry is much more concentrated with 85 percent of production accounted for by six large producers, each of which is part of a separate industrial group. Within each group in Japan the semiconductor producer has a "captive" market. Nevertheless, the Japanese semiconductor producers do specialize, so that there is trade among the industrial groups. The basis for specialization is not clear, but it could reflect scale economies. The competitive structure of the existing U.S industry does not indicate that these economies are significant, but it was suggested that the entire semiconductor market is undergoing a structural transformation, moving toward more vertically integrated firms. If this is true, then we may observe changes in the structure of the U.S. industry in the direction of the Japanese structure.

A potentially important aspect of the Japanese industry is the prominence of both government support of research in semiconductors and research joint ventures in the industry. The latter have the special feature that generally all members of the venture must agree before technology developed by the venture is licensed to others, and MITI is part of each joint venture, thereby potentially controlling licensing. Research joint ventures provide the possibility of gaining from sharing the costs of research and elimination of duplication, and from internalizing the benefits of research within the group. The ability to organize research joint ventures may have given the Japanese industry an advantage over the United States. These observations led to a separate discussion of research joint ventures.

Evidence developed in a study by Flaherty (1983) suggests that in the semiconductor industry research interacts strongly with applications engineering and the provision of conventional business services. For example, Flaherty's analysis of her data showed that a company with a two-year technology lead over its competitors has 15 percent more of the market if its applications engineering effort is one standard deviation above average than if that effort is just average.

There are some indications of informal protection in the Japanese semiconductor market. When import protection has been liberalized in the past, the U.S. share of the market has increased, but only temporarily. One can also recite two indirect pieces of evidence to support the view that this industry receives informal protection in Japan. The first is the Japanese Industry Structure Council's concern about the effects of particular trade liberalization steps. The second is the dominance of U.S. producers over the Japanese in Europe.

The analysis of the semiconductor industry indicates a potential issue of trade policy proper—limited access to Japanese markets. But the issues of U.S. government policy toward that industry range far more widely. They include science and technology policy generally (education of scientists and engineers) and antitrust policy, especially as it concerns research joint ventures.

Discussion of the data on the semiconductor industry raised two further analytical points on the effects of exchange rate changes and the use of market share data. First, the fall in the U.S. shares of the world market and the increase in the Japanese shares since 1981 partially reflect the real appreciation of the dollar. This makes it important to decompose overall changes into those due to macroeconomic policy and those resulting from structural aspects of the industry.

Second, the data as organized by USTR or the Department of Commerce tend to focus on market share rather than profits. The latter are the normal criterion of firm and industry success. Assessing success is further complicated because the time profile of profits is important. It may take years of investment before returns are realized, so that one should weigh the past costs as well as current profits in analyzing the industry.

To summarize, the analysis of semiconductors raised several issues. These include the antitrust treatment of research joint ventures, the seemingly limited access to the Japanese market, the ambiguity of market share as a measure of "success," and the importance of an intertemporal view of success criteria in an industry with heavy research and development costs.

Jet Transport Aircraft

The principal trade policy problem in the large civilian jet transport industry can be characterized as follows. A new generation of 150-seat aircraft is being developed. The timing of the introduction of the new plane by the aircraft manufacturers is an important strategic concern for them because, it is generally believed, the market has "room" for two actual producers, though there are three potential ones: Boeing, McDonnell-Douglas, and Airbus. In addition there is some concern within the industry about whether the market is ripe for such planes and some concern that an untimely introduction of the model might spoil the market.

Airbus is a European government cartel, which is directly and explicitly subsidized by the participating governments, whereas the U.S. producers are indirectly subsidized by military sales, by the ability to apply commercially the knowledge gained from military developments—particularly in the case of engine developments, and in Eximbank financing of sales. The participating European governments are pushing politically for national airlines to buy the Airbus products. How should the policy issues be analyzed in this case?

It is important, at the outset, to understand that it is difficult and indeed inappropriate to look at the problem as a one-time phenomenon because it is, in fact, one stage of a repeated game. There is always a new generation of aircraft coming on the scene. Historically there have always been three or four potential producers and entrants at the start of each race, and fewer—usually only two—efficient "winners" in each round. Hence the appropriate analytical framework for consideration of the aircraft industry's situation is a repeated game with strategic behavior at each stage and, in particular, the possibility of effective precommitment by governments. At any one time there is both ex post competition in the market for the current generation of aircraft and ex ante competition for the next one. It should be recognized that actions taken now will also affect future rounds in the aircraft industry.

The large fixed costs in the industry also generate elements of natural monopoly. Indeed, Dixit and Kyle (1984) introduce their paper on policy choice in the industry by observing that artificial barriers to international trade and natural barriers to entry are both important features of certain imperfectly competitive high-technology industries, such as aerospace and computers. The Dixit-Kyle paper analyzes the functioning of such markets and the role of policies toward them. To analyze the issues adequately, the potential for strategic behavior on the part of both governments and firms must be taken into the account. Furthermore it is important to recognize that the strategies of governments interact with those of firms. The appropriate analysis is therefore a game-theoretic one, with the governments and the firms as the players. The central issue in industries like aircraft is whether one government can make a strategic precommitment of policy choice that affects subsequent choices of others to its own advantage. The availability of such moves in practice will depend on particular features of governmental and international institutions.

The particular analysis presented by Dixit and Kyle is suggested by the Airbus example but is not to be taken as a literal representation of that case. They assume that there are only two countries and two firms. One of the firms is an incumbent (i.e., its sunk costs have already been incurred) located in one of the countries, the United States, whereas the other firm, Airbus, is a potential entrant located in the other country, the EC. The objective of each firm is to maximize its profit. The object of each government is taken to be the standard criterion of social welfare—the sum of domestic consumer and producer surpluses.

Dixit and Kyle show how and when policies to promote entry of a country's firm into the industry promote national advantage. They find that the EC gains from protection to promote entry if such a policy actually leads to entry. They also examine the implications for world welfare. As a general tendency, protection for entry promotion by the EC is harmful to the world, and U.S. countermeasures that deter such a policy are beneficial. Subsidies as instruments of entry promotion are generally more desirable from a world viewpoint; countermeasures against them are either ineffective or harmful.

Telecommunications

The trade policy problem in this industry is basically a by-product of the domestically oriented decision to break up AT&T. Because of the national telecommunications procurement policies of foreign governments, those markets have been closed to import competition, except in the case of special agreements (as the United States has had with Japan). The U.S. market has been nominally open, but prior to deregulation of telecommunications and the AT&T divestiture, self-sourcing by the principal companies—particularly, Bell System purchases from Western Electric—rendered the U.S. market basically closed as well. Deregulation of some parts of the telecommunications market, begun some years ago, opened the U.S. market to competition in private (business) switching equipment and consumer equipment, and there has been substantial import penetration in these sectors. But until the January 1, 1984, divestiture of the Bell System operating companies, the U.S. market for central switching equipment was essentially closed to foreign competition. With the breakup of AT&T the separate operating companies can now buy equipment from any source, including imports, where previously they bought from Western Electric. Hence the U.S. telecommunications market is now effectively open to foreign competition, while foreign markets remain essentially closed.

This shift in domestic policy effectively provides a tariff benefit to the rest of the world, which might be the basis for an argument for the United States to demand compensation through the GATT. The U.S. move might also give an impetus to liberalization abroad as foreign businesses exert pressure on governments to enable them to use equipment abroad that is compatible with U.S. equipment.

Telecommunications may be an example of an industry that currently faces an adjustment problem, but one that is not a case for trade policy action. Although an argument might be made for subsidizing the telecommunications industry on the grounds of technological externalities and strategic national security considerations, that is not an argument for trade policy action, as usually conceived.

Steel

The problems confronting the U.S. steel industry include, among others, the effects of the worldwide recession, the level of wages and rate of wage acceleration in the United States, unfavorable exchange rate movements, and competition from other materials. The industry has responded to these problems in a number of constructive ways, for example, undertaking cost reductions, plant modernizations, and joint production while simultaneously closing some inefficient plants.

The industry argues, however, that it is also being harmed by the operations of international markets. There are two different sets of complaints that should be sharply distinguished. First, the USTR materials characterized the U.S. market for steel as being relatively open. While the United States, until recently, provided periodic tariff or trigger-price protection, most other countries close their markets to significant import competition either formally (by tariff and nontariff barriers) or informally (through reliance on trading companies). Second, there is heavy foreign government involvement in steel production with the accompanying subsidization of the industry, and there are allegations that foreign firms receive export subsidies and "dump" on the U.S. market.

The data provided by USTR seem to show that the international recession beginning in 1981 had devastating effects on the steel industry, generating enormous excess capacity, and that U.S. companies had borne the brunt of the impact. In addition the econometric study by Grossman (1984) showed that though imports have contributed significantly to the pressure on U.S. steel companies, most of the increase in imports can be attributed to the real appreciation of the U.S. dollar. Again, as in the semiconductor case, decomposition of the sources of changes into macroeconomic factors and structural problems seems essential.

Steel is an example of an industry that may not be appropriately on the trade policy agenda beyond the need to open foreign markets. There is a general agreement that efforts to remove barriers to imports in foreign countries are definitely appropriate in the steel case. Part of such a program might entail short-run strategic responses with regard to the U.S. market. Any such steps would of course have the long-run goal of attaining open international markets.

There is less consensus on the appropriate way to view foreign subsidies. Should the United States, as a consumer, be delighted to enjoy the subsidized prices for as long as they last? Are the long-run implications of the subsidies detrimental to the United States? How do prescriptions based on consideration of strategic policy elements differ from the recommendations drawn from more conventional analyses? If the United States allows foreign steel producers to solve their excess capacity problem by selling cheaply in the U.S. market, future U.S. production capability may be reduced, and in the long run, the United States as consumer may be harmed as well. An alternative approach would be to use control over access to a very large market (the United States) to open up markets elsewhere to the kind of competitive structure that economists believe is conducive to efficient performance.

Three critical questions in assessing these policy issues are: How much pressure can the United States actually bring to bear on foreign governments to move toward open markets? Is domestic competition from mini-mills, and so on, sufficient to compensate for the loss of disciplining by foreign competition that comes with strategic protectionist responses? How do we extricate ourselves from a policy of strategic protectionism if our efforts fail?

Automobiles

A central problem in the U.S. auto industry is the existence of high relative costs of production, which are only partly due to the appreciation of the dollar. Some observers doubt whether the cost reductions of recent years can be maintained if pressure on the industry abates. Additional problems are a lag in product development in the face of shifts in consumers' tastes, particularly toward smaller, fuel-efficient cars, and the difficulties created by foreign governments' local content laws.

With regard to the overall problem of high costs, most economists in the group took the view that import competition in the U.S. automobile market has, in fact, been helpful. It has provided just the kind of disciplining function that is beneficial to the economy. They also agreed that efforts to have foreign local content laws eliminated were desirable, from a global point of view, as well as from a narrower U.S. perspective.

Despite the beneficial effects of import competition in autos, there might, however, be an argument for some short-term relief to enable the U.S. automobile industry to recover its strength, to give it some "breathing room," as it changes product mix. The argument is buttressed by concern that the U.S. automobile components be a viable competitor in the international market in the future. But such an enterprise entails a delicate balancing act. It would be undesirable for the U.S. industry to fall to such a reduced market share that it cannot recover. But it is important that the relief be explicitly temporary. If it is not, the risk is that the aid gets built into prices and wages, making the ultimate adjustment problem even more difficult.

Research Joint Ventures

Our discussion of the semiconductor industry highlighted the importance of research and development policy in any consideration of the international trade position of U.S. high-technology industries. The central role that research joint ventures (RJVs) have played in the Japanese semiconductor industry suggested an inquiry into the role of RJVs in the United States and American antitrust policy toward such undertakings.

Current antitrust policy gives mixed signals to the business community concerning the legal risks that cooperative efforts like RJVs run. This "antitrust risk," which could be reduced without harm, may discourage desirable cooperation. Furthermore current antitrust law need not stifle joint R&D projects. Cooperative R&D may well be pro-competitive, and the market implications of such projects are less worrisome when one recognizes that the relevant market for high-technology industries is the world market.

The principal reasons for supporting the undertaking of RJVs, from the social point of view, are the economies they generate. These include economies of scale in R&D, reduction of duplicative efforts, and the social benefits of risk sharing. But such economies are precisely the kinds of considerations that traditional antitrust jurisprudence has had trouble taking into account. Both the ambiguity of existing policy and the difficulty of taking these economies into account under existing law suggest the desirability of following the legislative route in formulating policy toward RJVs.

In a broader paper exploring the technology problems that lie behind the RJVs issue, Shapiro (1984) asks the fundamental question: What is special about "progressive" or "high-technology" industries that calls for special public policy? He gives two answers to the question. First, the output of research and development (R&D) is in many ways a public good. It is difficult for a private innovator to appropriate fully the benefits of his discoveries, and this problem is most marked for basic research activities. Second, private R&D activity is logically inconsistent with perfect competition. An innovation must confer market power in either the market for the innovation or in the market for final product if it is to offer sufficient expected reward to justify the R&D costs.

Once these features are recognized, a whole host of complexities enters the picture. Does our antitrust policy unintentionally discourage innovation? Should additional cooperation among competitors be permitted in the R&D arena? Should R&D be subsidized to promote more competition among innovators? How should patent lifetime and scope be determined? Does the presence of profits in progressive, oligopolistic industries call for a nationalistic policy designed to garner a greater share of those profits for domestic firms? The conjunction of appropriability and market power problems put us squarely in a second-best world when evaluating public policies toward R&D.

Private sector R&D is inherently a strategic endeavor, as firms vie for a technological lead. In addition, in industries where R&D plays a significant role, after the research results in an innovation, pure profits are the norm rather than the exception. The distribution of these profits across national borders is not a matter of indifference to U.S. policymakers adopting a national welfare objective. Government policy can change the rules by which strategic games are played, and this opens up a role for trade policy. Changing the rules in an effective manner, however, may require substantial information about firms' costs, the extent of spillovers, and the possibilities for industry profits.

Furthermore in industries where U.S. firms are the pioneers, it may be in the national interest to coordinate the licensing of domestic firms' patents to foreigners. This can be justified both on the ground of increasing incentives to innovation for domestic firms, and on the ground of exploiting domestic monopoly power (such as justifies the establishment of export trading associations).

In general, it is important to distinguish between appropriability by the firm and appropriability by a nation. The last example—coordination of domestic firms' licensing to foreigners—suggests a way to increase the degree to which the results of domestic R&D are appropriable by the nation. The argument underlying such coordinated restrictions on patent flows is analogous to the argument in Dixit and Grossman (1984) that an export subsidy given to domestic firms that compete for a common resource base may be detrimental. An alternative uncontrolled licensing policy may, in attempting to increase national appropriability, actually reduce the incentives to do R&D and cause some of the benefits to flow abroad. Thus the policy issues generated by the difficulties of appropriating of R&D output and by the market power that output confers can include questions of restrictions on trade in R&D output, if only national welfare is the object of policy.

Lessons Drawn from the Experiment

Perhaps the principal lesson to be drawn from our sessions is the importance of proceeding on a case-by-case basis to analyze the market organization and international trade aspects of items appearing on the trade policy agenda. The features of the sectors we discussed were so strikingly different, when examined with a sufficient degree of care, and the problems confronted by firms in those sectors were so disparate, that it made little sense to speak of a "U.S. trade policy problem." Indeed, even across areas that might be thought to have much in common as a class—"high-tech" industries or "smokestack" industries—careful consideration of market structure, conduct, and performance demonstrated clear and crucial differences. With the concerns arising about particular industries being so different, the approach required to each of them and the role for trade policy, if any, were also different.

For example, what might be needed to improve performance in the semiconductor industry, where rapid technological change and the attendant issues of research and development competition in the face of foreign government support are central, is quite different from what might be valuable in the telecommunications industry, where the major factor currently is the adjustment to deregulation in the U.S. combined with the procurement policies of foreign governments. Again, the government policy to be pursued when a smokestack industry such as steel is coping with the demand-side effects of a worldwide recession is quite different from what should be done when another smokestack industry such as autos is trying to regain its competitive footing, having initially missed out on product development in a rapidly growing segment of the market. It is important to understand the structure and behavior of the particular market before designating it as an area that government policy, and trade policy in particular, needs to address.

As noted several times in our discussion of the data of our experiment—our description of the sessions themselves—a recurrent question was whether a particular product or particular industry was appropriately on the trade policy agenda. What distinguishes, both positively and normatively, concern about the economic performance of a particular firm, industry, or sector as an appropriate target of concern by trade policymakers? Our discussions made clear the importance of distinguishing between the political process of formulating trade policy and the legal process of administering it. Starkly put, this is the difference between making trade law and enforcing it. Some participants in the sessions asserted that these functions are more merged and intertwined in foreign governments than in the United States. For example, the MITI in Japan regards itself as both maker and administrator of trade policy, whereas the USTR perceives itself as not taking policy initiatives but as only administering the law. In this sense the United States has a "reactive" trade policy in which industry or labor activate policy by bringing complaints to USTR, the

Department of Commerce, or the International Trade Commission. These concern lack of openness of foreign markets or harmful actions of foreign firms in U.S. markets, and these complaints require a response by the appropriate agency.

In the discussions of the sectors that we examined, the difficulties inherent in this basically reactive mode became apparent. A particular industry might be facing problems that merited the attention, and perhaps the intervention, of government as a matter of industrial or adjustment policy. The sector's concerns appeared on the trade policy agenda, however, not necessarily because the behavior of our trading partners was the "cause" of the industry's ills but because the industry could fashion its complaint as a trade complaint. As such, it would be entitled to consideration and perhaps action by a governmental agency. The trouble is that the USTR or another trade unit might not be at all the appropriate locus of an adequate overall policy response. For example, in the case of steel, and its presence on the trade policy "docket," it was observed that the United States had not come to grips with the problems engendered in restructuring an industry facing a significantly changed environment, and in particular, substantially reduced demand. The lack of directness and orderliness in addressing the industry's situation leaves it in a difficult position. Since the industry can formulate its complaint as a trade complaint, it comes into the trade policy agenda.

The problem of such industries are real and of serious concern, and aspects of foreign countries' behavior—import barriers or export subsidies—may contribute to them. By placing the burden on relief on trade policy, however, we risk moving from second best to Nth best by our use of an inappropriate policy tool. A technological development—for example, the appearance of new or cheaper alternative materials—may place a particular industry in a less than ideal world. But it may be a political problem—a failure of better-suited political institutions to fashion an appropriate response—that causes the industry's difficulties to be presented as a trade policy problem.

In addition this reactive mode of U.S. trade policy gives rise to a possibly inaccurate measure of success for such a policy. First, in terms of the data that are used to identify a detrimental situation or to determine the legitimacy of a complaint, the case materials with which our discussions opened put the greatest emphasis on market shares. The concern was with how U.S. penetration of foreign markets compared with the share of the U.S. market taken up by other countries' exports. In some instances there were also comparisons, though featured less prominently, of the relative shares of the United States and its competitors in third markets. But more appropriate indicia of concern about an industry—its profitability, the intertemporal profile of profits, the market's efficiency, conditions of entry, and technological features like economies of scale or spillovers from one firm to another or one country to another—received less attention.

Second, when a policy is founded on reaction to complaints, it is only natural to measure success by the absence of complaints. Viewing trade policy as one part of overall U.S. economic policy, as it should be viewed, better gauges of success are the profitability of the industries involved and the efficiency of the markets that they serve. The relationship between the absence of trade-related complaints from an industry and the performance of that industry as measured by any of the conventional standards of market organization is tenuous.

The discussion of the various sectoral issues in conjunction with relevant analytical frameworks brought to light another concern about U.S. trade policy as it is currently administered. Specifically, not only is the policy principally reactive in character, but it also allows for a substantial degree of administrative discretion, in both determining whether a complaint is well-founded and in prescribing corrective or retaliatory measures. But one of the principal lessons of several of the recent contributions to the theory of strategic behavior in an international trade setting—for example, the work of Brander and Spencer (1983), Dixit and Kyle (1984), Dixit and Grossman (1984), and others—is that the policy's effect is greatest when it sets in motion predictable responses to a given stimulus. It is the knowledge that if country X provides an export subsidy, country Y will definitely retaliate in a clearly prescribed way, which gives Y's policy its strength in affecting other countries' behavior. If all that is known is that if X subsidizes a particular export, Y will consider whether harm has been done to its industry and will ponder how to respond, these recent contributions teach us that Y's strategic power is drastically reduced. Hence, even where government intervention in trade is appropriate, the way in which that role is currently played may not be providing the benefits we seek.

A final theme that emerged was that for a sound and effective trade policy, it is imperative to consider responses to particular complaints in the context of the full international trading system. There are two dimensions to this need for peripheral vision in policymaking. First, U.S. responses to foreign government actions with regard to a particular industry or product can serve as deterrents to those countries' protectionist measures vis-à-vis other U.S. producers and products. In particular, although much of the recent literature on strategic behavior in trade policy has focused on the possibility of solely nationalistic gains from protectionist measures, strategic use of retaliatory measures can provide a spur to other countries to attain a world surplus-maximizing system of competition. Second, in considering how the U.S. will respond to one foreign government's action—be it an export subsidy, an import barrier, support of R&D, and so on—we should take account of how this policy will affect our other trading partners as well. Nor is this a rather empty counsel of perfection. On the contrary, unless trade policymakers retain broad perspective even when making specific decisions, they may regrettably find the effectiveness of their efforts undermined.

Note

This project has been sponsored by the National Bureau of Economic Research and supported by a grant from the National Science Foundation, Division of Policy Research and Analysis.

References

Brander, J. A., and B. J. Spencer. 1983. "International R&D Rivalry and Industrial Strategy." *Review of Economic Studies* L4 (October), 707–722.

Dixit, A. K., and G. M. Grossman. 1984. "Targeted Export Promotion with Several Oligopolistic Industries." National Bureau of Economic Research Working Paper No. 1344, May.

Dixit, A. K., and A. S. Kyle. 1985. "The Use of Protection and Subsidies for Entry Promotion and Deterrence." *American Economic Review.*

Flaherty, M. T. 1983. "Technology Leadership and Market Share Determination." Mimeo, Harvard University. April.

Grossman, G. 1984. "Imports as a Cause of Injury: The Case of the U.S. Steel Industry." Woodrow Wilson School Discussion Paper No. 78. Princeton University, September.

Shapiro, C. 1984. "Strategic Behavior and R&D Competition." Mimeo, Princeton University. April.

11

The New Political Economy of Trade Policy

J. David Richardson

This paper describes recent politico-economic trends in U.S. trade policy and shows how many can be viewed from the perspective of conflict and cooperation in "strategic" environments. This section of the paper introduces some of the terminology associated with strategic environments.

Strategic environments are those where the number of economic agents making interdependent decisions is relatively small. Each agent takes into account some counterresponse from rivals in calculating its best course of action. Actions include threats and promises, bluffs and commitments, all aimed at influencing the outcome of a conflict in one's own favor. These are familiar features of games and war. They have little place in the perfectly competitive environment usually employed to analyze trade policy.

In the perfectly competitive environment each of many agents considers itself too small to influence market outcomes. Each therefore makes choices assuming that all rivals' variables are given. Governments in this familiar framework presume that their policies affect market equilibrium but do not account for the way they may affect the behavior of other governments. When agents take the actions of their rivals to be immutable, strategic behavior plays no role. And when the behavior of agents is sufficiently competitive, then there are only weak analytical defenses for trade policy intervention. In the absence of market distortions market-determined trade wastes fewest resources; in the presence of market distortions corrective policies other than trade policy waste fewest resources. Such need not be the case in the strategic environments described in this paper, where trade policy can alter the entire set of preconditions on which large firms and governments base their strategic decisions.

Trade issues increasingly arise in environments that seem strategic

and that do not fit the orthodox paradigm. Firms have grown multinationally over the past few decades. The European Community,
coproduction, joint ventures, and ambitious development plans have
all encouraged their global identity. In some national markets a small
number of firms compete for a "prize" that is essentially control of the
whole nation's industry. In such concentrated environments firms
clearly recognize the effect that their actions have on the behavior of
other firms. In addition each firm conjectures how its rivals will react
to its own decisions. These same features make governments participants in a strategic "game" among themselves. Their choices regarding trade policy influence global market decisions and may induce
either retaliation or cooperation from rival governments. Governments furthermore are sometimes the owners and indirect managers
of firms.

Strategic trade policy is both topical and controversial. It is topical
in the United States because of the perception that governments
abroad are taking unfair advantage of U.S. commitment to open
trade. This perception underlies sentiment for a new and aggressive
"reciprocity" requirement in U.S. trade policy. It is also topical because strategic moves by foreign firms, often with support of their
governments, seem to some observers to be placing U.S. firms under
unprecedented pressures. These pressures lie behind many of the
recent demands for a U.S. industrial policy, to prevent U.S. sectoral
structure from becoming the cast-away residual from world sectoral
planning.

Strategic trade policy is controversial, too. Careful critics wonder
whether strategic policy will lead to mutually destructive trade wars
or to unproductive windfall seeking by special-interest groups. They
wonder further whether strategic trade policy is likely to require a
case-by-case evaluation that government may be ill-equipped to carry
out.

Outcomes from strategic interplay among governments may be
either cooperative or noncooperative. In the cooperative case com-
munication, agreements, monitoring, sanctions, and reputation may
all feature in establishing an equilibrium in which each participant
gains. In the absence of some of these features it is often in a government's interest to "cheat" on a cooperative agreement. Widespread
cheating or inability to communicate often lead to a noncooperative
outcome known as the "prisoner's dilemma." The unfortunate feature of this outcome is that every government would prefer the

cooperative outcome—if only there were some credible mechanism to preclude cheating. In the absence of such a mechanism each government sees "beggar-your-neighbor" policies as rational. There are, however, two kinds in recurrent conflict. Aggressive beggar-your-neighbor policies look for chances to exploit by initiating cheating. Defensive beggar-avoidance policies attempt to deter beggar-your-neighbor policies abroad by responding when provoked. Aggressive policies are active; defensive policies are reactive.

These concepts are employed in a discussion of recent trade-policy trends. Many of the insights from strategic trade-policy analysis appear to be impractical or undesirable for the United States. Several, however, have practical promise and are summarized in this paper. One is that completely passive U.S. trade policies invite predation. Credible dissuasionary policies would be preferable. A second is that conciliative initiatives from abroad might be able to restore a cooperative U.S. trade-policy posture. A third is that a generally cooperative posture is itself often clever strategy because of the favorable response it can encourage from rivals.

Recent Environmental Trends

Adaptability and Strategy

The intrinsic adaptability of an economy is one of the deep fundamentals underlying its ability to engage in effective strategic policy. Sports metaphors such as "rolling with the punches" and "checking off at the line of scrimmage" convey this link between adaptability and strategy. So does the insight that extreme rigidity, the opposite of adaptability, practically invites predatory actions by rivals (they have nothing to lose, so nothing they do can prompt any change in our rigid response). Adaptability may also facilitate cooperative rather than noncooperative initiatives by minimizing a sense of victimization that raises "punishment" of rivals above working with them as partners for mutual gain.

U.S. Adaptability to Global Change

The sensitivity of the U.S. economy to global trends and shocks increased markedly in the past fifteen years. This increased sensitivity is widely recognized for commodity markets. Yet it is much more pervasive than that. Many U.S. asset markets are now inter-nationalized. Trade in services is mushrooming. Much U.S. produc-tion has become sensitive to international events, as multinational corporations account for larger and larger shares of economic activity, even within U.S. borders. This leads in turn to increased sensitivity of U.S. workers to international events—not because they themselves have broadened horizons and increased mobility but because the firms for which they work have done so. The natural consequence of these trends is that U.S. economic policies, and even attitudes, are shaped more and more by international events.

By some measures U.S. adaptability to global economic change is impressive. U.S. firms spearheaded the multinational corporate movement. U.S. financial intermediaries are in the forefront of the global financial integration that—for all its excesses—made "newly industrializing countries" possible and concern over "recycling pet-rodollars" irrelevant. The United States has shown little slippage in technological impetus, even though its relative leadership has nar-rowed due to exceptional technological dynamism in Japan espe-cially. U.S. employment growth over the past fifteen years has been astounding and is due in part to international pressures (e.g., energy price shocks). U.S. real wages have shown far more flexibility than those of Europe and Canada, although not perhaps as much as those of Japan.

By other measures U.S. adaptability to global economic change may be waning. The very success that the U.S. has enjoyed in liberalizing trade may reduce adaptability—by increasing specializa-tion according to comparative advantage (Grossman and Richardson 1982, pp. 19–24). Specialized workers and specialized firms are by nature not notably adaptable. U.S. commodity imports have become more complementary to domestic production (Branson 1983, 1984). Skills, technology, and equipment differ more radically between im-port-competing industries and the rest of the economy than in the past. This makes for more difficult intersectoral adjustments in re-sponse to international change. Adjustment stimuli from the inter-national economy are heightened by increased U.S. export specialization on capital goods, which are hypersensitive to world cyclical swings.

Recent U.S. social trends, although hard to measure, may also impede economic adaptability (Richardson 1983, pp. 301–302). They include declines in the quality of U.S. education and militant pursuit of rights at the expense of contingent privileges. These aggravate market problems such as imperfect information, incomplete factor mobility, and insufficient wage-price flexibility. Other trends include increasing acceptance of trade policy as a kind of social insurance (Richardson 1983, pp. 283, 295–298), aimed at insulating the U.S. economy from injury caused by adjustment stimuli abroad. Unintended side effects include reduced economic adaptability and an undermining of some outward-looking "strategic" trade policy.

Some trends in the United States increase adaptability for certain groups and reduce it for others. Almost ten years of deregulation has made it easier for the most successful U.S. firms to respond to international change. The same deregulation may have made responsiveness harder, however, for labor, consumer groups, and marginal firms that rely on regulatory agencies for information and protection. Deregulation has almost certainly made government's trade-policy reaction more problematic. The removal of regulations forces a trade-policy question: Should the regulations be removed for all agents, or only for domestic agents? Taking the latter route implies special treatment for foreign sellers or buyers, and is by its discriminatory nature a trade policy. Taking the former route might be seen correspondingly as a trade concession. But the initiating authority may be none of the traditional trade-policy centers. It may be rather the Department of Energy, the Federal Communications Commission, or the Senate Committee on Commerce, Science and Transportation, none of which have any extraordinary experience or sensitivity in trade-policy matters.[1]

Adaptability, Trade Policy, and the Dollar

U.S. trade policy is in transition. Many forces undercut its traditional foundation and push it in the direction of noncooperative "activism." We will describe the traditional foundation first and then the new forces.

Adaptability to global economic trends has been facilitated in the United States in the past forty years by consistent advocacy of "open" trade. Protectionist forces that attempt to insulate the U.S. economy (at least temporarily) from the need to adapt have been held at bay. This consistency has been maintained in part by the ingenious institutional design of U.S. trade policy. After the 1930s Congress seemed almost to fear becoming the captive of its (voting) domestic constituency alone and recognized the importance of its (nonvoting) "foreign constituencies" by delegating significant trade-policy powers to the executive branch, just as with foreign policy.[2] The executive branch has for its part made policy administration a multiagency process, so that typically pro-trade interests (State, and parts of Commerce and Agriculture) balance typically insulative interests (Labor, and different parts of Commerce and Agriculture). What appears chaotic and unfocused has often been an implicit balancing of competing foreign- and domestic-policy concerns, moderated by the Office of the U.S. Trade Representative, the system's "broker" since the early 1960s.

In this light, adaptability of the U.S. economy to global change has suffered badly from the strong dollar of the past few years. The strong dollar has destroyed the traditional balancing of pro-trade and insulative interests—by undermining the international competitive position of even the most prosperous U.S. export sectors. It has been persuasively argued that the strongest single correlative of protectionist progress in the United States is the strength of the dollar, not the unemployment rate (Bergsten and Williamson 1983).

Adaptability problems due to the strong dollar may persist (and perhaps cumulate) for some time, especially vis-à-vis Japan. The persistence will be due to savings-investment alignments that are among the most sluggishly adjusting of all economic variables. Countries with chronically large demands for claims on the future compared with domestic supplies will have sustained net imports of them. Japan is a prime example due to its relatively high level of national savings and undistinguished availability of competitive savings instruments (i.e., high excess demand for claims on the future). Such chronic net importers of claims on the future will tend to have chronic current-account surpluses and currencies that appear to be chronically undervalued in current trade alone. The United States seems increasingly to be in the converse competitive position, with low levels of national savings and wide availability of high-return, low-risk savings instruments due to its well-developed capital markets, financial deregulation, and stable economy. It should tend to have chronic current-account deficits, and what would appear to be a chronically overvalued dollar in the light of current trade alone.

Recent U.S. Trade Initiatives and Pressures for Transition

The GATT (General Agreement on Tariffs and Trade) Ministerial Meeting of November 1982 was a highly publicized initiative by the United States to reassert cooperative global leadership in adapting to global change. It was, however, poorly executed. In the meantime other U.S. initiatives have gone in an opposite noncooperative direction. These are less broadly publicized but are obvious to those most affected. In procurement, four important bills passed in 1978–79 attaching Buy-American strictures to federal purchases totaling $18 billion. Since then at least six more procurement bills with Buy-American restrictions have become U.S. law, covering even more trade. The conformity of these laws to the Tokyo Round code on procurement is not at all clear, though the signal they send to trading partners is probably all too clear. In agriculture the United States has recently mounted retaliatory challenges to European subsidized export sales. Credit subsidies and guarantees for exports of agricultural products have been expanded greatly. The Senate Agricultural Committee has reported out a bill that would regularize U.S. agricultural export promotion using all of the tools that the European Community uses—subsidies, credit, dumping of surpluses, cargo preference, and so on. In export financing the U.S. Export-Import Bank in March approved its first two cases of retaliatory "mixed credits" (a mix of nonconcessional export financing and concessional foreign aid) to Cyprus and Indonesia.

Underlying these examples of noncooperative activism in U.S. trade policy are economic, institutional, perceptual, and intellectual changes. Intellectual changes are described in the next two sections of this paper. The others are described here.

Economic Change: The Domestication of U.S. Trade Policy
U.S. trade policy has always served two masters, and is in fact a way of discriminating between them. For the U.S. in recent years, one master has grown in relative influence. Domestic economic prosperity has become increasingly sensitive to trade policy, which has been turned more and more toward meeting its demands. International and national security goals of U.S. trade policy have declined in relative importance. Ahearn and Reifman (1983) describe this as the "domestication" of trade issues.

Domestication is a predictable result of growing U.S. dependence on international markets and of decline in U.S. hegemony. Growing U.S. trade dependence increases the influence of the country's trade policy on domestic economic variables. Responsiveness (elasticity) of sectoral output, employment, and profit with respect to trade policy rises as import and export shares rise. When trade shares were small, even export and import embargoes had only modest impacts on domestic industries. As trade shares have grown, so has the attractiveness of trade policy to attain domestic goals and to defend against "unfair" trade practices of foreign firms that are no longer just token competitors for U.S. giants.

Correspondingly, as the rest of the world has grown relative to the United States, its trade dependence on the United States has declined. Responsiveness (elasticity) of global output, employment, and profit with respect to U.S. trade policy has become smaller. U.S. strategic ability to influence world economic prosperity has therefore declined and so has the importance of this goal in shaping U.S. trade policy. The United States is a "smaller player" than it once was. Nonvoting foreign "constituents" of U.S. trade policy have taken careful note of its reduced influence on them at the same time as voting U.S. constituents have awakened to its growing influence on them.

Institutional Changes: Concentration and Politicization in the Markets, Diffusion in the GATT

Global industrial structure is moving toward rationalization. Firms have grown multinationally, and national markets have acquired an increasingly similar industrial structure, with the same firms in each.

As global industries become more concentrated (even if national markets do not), strategic government leverage over firm decisions may increase. Bargaining and monitoring costs are low because of the small numbers of "players" involved, and little effort need be spent on educating firms that are already globally informed. Performance requirements toward exports and local content may be easier to negotiate and police than tariffs and other standard instruments.

Furthermore foreign governments are acquiring increasing ownership stakes in corporate activity. Public corporations have grown, private corporations have been nationalized, and governments have acquired equity shares in both new and old ventures (Vernon 1983a, 1983b, pp. 31–34; Vernon and Aharoni 1981; Kostecki 1982). Trade policy abroad is inevitably tugged in the direction of promoting growth and preserving employment and the capital value of publically owned equity—especially at the expense of growth, employment, and equity value in the firms of foreign, often U.S., competitors. Trade policy takes on aspects of boardroom policy as trade itself includes more state trading. And state trading is inevitably more "politicized" than market trading.

GATT forums for cooperative policy initiative and conflict resolution have in the meantime grown more cumbersome. Administrative trade policies are inherently more difficult than tariffs to monitor, harmonize, or challenge. Investment-related trade policies (performance requirements) are even more difficult for GATT to consider because of the absence of codes on policy toward investment (Bale 1984). The increasing number of GATT participants makes negotiation more costly and reduces the relevance of strategic perspective. Each government is less confident that its initiatives will significantly alter the policy choices of the many other governments. It is more likely to "play independently" in GATT forums, not cooperatively, taking rivals' policies as given (and sometimes beyond hope). Bilateral trade initiatives may appear to governments, by contrast, to be much more promising.

Perceptual Changes: Inequity and Grievance
Increasingly active, even aggressive, trade policies abroad and ineffective GATT oversight lead easily to the perception that the United States is a beleaguered victim in these matters. The perception has grown that foreign governments are preying on U.S. openness and democratic due process. Increased use abroad of opaque administrative policies heightens U.S. suspicions that something discriminatory and unfair is going on below surface appearances. This makes it increasingly difficult for the United States to defend its traditional position that trade should be "free but fair."

A sense of grievance and injustice stands in the way of U.S. adaptability and cooperative initiative. In popular opinion and in policy there seem to be sporadic "withdrawal" and "lashing out." Withdrawal might be illustrated by grudging U.S. support for the International Monetary Fund and the World Bank, or by the administration's refusal to allow global real interest rates and the exchange value of the dollar to influence its macro policy mix. "Lashing out" might be illustrated by U.S. trade policy toward European export credits and agricultural policy and by legislative initiatives that demand reciprocal "fair" treatment from all trading partners. Such collective withdrawal and lashing out are almost the antithesis of cooperative adaptability, in the same way as is true in interpersonal conflicts.

There seems also to be a historical root to this collective nursing of grievance. There is a popular perception that U.S. forbearance and generosity were crucial to the reconstruction of Europe and Japan after World War II and that what the United States received in return was ruinous competition, not appreciation.[3]

"New" U.S. Trade Policy: Preliminary Considerations and Concerns

In light of these pressures it is no wonder that the conviction has grown that the United States needs a "new" and more "active" trade policy.

Recent policy initiatives, especially from Congress, reveal an anomalous division of opinion concerning the proper new strategy. Some initiatives attempt to export U.S. policy tradition to the rest of the world. Others attempt to import policy tradition abroad to the United States. Illustrating the first are new conceptions of "reciprocity"— notions that policy abroad must provide U.S. firms with the same market opportunities as our policies provide to their firms . . . or else! Illustrating the second are new conceptions of trade policy as active industrial policy—notions that U.S. trade policy should be marshaled as an important tool in striving for an optimal industrial structure.

These two strategies are not inconsistent of course—trade policy abroad could become like ours at the same time as ours became like others. The result of both strategies would be policy convergence. Thus both represent a departure from the historical U.S. approach, which is more aptly characterized as cooperative policy tolerance— accept policy differences in general, and at the margins exchange policy concessions for mutual gain. The recent appeal in the United States of policy convergence over policy tolerance appears to rest in suspicions of unfairness. One might typify it as, "If they only stopped cheating on the system and played like we do, then the field would be more level; if we only 'wised up' and played like they do, we could share all their advantages."

The issue of rules versus discretion in trade policy is closely related. U.S. tradition is rules based and ultimately subject to litigation. Tradition abroad is much more discretionary—flexible, managerial, and administrative, with negotiation rather than litigation as the vehicle for resolving differences. Here is another conflict for U.S. trade policy. Movement toward an even greater use of rules can satisfy domestic constituencies but isolate the United States in international negotiations. A good example is changes in countervailing-duty law and its administration (Shuman and Verrill 1984). Although the rules are now clearer than ever, there is still marked sensitivity in the executive branch to foreign objections when countervailing-duty cases are aggressively pursued. Negotiations with industry and foreign governments often ensue, with the result that the admittedly clear rules are bypassed by discretionary negotiation among the participants. Movement away from the rules toward discretion may, however, aggravate the widespread sense that the U.S. government is not actively pursuing American interests and undermine domestic support for all U.S. trade policy. In recent years most initiatives in U.S. trade policy might be described as "rules with discretionary overrides." Orderly marketing arrangements in footwear, television equipment, and steel can be described in this way, as can the Tokyo Round codes on subsidization, dumping, and government procurement.

These initiatives are also administrative, not implemented by taxes. Increased recourse to such administrative trade policy in the United States has led to unfortunate unpredictability as forecasts become more complex and costly. Forecasts of congressional action are less accurate and more costly because nontax initiatives involve multiple committee referrals, because cross-committee congressional discipline has waned, and because trade has provided popular "platform issues" on which to posture for constituent consumption (Ahearn and Reifman 1984). Nontax trade initiatives also cut across executive departments, causing proliferation of interest groups and diffusion of influence. Forecasts of executive action are less accurate and more costly because complex issues remain unresolved (e.g., the role of recession relative to foreign competition in the import-injury decisions of the International Trade Commission). Forecasts of action by untypically trade-oriented agencies such as the Federal Communications Commission and the Federal Maritime Commission may soon become necessary, as each is charged with scrutinizing reciprocal market access. Forecasts of judicial action may also become necessary due to increased review responsibility in countervailing-duty cases and to proposals for initiating injunctions against dumping.

Complexity and unpredictability such as this causes obvious problems for U.S. firms. Yet it also causes a strategic problem. It makes it hard for rivals abroad to read U.S. intentions, and especially hard for them to be credibly dissuaded from injurious initiatives by U.S. trade-policy deterrence. From their perspective U.S. trade policy may look essentially capricious. The best course of action for foreign rivals in that case is to take whatever actions that satisfy their narrow self-interest and to abandon efforts to curry U.S. trade-policy favor. Currying favor is too much like a crap shoot.

Unpredictability and the proliferation of trade policy turfs help to explain the initial appeal of a consolidated Executive Department of International Trade and Industry (DITI) with centralized discretion over trade policy. Yet the attitude of most commentators toward a DITI is skepticism. There seems a consensus that the most fundamental issues confronting U.S. trade policy would be just as vexing with a DITI as without.

One issue, though, would almost surely stand out more clearly with a DITI. It is the trade-off between effective discretion and participatory decision making. To exercise effective strategic discretion over trade policy would seem to require a corporate managerial style of government decision making. Such managerial decision making is typically hierarchal, not "democratic," "representative," "participatory," or "multiagency" (multidivisional). "Democracy" within a large firm seems incompatible with its competitive survival. If this is inevitable, then the cost of pursuing effective discretionary trade policy may be a decline in participatory democracy. In that light at least some governments, the United States especially, might eschew such policy for political reasons.

Successful trade or industrial policy along managerial lines would also seem to require the same flexibility and criteria for evaluation as are found in firms. It is not clear that any representative government can feasibly adopt these characteristics, especially if its functions are constitutionally delineated, legislatively detailed, and judicially defended, as in the United States. Constitutional, legislative, and judicial checks and balances are built into the U.S. political system precisely in order to make U.S. government less flexible. Americans fear more than most that flexible governments can become capricious and tyrannical. The most flexible of all firms are monopolists. The most flexible of all governments are dictatorships.

Stylized Strategic Environments and Some Implications for Trade Policy

Intellectual changes also underlie the shift toward noncooperative activism in U.S. trade policy. The new analysis of trade policy in strategic environments has provided many suggestive insights, some of which differ drastically from conclusions out of traditional analysis. The new analysis has at the same time reinforced many traditional conclusions, by providing new reasons why they apply, even to strategic environments. In this section I offer a very brief summary of the suggestive insights. In the next section I describe reasons for caution in implementing these insights, discussing both analytical and environmental considerations. In both sections I emphasize politico-economic insights and conditioning factors. Other papers in this volume describe their technical aspects in greater detail.

Stylized Strategic Trade Policy in Imperfectly Competitive Markets

One illustration of the potential for strategic trade policy is described in the work of Brander, Spencer, and Krugman, chapters 1, 2, and 4 of this volume. In their stylizations imperfect competition among small numbers of large firms make above-normal profit a fact of life. Taking such profit as given, then trade patterns that give a nation larger access to it are economically superior to other trade patterns. Trade policy can potentially achieve such desirable trade patterns. Or it can deter other nations from gaining such patterns at "our" nation's expense. The former is an aggressive trade policy, the latter a defensive trade policy.

Active trade policy can thus be defended as a profit-shifting device in imperfectly competitive environments. Aggressive variants shift global profits to "us"; defensive variants deter foreign predation on our profits. The reason trade policy has this power in these stylizations is that it alters the preconditions of imperfect competition. Our export subsidies, for example, may be seen by firms as equivalent to domestic cost-reducing innovations. They may preempt or deter foreign firms from profit-draining expansion in third-country markets. An import tariff may do the same at home. To alter rival decisions in this way, of course, foreign firms must understand such domestic policy to be a credible precommitment, giving domestic firms so-called "first-mover advantage."

Stylized Strategic Trade Policy Among Governments

Recognition of strategic interplay among firms of different na-
tionalities leads naturally to consideration of strategic interplay
among governments. Whether product markets are perfectly or imperfectly competitive, policy can potentially be used by "us" to
improve "their" calculation of optimal policy, (Grossman and
Richardson 1984, secs. 2 and 4). In other words, we may be able to
choose some active policy, or menu of active policies (contingent
on foreign response), that would shift optimal policy abroad to an
outcome more desirable to us than the outcome under policy
independence.

Aggressive illustrations include threats of new trade barriers to
force foreign governments into "reciprocity"—access for our products that matches our markets' access for theirs. Defensive illustrations include countervailing-duty provisions that are aimed at making
beggar-the-U.S. policies ineffective from a foreign government's perspective—and hence never practiced.

With imperfectly competitive product markets the potential for
policy-versus-policy strategy may be even stronger. Being "first" with
policy precommitments, or threats of such, may reduce the payoff to
reactive foreign policies of a profit-shifting sort (Macdonald 1983, pp.
13–15) and may also deter firms abroad from attempts at market
preemption.

Stylized Strategic Policy as a "Prisoner's Dilemma"

Many of the illustrations of the potential merits of strategic trade
policy share a common structure. The structure is known as the "prisoner's dilemma," based on a fable often employed to introduce it.
The structure can be described by the matrix in table 11-1. Its most
important insight is that under certain conditions cooperative outcomes are not chosen by rational "players" (governments), even
though each would prefer the cooperative outcome if it could be sure
its rival would not "cheat."

The insight can be illustrated for the imperfectly competitive market settings and policy conflicts described previously. For example,
Brander, Spencer, and others show how export subsidies abroad
might give foreign firms "first-mover advantage" over ours.[4] If we
were passive, maintaining our traditional cooperative stance, the up-

Table 11.1
Gains and losses in the status quo and from alternative active trade policies in a "prisoner's dilemma"

"Our" nation's trade policy	"Their" nation's trade policy	
	Cooperative initiative (refrain from active trade policy)	Noncooperative initiative (actively protect or promote)
Cooperative initiative (refrain from active trade policy)	0 for us 0 for them	−3 for us +2 for them
Noncooperative initiative (actively protect or promote)	+2 for us −3 for them	−2 for us −2 for them

per right outcome would result. Foreign firms would gain at the expense of ours and shift profits in their nation's favor. If foreign governments suspect that we will remain passive, then their self-interest suggests active export subsidization (they gain 2 rather than 0). There are, however, even more unpleasant implications of the matrix. Foreign self-interest suggests active export subsidization even if we ourselves subsidize (they lose only −2 instead of −3). Our self-interest suggests the same! Active subsidization is best whether foreign nations subsidize (we lose −2 instead of −3) or cooperate (we gain 2 rather than 0).[5] In the former case we would presumably defend such action as defensive strategic policy. Why allow ourselves to be exploited?

Rational self-interest thus leads both nations to choose export subsidization. The outcome (−2, −2) is attained whether strategic motives are aggressive or honorably defensive. Rationality rules out a much better outcome, not only for the two nations as a collective but for each individually. Each would prefer the jointly cooperative outcome (0, 0) to the noncooperative outcome (−2, −2).[6] Each would choose a cooperative strategy if only its rival could precommit or credibly promise to play cooperatively. In the absence of such, the inevitable outcome is a devolution to noncooperative trade-policy war.[7]

Recurring Prisoner's Dilemmas: Stylized Insights from Simulations by Axelrod (1983)

The grim inevitability of a trade-policy war in the stylized prisoner's dilemma is due principally to its one-shot, one-choice, snapshot character. Matters appear to become less grim and more revealing in a setting where prisoner's-dilemma decisions confront the same policy authorities recurrently. Skirmishes are a natural part of this more realistic setting, but not necessarily enduring pitched battles. Long periods in which the cooperative outcome obtains are still possible. In fact cooperation may actually evolve out of conflict through natural forces.

All these are broad conclusions from recent research by political scientist Robert Axelrod (1983). The research was not applied directly to strategic trade policy, but has suggestive implications for any prisoner's dilemma.[8]

Axelrod simulated the results of repeated plays of a prisoner's dilemma game. He solicited strategies from a large number of participants and played them off against each other. Each player/strategy was able to recognize others and recall what the history of their contact had been, specifically whether the rival had cooperated or cheated in each prior meeting. Strategies were "graded" on their cumulated point totals (numerical gains and losses in table 11.1 added together over repeated plays).

The results were quite definitive, even after Axelrod re-ran the simulations to allow new strategies to take advantage of strategies that won and lost the first time round.

The strategy that consistently amassed the greatest points was a very simple one, named "tit for tat." Its character was always to cooperate until cheated by some rival, then to retaliate (i.e., defect from cooperation) against that rival at the next opportunity, but only once. In essence tit for tat chose whatever action a rival took the previous play.

The trade-policy analog to this winning strategy is a clear inclination to cooperate coupled with a completely predictable willingness to retaliate when cheated. The implied trade policy is cooperative when possible, defensive when necessary, and never aggressive. This last trait means it never takes the initiative to abandon cooperation for the chance at beggar-your-neighbor exploitation. Axelrod describes this trait by the adjective "nice."

Axelrod's explanation for the stellar performance of tit for tat is that it elicited the greatest inducement among rivals to cooperate. This of course is the essential goal of all strategic policy—to prompt the most favorable response from an interdependent rival. Being "nice" helped tit for tat by assuring rivals that cooperation was always forthcoming unless the rival had cheated the previous time. Unexpected cheating by tit for tat was out of the question. Cooperation could be credibly expected. But so could retaliation. So the best a rival could do by cheating was to get "one move ahead" of tit for tat. But a return to cooperation by the aggressive rival was encouraged by tit for tat's "forgiving" (or just) character—the one-period (only) punishment fit the crime (one period's cheating), an eye for an eye, but a kiss for a kiss. Thus the rival was encouraged to ensure a return to cooperation from tit for tat by itself playing cooperatively (submissively) even during the period that tit for tat retaliated.

Finally, tit for tat encouraged cooperation by simply being clear, easily figured out by rivals in the recurrent meetings. Highly complex strategies fared poorly in contrast to tit for tat. They appeared inscrutable to rivals, even though there was in fact method in their (apparent) madness. The mere appearance of inscrutability is sufficient to leave a rival ignorant of how to respond and hence tempted not to respond at all. Inscrutable strategic policies fail precisely because they elicit no response from rivals.

The analog to trade policy is instructive. Overly complex trade policies, such as might characterize ambitious attempts to use trade policy as industrial policy, may appear inscrutable to other governments. High admixtures of discretion in trade policy may also appear inscrutable, unless the criteria underlying discretionary decisions are decipherable. The problem with highly complex, inscrutable trade policies is that rivals get the (mis-)impression that it may be worth gambling on no retaliation from their own aggressive beggar-their-neighbor actions. "Keeping 'em guessing" keeps them cheating.

Not that the clearest of all strategies is best. The clearest of all are unresponsive, unprovocable strategies. In the trade-policy milieu they are illustrated by rigid strategies such as: "free trade is always best"; "always maintain the status quo"; "always cooperate, do unto others . . ."; and "always cheat, that's all you can expect from them after all." The trouble with all these rigid strategies, whether noble or ignoble, is that the best response to them from a rival's point of view is always to cheat. Inducements for rivals to cooperate are completely absent.

In sum, using Axelrod's language to summarize the suggestiveness of his work for strategic trade policy: the best kind of strategy over repeated play is "nice, forgiving, clear, and provocable." It plays cooperatively until provoked, retaliates then but quickly returns to cooperation unless provoked again, and does all this unfailingly and transparently so that rivals are never surprised. One might capsulize the strategy as "speak (act) cooperatively and carry a clear stick."

One final feature of tit for tat is notable. It is vulnerable to the initiation of cheating, and at best just "gets even" by retaliating. Hence by comparison to every other strategy, it loses or ties in every pair of "plays of the game." It never "wins," in the sense of cheating some rival successfully more times than it itself has been cheated. It nevertheless wins the most points in repeated play because it encourages the most cooperative response from all its rivals. The implication for trade policy is that the ideal strategy may appear vulnerable in a bilateral comparison. Some particular trading partner may be able to get ahead of or beat "us" bilaterally. Yet in the multilateral competition against all other strategies, the tit for tat approach nevertheless may work best by encouraging cooperation best across the board.

Some Cautionary Conditioning Factors

If to do were as easy as to know what were good to do, chapels had been churches, and poor men's cottages princes' palaces. . . . I can easier teach twenty what were good to be done, than be one of the twenty to follow mine own teaching.
William Shakespeare, *The Merchant of Venice*, quoted by Wolf (1979, p. 135).

Many changes, environmental and intellectual, propel the United States toward a more active, strategic trade policy. Yet some aspects of environment and analysis are unchanging and provide ample reason for caution before implementing any of these strategic insights. Having described the analysis of strategic trade policy in the previous section, we begin with analytical reasons for caution, then move to environmental reasons.

How Pervasive the Strategic Gaming?

Most of the stylized descriptions of strategic trade policy are very limiting in delineating the locus for strategic action. Firm strategizes against firm, perhaps with the assistance of respective governments, or government strategizes against government. A more accurate stylization may be less limiting and more worrisome. Who, one might ask, is the game-er, and who is the game-ee? For example, firms may strategize against governments, in the attempt to capture their regulators so as to create extra profits out of the pockets of consumers (as well as shift them from foreign competitors). Such windfall-seeking games are well known to undermine productivity, and are usually thought to pervert the income distribution. Or, for example, large unions may strategize against firms or against governments, seeking again to transfer windfalls to themselves.[9] Most early analysis has ignored the large-firm-versus-government conflict and implicitly assumed labor markets to be competitive.[10] So caution needs to be exercised in applying conclusions from a "spy-versus-spy" analysis to a "spy-versus-spy-versus-spy" reality, as readers of *Mad* magazine will appreciate.[11]

The Uncertainty of What Exactly to Do

Furthermore conclusions from even the simplest strategic analysis are sometimes quite uncertain, as Grossman's paper for the conference observes. He shows, for example, how the ideal type of strategic trade policy may depend on subjective conjectures by firms of rival behavior, or even on numbers of firms. Conjectured aggressiveness in a foreign rival suggests that export subsidies would shift profits desirably; conjectured timidity in the same rival suggests export taxes instead. Regardless of subjective conjectures, export taxes replace export subsidies as the ideal profit-shifting policy as the number of domestic firms grows. Grossman shows furthermore how complicated is the calculation of ideal profit-shifting trade policy when many different sectors have above-average profits. Not all should be encouraged to expand, nor should those expanding expand to the same degree. Encouraging some sectors may tax others as they draw on scarce resources for which they all compete. The cautions are very similar when a single sector's products undergo a life cycle. Early stages of a product's life may be characterized by intense competition and sub-normal profits among firms. Yet active trade policy may be desirable at that time in order to establish the capacity to earn above-normal profits as the product matures (during which time ideal trade policy may be passive).

Burdensome Informational Requirements

In principle these uncertainties and intricacies could be resolved by adequate data collection and analysis. That was the motivation for David R. Macdonald, then Deputy United States Trade Representative, to suggest the working group on strategic behavior and trade policy that is described by Branson and Klevorick in their paper for this conference. In practice, constructing an adequate data set would be a gargantuan endeavor.[12] There are many, many relevant strategic environments that depend on circumstances such as those just described. There is, by contrast, only one perfectly competitive environment (which may explain why economists have such fondness for working with it). Practical trade policy in strategic environments is almost certainly more complex and variegated than in the perfectly competitive environment.

Undesirable Side Effects

Strategic trade policy of the type described in this paper may have unfortunate and sometimes unexpected side effects. One possible outcome is cartelization of the global industrial structure. This in turn illustrates a more general caution. The very existence of strategic trade policy can aggravate unwanted distortions to market norms.[13]

Most of the literature on strategic trade policy accepts imperfect competition as a fact of life. As an admission of reality this is no doubt good. Yet much of the literature also takes the degree of imperfect competition as a given (measured, say, by numbers of firms, or abilities to collude). This is less praiseworthy. Strategic trade policy can realistically affect both the number of rivals (Dixit and Kyle 1984) and their ability to collude. In the latter case cartelization can easily result. Krishna (1983) has demonstrated how voluntary export restraints (VERs) act as "facilitating" devices for implicit collusion between imperfectly competitive firms (at the expense of consumers in the importing country). VERs and import quotas that prescribe permissible market shares heighten the stability of any cartel-like collusion by making it illegal for a firm to "cheat" its rivals (possibly better described as partners).[14]

Along similar lines, it is worth mentioning again that a bureaucratic agency charged with facilitating its own firms' survival and profit may be ripe for "capture," as described previously, with the potential for undesired windfall-seeking and income-distributional by-products.

The income-distributional consequences of even an uncorrupted strategic policy may be an unwelcome side effect. Most strategic trade policy redistributes income from foreign firms, and from consumers worldwide, to large national corporations. Even if this redistribution yields an increase in overall national welfare, it might nevertheless be opposed. The oft-noted tension between efficiency and equity objectives of trade policy becomes all the more dramatic when the beneficiaries of policy are those firms already earning above-normal profits.

Government and Firms: Asymmetries, Character Incompatibilities, and Conflicting Mandates

One of the most significant reasons for caution in applying strategic insights to U.S. trade policy is that the government may be ill-equipped to manage some of its aspects. This seems especially true in the case of aggressive profit-shifting initiatives and other attempts to capitalize on attractive trading opportunities by policy. The U.S. government seems better equipped, by contrast, to manage defensively strategic policy—retaliation, threats, and exhortations to behave cooperatively. Such defensive policies require reactive rather than active administration, and U.S. trade laws and agencies are both inherently reactive.

The difference between managerial and democratic styles of administration has already been discussed. It is one asymmetry between government and firms. Other asymmetries include differing primary mandates (justice, infrastructure, and other public goods versus efficiency and technological frontiersmanship); differing monitoring/accountability arrangements (voters motivated by responsibility to evaluate in periodic elections versus shareholders motivated by money on the line to evaluate continuously);[15] and differing abilities to experiment (due to risk aversion on the part of the general public that inevitably exceeds the risk aversion, if any, of venture capitalists, entrepreneurs, and innovators). Each of these asymmetries provides an important practical barrier to aggressive strategic trade policy. Its attractiveness rests by contrast on government becoming "like" its firms—at least a facilitator, perhaps an underwriter, and possibly even a coparticipant in corporate planning. Such convergence of character may in the long run be beneficial. Government was no doubt wise to adopt some traits of large firms as it became larger while abandoning some traits of town meetings. Yet the benefits are by no means certain, and institutional inertia makes any short-run realization very costly.[16]

Anecdotal Reasoning and Circumstantial Leaps of Faith

Two final reasons for caution in applying strategic perspectives relate to the process by which they are often evaluated.

There is first a dangerous tendency to use anecdotal argument to document the alleged success of strategic trade policy. Its apparent reality and clarity, however, disguise its inherent lack of integrity. Anecdotal argument draws a sample consistent with a predetermined conclusion. It cannot thereby solidify the conclusion's accuracy. Repetition of the same anecdote does not add authority to its applicability—any more than repeated sampling of the same observation in a data set adds to its ability to explain.

Second, there is a tendency toward circumstantial leaps of faith in assessing strategic trade policy. Apparent pressures to "do something (anything)" make commentators jump from a demonstration that some strategic initiative might work to the conclusion that "it does, and we should adopt it." Conditioning circumstances are neglected, as is the hard empirical work of figuring out if they hold. It is perhaps helpful to remember how often doing nothing is better than doing something, even in the middle of turmoil.

A Summing Up

What conclusions come from this assessment of the new political economy of trade policy? A tentative summary might be that the only sensible offense is a good defense and might include the following:

1. Cooperative trade-policy initiatives still appear worthwhile, even from a strategic perspective—not just good but smart. The strategic reason for cooperative initiatives is to encourage cooperative responses from rivals-turned-partners.

2. Cooperative initiatives and responses are not appropriate in every case, however. Retaliation, that is, defensive noncooperation, is a powerful instrument for encouraging cooperation from trading part-

ners. That is why it is strategically sensible. But to be maximally effective, it must be utterly transparent and predictable and also temporary, measured, and not unduly punitive. These requirements buttress the case for rules-based retaliation and suggest unsatisfactory consequences from discretionary retaliation.

3. Cooperative trade-policy initiatives from abroad make a cooperative response from the United States economically more likely and politically more attractive. This is really just the foreign application of point 1. Yet it affects U.S. policy insofar as strategic noneconomic initiatives by the United States (e.g., with regard to defense-sharing, foreign policy, or cultural and education exchanges) might be used to encourage cooperative trade-policy initiatives abroad, especially from like-minded trading partners.

4. Aggressively noncooperative initiatives can work to a nation's benefit in some circumstances but have significant weaknesses. Their chief strategic weakness is to undermine the case for cooperative trade-policy responses from trading partners, cooperation from which "we" gain. Their chief economic weaknesses include uncertainty even in principle about whether trade policy should promote trade or restrict it, dependence on subjective conjectures of rivals' responses, and undesirable potential side effects. Their chief administrative and political weaknesses include onerous information requirements and (for the United States) the unsuitability of traditions and institutions for effective implementation of such policy.

Notes

This paper has benefited greatly from comments by Doral Cooper, Daniel Littman, Mark Sniderman, and participants in the National Bureau of Economic Research (NBER) Summer Institute in International Studies. Some of the research that underlies it has been supported by National Science Foundation Grant PRA-8116459 to the NBER. Shortcomings that remain are the author's full responsibility. Neither they nor any opinions expressed herein should be associated with the persons or institutions acknowledged above with appreciation.

1. A corollary to this observation is that new trade policy initiatives in regulated areas, such as services trade with Israel (*Wall Street Journal*, October 12, 1984, p. 33), have almost certainly made government's regulatory oversight more problematic for similar reasons.

2. The language "fear becoming the captive" is chosen to reflect an important aspect of political economy—the rivalry between a government charged with

regulating a private sector and a private sector tempted to co-opt (capture) its regulators. For an expansion of the points in this paragraph, see Destler (1984, ch. 2).

3. That perception of course disregards the benefits of the long period of U.S. hegemony.

4. The example may apply quite closely to the OECD Guidelines for Officially Supported Export Credits, showing the incentives for cheating to undermine the cooperative agreement.

5. A matrix where our gains and losses are not symmetric to theirs can be easily constructed, yielding the same qualitative results.

6. The numbers illustrate the likely characteristic that the losses to both nations together increase with the number of distortions. Collective losses are -1 with one nation choosing active policy, and -4 when both do.

7. For tariffs, GATT bindings illustrate (more-or-less) credible commitments to play cooperatively. Rights to compensation help to buttress these commitments.

8. Otherwise the analysis of dynamic, repeated trade-policy conflict is still in its infancy. Jensen and Thursby (1983) is one example.

9. It is the rent-seeking part of this activity that is undesirable. Jon Eaton and Paul Krugman have both observed that the pure profit-shifting argument for strategic trade policy could be recast as a wage-shifting argument in the case where concentrated labor groups bargain successfully with firms to pay out above-normal profits as wages.

10. Brander and Spencer (1984) is an exception in the latter regard.

11. For example, Paul Krugman (1984, p. 103) and others have pointed out that a government may find it best to abjure seemingly desirable strategic discretion, say in export policy, if too much governmental freedom of action there birthes a Pandora's box of irresistible pressures for similar "strategic" favors to all special interests. The point has its analog in parenting. Favors one does for the benefit of a responsible child (and the whole family) may not appear so beneficial when irresponsible children exploit them as precedents. Tying one's hands may be better than discretion in a multiagent game. This is not to be taken as a presumption, however, only as a possibility. It will at other times be true that a government's discretionary strategy can be enhanced by playing one of its several rivals off against others. The Organization of Petroleum Exporting Countries in the 1970s would seem to have neutralized both oil companies and their governments in somewhat this way. U.S. trade policy itself has traditionally rested on a "playing off" of competing domestic interests internally, as described earlier.

12. It would also have some distinct subtleties. To the extent that profit is an important variable, for example, one would need a precise answer to the age-old questions, "What is profit? . . . normal profit? . . . above-normal profit? Is it adequate to measure it as a residual? . . . over what period of time? What

about expected profit? What about risk premiums that cause profit to differ naturally across activities?"

13. Krugman (1984, pp. 96–97) illustrates and discusses this caution for distortions that increase a sector's wages above the national average.

14. Proposed U.S. marketing agreements with foreign steel producers are illustrations. They implicitly grant "first-mover advantage" to U.S. firms by setting imports as a share of U.S. market size. The nature of competitive interchange will change. Conjectures of rival responses are no longer needed. Implicit collusion and so-called "leader-follower" behavior are encouraged.

15. The fundamental agency problem for government is more severe than it is for firms. There are furthermore several other layers of agency problems involved in implementing an aggressive trade or industrial policy. These are discussed in, for example, Littman (1984). Monitoring/accountability arrangements among layers of government differ significantly from those among divisions of firms.

16. Examples may just belabor the obvious. It seems almost impossible, for example, to imagine quickly reversing a selection bias that propels the best industrial planners toward private firms (rather than toward a DITI) where they rub shoulders with the best industrial planners of preceding cohorts and generations. Within government, mid-life, mid-level personnel cannot be easily moved or displaced. Government institutions inevitably reflect their character and tradition.

References

Ahearn, Raymond J., and Alfred Reifman. 1984. "Trade Policy Making in the Congress." In R. E. Baldwin, ed., "Recent Issues and Initiatives in U.S. Trade Policy." NBER Conference Report.

Axelrod, Robert. 1983. *The Evolution of Cooperation.* New York: Basic Books.

Baldwin, Robert E., ed. 1984. "Recent Issues and Initiatives in U.S. Trade Policy." NBER Conference Report.

Bale, Harvey E., Jr. 1984. "Trade Policy Aspects of International Direct Investment Policies." In R. E. Baldwin, ed., "Recent Issues and Initiatives in U.S. Trade Policy." NBER Conference Report.

Bergsten, C. Fred, and John Williamson. 1983. "Exchange Rates and Trade Policy." In R. Cline, ed., *Trade Policy in the Eighties.* Washington, D.C.: Institute for International Economics.

Brander, James A., and Barbara Spencer. 1984. "International Markets with Asymmetric Labor Commitment and Union Power."

Branson, William H. 1983. "Trade and Structural Adjustment in the U.S. Economy." Mimeo.

Branson, William H. 1984. "The Changing Structure of U.S. Trade: Implications for Research and Policy." Mimeo, March.

Destler, I. M. 1984. *The American Trade Policy System.*

Dixit, Avinash K., and Albert S. Kyle. 1984. "On the Use of Trade Restrictions for Entry Promotion and Deterrence." Discussion Papers in Economics No. 56. Woodrow Wilson School of Public and International Affairs, Princeton University.

Jensen, Richard, and Marie Thursby. 1983. "Free Trade: Two Noncooperative Equilibrium Approaches." Mimeo, Ohio State University.

Grossman, Gene M., and J. David Richardson. 1982. "Issues and Options for U.S. Trade Policy in the 1980s: Some Research Perspectives." NBER Research Progress Report.

Grossman, Gene M., and J. David Richardson. 1984. "Strategic Trade Policy: A Survey of Issues and Early Analysis." NBER Research Progress Report. Forthcoming as Princeton University *Special Paper in International Economics.*

Kostecki, M. M., ed. 1982. *State Trading in International Markets.* London: Macmillan.

Krishna, Kala. 1983. "Trade Restrictions as Facilitating Practices." Discussion Papers in Economics No. 55. Woodrow Wilson School of Public and International Affairs, Princeton University.

Krugman, Paul. 1984. "The U.S. Response to Foreign Industrial Targeting." *Brookings Papers on Economic Activity.* Washington, D.C.: Brookings Institution.

Littman, Daniel A. 1984. "The Implementation of Industrial Policy." Draft article under consideration for Federal Reserve Bank of Cleveland, *Economic Review.*

Macdonald, David R. 1983. "A Washington Perspective on Strategic Behavior and Trade Policy." Mimeo, March 17.

Richardson, J. David. 1983. "International Trade Policies in a World of Industrial Change." In Federal Reserve Bank of Kansas City, *Industrial Change and Public Policy.*

Shuman, Shannon Stock, and Charles Owen Verrill, Jr. 1984. "Recent Developments in Countervailing Duty Law and Policy." in R. E. Baldwin, ed., "Recent Issues and Initiatives in U.S. Trade Policy." NBER Conference Report.

Vernon, Raymond. 1983a. *Two Hungry Giants.* Cambridge, Mass.: Harvard University Press.

Vernon, Raymond. 1983b. "Old Rules and New Players: GATT in the World Trading System." Mimeo, May 11.

Vernon, Raymond, and Yair Aharoni. 1981. *State-Owned Enterprise in the Western Economies.* London: Croom Helm.

Wolf, Charles, Jr. 1979. "A Theory of Nonmarket Failure: Framework for Implementation Analysis," *The Journal of Law and Economics* 22 (April), 107–139.

12

Trade Policy: An Agenda for Research

Avinash K. Dixit

Consumers of academic economic research in the real world rightly judge it by the criterion of how well it helps them in their own endeavors. The loud reaction to a paper that puts forward an agenda for further research on trade policy is therefore likely to be "Why?" Recent research contains support for almost all the vocal and popular views on trade policy that only a few years ago struggled against the economists' conventional wisdom of free trade. Now the mercantilist arguments for restricting imports and promoting exports are being justified on grounds of "profit shifting." The fears that other governments could capture permanent advantage in industry after industry by giving each a small initial impetus down the learning curve now emerge as results of impeccable formal models. The claim that one's own government should be aggressive in the pursuit of such policies because other governments do the same is no longer dismissed as a non sequitur. Numerous advocates of such policies, from business, labor, and government, are likely to react to my title by saying, "Why not stop right here and leave a good thing alone?"

The answer is that academic economists are not going to leave it alone, and it is well to be forewarned about the questions they are likely to investigate. Academics are unwilling, by inclination as well as training, to accept any answers as final. They are going to examine the new wisdom carefully and ask if it has a sound basis. They are going to ask if the assumptions made by the theorists of the new wisdom correspond to reality. And they are going to ask whether the policies of the new mercantilists serve the general interest, or whether John Stuart Mill's verdict on the old mercantilists—"When they say country, read aristocracy, and you will never be far from the truth."—still holds, with "aristocracy" replaced by "business" or "organized labor."[1]

Of course, academic economists have their own selfish reasons for continuing research. Graduate students want to get Ph.D.s, assistant professors want to get tenure, and as for professors, "All professors are ambitious—ambitious to become professors somewhere else."[2]

My task here is to speculate on the kind of research we academic economists are likely to do in this area over the next five years. This picture is of course limited by my vision and not unmixed with my judgment as to what we should do. Nevertheless, I hope it will be useful. To set the stage for it, I shall begin with a general discussion of the principles governing the conduct of economic policy in a market economy. Then I shall examine how well the new mercantilism conforms to these principles. The gaps that remain, or the conflicts that emerge, gives us the issues and questions for future research. In the concluding section, I shall bring these items together into a research agenda.

The discussion will not be separated into theoretical and empirical issues but according to the nature of the economic problem that is at stake. However, it is worth pointing out that most of the recent research, which has altered many views on the role of trade policy, has been purely theoretical. It has pointed out certain logical possibilities, without asking about the empirical likelihood of the stipulated circumstances. To correct this imbalance must be a high priority for future research. Variations on this theme will recur throughout my discussion.

Some Principles of Economic Policy

Economic policy in a market-oriented economy works by changing the trading opportunities and the incentives of the market participants who make the decisions about production, labor supply, consumption, and so on. Most such policies affect both the general interest (i.e., the total real value of goods and services at the command of the whole society) and various special interests (i.e., the distribution of the goods and services among individuals and groups).

Details of the effects are complex and subtle because the economy is a complex and subtly interlinked mechanism. But some general principles to guide policy stand out. Considering the general interest, the following two are probably the most important. For ease of future reference, I shall number them, and cast them in the form of questions that should confront any proposed policy intervention. The statement of each question is followed by a brief explanation and discussion.

Question 1 Does the social benefit-cost calculation differ from the private profitability calculation of participants in the market?

The mere fact that an economic activity or project has benefits in excess of its costs does not justify a policy to encourage it; nor does the opposite automatically argue for restrictions. If the private decision maker can capture or appropriate the full benefits in the form of prices received for the outputs of the project and bears the full cost in the form of prices paid for the inputs, then his private profitability calculation will work out just right from society's viewpoint. This is exactly the invisible hand of the price mechanism guiding resource allocation.

When market prices do not correspond to social values, economists speak of a "market failure." As an illustration, consider research in a society where patent protection is imperfect. Then an inventor or innovator can capture only a part of the profit his research generates. As another example leading to the opposite bias, consider activities that inflict congestion or pollution on others. Here the net social benefit is less than the gain to the individual or the firm that performs the action.

Such market failures are the basic justification for all economic policies in the general interest. If the government can measure the discrepancy between social and private costs and benefits, it can calculate subsidies for research, taxes on pollution, or other policies that will close the gap and restore the private decision makers' incentives to the right social level. Even without precise measurement a step in the right direction can often be taken.

However, it is one thing for an economist to think of an abstract policy measure; it can be quite another matter to implement it in a political world. There is considerable danger that special interests will capture the policy process and design it to serve their own ends, often at considerable cost to the rest of society.[3] Therefore, even in relatively clear-cut cases of market failures, it is no easy matter to design a realistic, implementable policy that serves the general interest.

Question 2 Is the policy being proposed the best way of solving the problem at hand, or are there better measures available?

The mere fact that the proposed policy brings social and private benefit-cost calculations into closer alignment does not clinch the argument. It is important to compare it with other policies that have a bearing on the problem. They may yield an even better alignment or have fewer harmful side effects elsewhere in the economy. In some cases the root cause of the problem may be some other action of the government itself; then the alternative to be considered should be the repeal of that other measure. A typical instance is where a group of firms could get together and jointly capture the full benefits of their actions but are prevented from doing so by antitrust policies. Then a reform of these restrictive measures, or a suitably designed exception to them, should be considered.[4]

The traditional mercantilist arguments for export promotion and protection did not perform well against these two questions. I can illustrate the point, and at the same time illustrate the questions in action, by considering one of the stronger arguments for protection— the infant-industry argument.[5] This argument was once limited to developing countries but is often made nowadays by U.S. industries in their second infancy; therefore it has immediate relevance here.

The argument is that protection will enable the industry to achieve dynamic economies of scale, to lower its costs, and to become competitive in world markets. Let us begin by asking question 1: Do private firms have the right incentives anyway? They can make an "investment" by continuing the high-cost production in the short run and get the "returns" in the form of higher future profits when the costs have fallen. If these costs and profits accurately reflect the social costs and benefits, then no policy intervention is necessary.

To keep the argument going, let us consider a case where there is a difference between private and social rewards. The typical problem is that workers trained by one firm at a cost in the early years are bid for by other firms as soon as their productivity rises sufficiently. The wages of such workers therefore rise. If is is to keep them, the first firm must pay matching higher wages. Thus the firm doing the training cannot capture the resulting profits and has no incentive to train.

Now there is scope for a policy to serve the general interest. Let us see how protection performs in this role. Protection increases the profitability of production in this industry but does nothing whatever to increase a firm's return from training a worker. Any expansion of this industry occurs by increasing the use of nonlabor inputs or unskilled labor. If protection is to be continued, the incentive to poach workers trained by another firm, rather than to train your own, is if anything greater. The policy of protection for such an industry therefore fails the test of question 2 in a truly abysmal way.

What alternative policies might do better? One might give a firm the right to the increase in future wages of a worker it has trained. But this is tantamount to a repeal of the Thirteenth Amendment, and there are compelling noneconomic reasons against such a step. One might offer direct subsidies for training. But one might also notice that there is the right market incentive within the system. If competition among firms raises the wages available to trained workers, then they capture the benefits of training and have the correct incentives to "invest" in this process. This might be done by means of an apprenticeship scheme, with appropriately lower wages for the training period. We are back to question 1, and perhaps no policy is necessary.

Of course special interests would argue differently. Firms would want to conceal or obfuscate the issues raised by the two questions and collect the special benefits conferred on them by protection. Labor might share in the benefits of protection. And it would prefer to collect training subsidies rather than sacrifice any wages. In all these cases the rest of society would pay the cost, and since the underlying problem would not be solved efficiently, the general interest would suffer.

The only old argument that passes the scrutiny of the two questions is at least in part, antimercantilist. It says that a country acting in its general interest, but not caring about other countries, should restrict its exports as well as its imports below their free-trade levels if it is sufficiently large in world markets to obtain more favorable prices by so doing (i.e., if it has monopoly power in trade, and individual competitive firms cannot exploit it).

The reasoning fits nicely into the framework of question 1. Consider one exporter from this large country. As he exports more, the world market price of the product falls, and the profits of his compatriot exporters go down. This is against the general interest of that country (i.e., each exporter is capturing more than 100 percent of the social benefit of his action). An export tax or other restriction is called for. The case of imports is argued analogously. Although it is more difficult to see, the test of question 2 is also passed in this instance, and trade restrictions are the best way a large country can exploit its monopoly power in trade.

Observe why the argument would not work for sales to consumers in your own economy. One producer's extra output lowers the price and so the profits of his competitors, but the lower price is good for the consumers. A general-interest calculation takes both into account, when they just cancel each other, and the one producer's private profit calculation correctly measures the net social benefit of his action. The case of the trading economy is different because it does not care about the benefit of the lower price to foreign consumers.

But this points out that a large country's exercise of monopoly power in trade is contrary to the general interest of the world as a whole. If the world has two large blocs, each has a selfish interest to restrict its trade, and their actions can trap them in a prisoner's dilemma where both are worse off than they would be under mutual free trade. Note that the incentive of one to restrict trade does not arise because the other is doing so; the same incentive would exist even if the other were practicing free trade and might even be stronger since there is a larger base of trade on which to extract monopoly profits. If the countries are to extricate themselves from the dilemma, they have to be able to make mutually credible promises of avoiding the restrictive temptation. This is difficult in a world with little supranational authority. But opportunities for an open or tacit agreement exist if the blocs interact repeatedly, thereby allowing threats of retaliation and the opportunity to build up trust.[6] I shall return to the issues of policy dilemmas and negotiations in a later section.

Profit Shifting

Let me now consider how the arguments of the new mercantilists have fared better. A good starting point is a statement wrongly attributed to an eminent old protectionist, Abraham Lincoln: "When I buy a coat from England, I have the coat and England has the money. But when I buy a coat in America, I have the coat and America has the money."[7] One does not have to be a professional economist to realize that there must be more to the state of affairs than that. One wonders: What does England not have in the one case, and America in the other? The answer is immediate: The resources that went into making the coat. The labor and capital whose services were engaged in the process of production could have been doing something else, the cost of the materials could have been saved, and so on. Only if the price of the coat exceeds the value of these resources in their best alternative uses can we speak of a net gain from having or seizing the opportunity to produce the coat.

This argument reveals an important general principle, which supplements our question 1 by giving us a criterion for measuring the costs in our calculation of net social desirability. The cost of an input is the value of the forgone opportunity to put it to the next best available use, what economists call "opportunity cost." If markets are functioning efficiently, bids from those alternative users will ensure that the prices of inputs will equal their opportunity costs, and the question of social desirability will boil down to that of an excess of the price of the coat over the costs of all inputs that go toward producing it—that is, the true economic profit. (Note that we must count the normal return required to attract capital as an input cost, and any returns in excess of this qualify as true or pure or excess profits.)

The word "money" in Lincoln's statement should therefore properly be replaced by "profit." We should also add, "if any." The qualification is important because, in competitive markets with free entry, pure profits disappear as eager new entrants to the tailoring industry bid for inputs and raise their prices, or put more coats on the market and lower their price.

This was in fact the major stumbling block for the arguments of the old mercantilists. Since their underlying model of the economy was one of perfect competition, there were no excess profits. Thus there was no special net benefit to American from supplying Lincoln's coat. The resources it would use up could instead have done something else just as valuable. Therefore there was no mercantilist case for policy to encourage purchase of American coats or to discourage purchase of English ones (whether by Lincoln or by Mr. Gladstone).

The prognosis was even worse for the old mercantilist policy. At the margin, producing just one extra coat might be a matter of indifference, as the cost of production just matched the price. Push this policy to increase coat production by ten thousand, and diminishing returns might raise the cost of production above the price. From the point of view of American society as a whole, this would be a loss-making proposition. If in the process the world price of coats fell, the losses would be compounded. In those circumstances American general interest would require an antimercantilist policy of export restraint, as was explained earlier.

Now consider the new mercantilists. They have a very different view of the economic world. Their basic model of the economy is one of imperfect competition, or more specifically, one with entry barriers. Firms operating behind these barriers are able to keep prices in excess of costs—that is, there are pure profits. Since these can be thought of as scarcity values of the restricted positions or slots in the industry, economists call them monopoly rents.

These profits or rents change the benefit-cost calculus of international trade considerably. It is in America's general interest if American firms get these rents instead of foreign ones. Many recent articles in the professional literature advocating the use of trade policy have been based on this idea of shifting the profit to one's own country's firms or away from foreign ones. Here are some examples: (1) If a foreign firm is making profits in a monopolized market in our country, a tariff can act somewhat like a tax on its profits.[8] (2) If home and foreign firms are involved together in an imperfectly competitive market, a policy of import restriction (if the market is in our country) or export promotion (if it is in another country) can in some circumstances increase the profits of our firms at the expense of foreign ones.[9] (3) If our firm has an entrenched monopoly position in the world market, foreign governments might try to aid their firms to break in, and our government could try to deter this attempt. Thus the need for our trade policy would arise because of theirs.[10] In each of these models other aspects of the general interest, notably the prices paid by our consumers, can enter the picture and modify it to some extent, but profit shifting remains the basic idea. Some other writers confine themselves to "positive" arguments, merely showing how trade policy could aid domestic firms and industries, but any "normative" use of their results to recommend such policies as desirable would have to invoke the same idea of profit shifting.[11]

Since the difference in assumptions about the nature and the degree of competition in markets causes such a difference in the implications for policy, the logical place to begin our scrutiny of the new mercantilism is by examining the empirical relevance of its assumption. The question is: In which industries are there imperfections of competition or entry barriers, and how significant are they? Or, to re-coin a phrase, "Where's the rent?"

In fact the research on profit shifting, including my own, has been purely theoretical. The question of the actual prevalence of rents in the world economy has been badly neglected and should be a high priority for future research. There are several difficulties that confront us in this task. Calculating true economic profit is never easy. We may have to use proxies like concentration to infer monopolistic profit potential. To make matters worse, we want to know what would happen in the absence of trade policy. We observe much monopoly rent in the world whose presence is due to trade restrictions, for example, the Japanese auto industry's profits due to the VERs and the Hong Kong textile and garment exporters' rents under the MFA. Those are not the kinds of rents the new mercantilists are talking about. They are products of the policy itself. We want to know whether the world markets would have monopoly rents even in a hypothetical free-trade regime, for these are the profits, according to the new mercantilist doctrine, that each national government would find in its general interest to capture.

It is my belief that research will reveal the profit-shifting argument to be of significance in only a small number of selected industries. Here are a few examples and arguments in support of this claim.

The auto industry is probably a good test case. Transport costs are not a significant barrier, and we should treat the world market as one. If we take the 1982 production figures by companies (treating all national subsidiaries of each multinational together) and measure passenger cars in units, the Herfindahl index of concentration is under 0.11, which is very competitive.[12] This simple procedure is flawed in many ways—we are looking at production figures in a regime that is far from free trade, we cannot treat all passenger cars as homogeneous units, and we should divide the market into subcompacts, luxury cars, and so on. But I think these improvements will leave the basic picture of competition unchanged.

In primary products and commodities, and at the national level, there are many instances of high concentration. In 1982 the United States produced 66 percent of the world's soybeans. At the height of its monopoly power in 1973 OPEC produced 54 percent of the world's crude petroleum. South Africa produces about 75 percent of the world's chromite. But once again, this is not the relevant monopoly power, at least in the first instance. The soybean market is almost perfectly competitive. The United States may want its exporters to act jointly like a cartel to drive up the price in the rest of the world and may achieve this my means of an export tax. But, as I said earlier, that is if anything an antimercantilist policy. Once one country has created such a monopoly position, other countries may want to shift some of this profit; that is a "second-round" new mercantilist effect, and the overall result is usually a prisoner's dilemma of policies. Such a policy was proposed in the United States as a countermeasure against OPEC.

The civilian jet aircraft industry is highly concentrated. It need not have commensurate monopoly rents, however, since competition among the few firms seems quite fierce. This highlights the importance of examining market conduct in addition to structure. Given the importance of this industry in the Eximbank's activities, I need hardly stress the importance of understanding its potential for profit shifting by conducting a thorough empirical study.

The market for top-of-the-line mainframe computers is quite concentrated; that for personal computers seems quite competitive. The pharmaceutical industry has a lot of monopoly rent, and high concentration if we break it down into its component parts each of which must be regarded as a market in its own right. In many cases this means an individual drug.

Generally, in any project where substantial amounts have to be sunk into research and development, and only one or a few firms succeed and go on to the production stage, we should expect to see the successful firms enjoying large monopoly profits. Without the prospect of such a reward they would not have undertaken the investment. But the profit-shifting argument must not be employed uncritically to such industries. It is important to look at the whole process of research and development followed by production, and such analysis brings some complications to light.

After successful firms have become entrenched in the industry, the sunk costs will constitute an entry barrier for new firms. But, before the fact, there is usually free entry to the whole process. Consider a firm contemplating the investment into research and development during this early stage of the industry's evolution. The expected actuarial value of the endeavor is

(Profit if successful) × (Probability of success) − (Cost of R&D).

Firms will enter until this actuarial value is reduced to zero. If their estimate of the probability of success is rational (i.e., equal to the number of successful firms divided by the number of entrants), then we will find that

(Profit if successful) × (Number of successful firms) − (Cost of R&D) × (Number of entrants) = 0.

There will be zero excess profit for the process as a whole; the profits of successful firms will just match the losses of the rest.

Now suppose the U.S. government announces the policy of offering import protection or export promotion to U.S. firms in such an emerging industry. This will increase the size of the prize available to a successful U.S. firm, and that will attract additional entry. In the final analysis, there will be a larger number of successful U.S. firms, but in the background there will be more losers, too. The group as a whole will get zero rent—that is, the resources used up in the whole process would have been just as valuable engaged in the best alternative opportunity. This U.S. policy will also reduce the prize available to foreign firms and discourage some entry. Since the group of foreign entrants as a whole also has zero rent, those resources are redeployed to other equally valuable uses. If the policy is pushed beyond the small marginal scale, it will actually harm the general interest in the manner that was discussed earlier in the context of Lincoln's coat.

Of course, if the U.S. government waits for the industry to settle down and then springs a surprise policy of profit shifting, the new mercantilist argument will work. But a better-known, and somewhat better-founded, dictum of Abraham Lincoln rules out any systematic use of this kind of policy: "You cannot surprise all of the firms all of the time." The industry will come to anticipate the policy, and firms will make their entry decisions accordingly. This will transform the story of an ex post oligopoly with profit to be shifted into one of ex ante competition with zero rent. I therefore believe that the applicability of the profit-shifting argument is questionable even in the context of dynamic, research-intensive, high-technology industries where it is supposed to hold sway.

The model of the process of research and development I have sketched is not meant to be definitive. Consideration of risk aversion should be introduced if there is systematic risk. The choice of intensity of research effort, and the races to be first and secure a patent, should be analyzed. Then there is an argument similar to a large country's national monopoly power case: the United States may benefit if it allows its firms to pool their R&D efforts and avoid mutually harmful competition. The effect again runs counter to mercantilist presumptions and has to be balanced against any domestic antitrust considerations.

Research along these lines should be a high priority for theorists. Some beginnings have been made, but they are not yet commensurate with the policy importance of the issues in many high-technology industries.[13] Lacking better analysis, the danger of misapplication of the new mercantilist doctrines to such trade seems a real one.

The foregoing remarks call into question the scope and significance of the profit-shifting argument and suggest empirical and theoretical work to settle the issues. Even when there are rents that a country's trade policy can capture, we must subject such policy to the test of our two questions before recommending it.

The first question points out that it is not enough that there are monopoly rents; role for policy is limited to situations where our firms are unable to capture these rents by their own actions. The usual answer given by the neomercantilists is that the government is able to make irreversible commitments that give the firms a strategic advantage against foreign ones and that the firms would be unable to replicate such strategic moves by themselves.[14] To my knowledge, the empirical validity of these assertions has never been tested. The answers will vary from one industry to another, and some case studies to help us understand the realities are badly needed.

The second question asks whether trade policy is the best way to achieve the aim of profit shifting. This issue has been badly neglected in research. There are few attempts to answer it in specific instances, and the results are generally unfavorable to trade policy. For example, rent is better captured from a foreign monopolist selling in your market by imposing a price ceiling or a profit repatriation tax.[15] Promotion of entry is generally better pursued by means of subsidies.[16] But in many other instances alternatives to trade policy have not been examined and ranked. This is clearly an important research question, especially in view of the strong results of this kind we have for competitive economies, where trade policy is generally inferior to other tax or subsidy policies.[17]

Other Issues

The argument of profit shifting is central to much of the recent research on trade policy, and that is why I spent so much time discussing it in detail. But there are some other arguments that deserve at least a brief mention.

Unemployment

In the discussion leading up to the role of rent, I explained that costs of a resource should be measured by its value in the best alternative use and that in a well-functioning market the price of the resource will equal this opportunity cost. Many people would argue that the labor market functions particularly poorly in this respect and the only alternative to the job at hand is unemployment. They would value this close to zero and would therefore regard a job-creating project as highly beneficial.

Our scrutiny of this argument follows the familiar pattern. First, we ask if the assumption is empirically valid; in practice there are many productive alternatives available to most workers. Next, we ask if this is a genuine market failure or a product of some deliberate policy such as an anti-inflation policy that works, creating a recession. If the latter, then another branch of the government will respond to our job-creating policy by generating further deflation that defeats our goal. Finally, we ask if trade policy is the right way to create jobs. If U.S. exports are highly technological, skill or capital intensive, then export promotion will be a poor policy in this respect. Good answers to all these questions require good empirical research.

Market Structure

I argued earlier that in many instances, barriers to entry and monopolization of national markets are the results of restrictive trade policies themselves. Such policies are usually followed not in the general interest but in response to pressures by some special interest groups. It is important to assess how they affect the general interest.

One line of research is theoretical, and asks how trade restrictions affect the structure and conduct in the domestic market. The general conclusion from the studies so far is that quantitative restrictions are particularly pernicious in their effect on domestic competition.[18] Another line is empirical, and finds that substantial amounts of rents created by these restrictions are lost to foreign firms or governments.[19] Both lines are well researched and yield significant conclusions, but continued studies to buttress the argument, especially on the empirical side, would be welcome.

Monopolistic Competition

Quite a few industries fall in an area between competition and monopoly, where products are sufficiently differentiated to give each firm some monopoly power but entry is sufficiently free to eliminate the monopoly rents. This is the case of Chamberlinian monopolistic competition. The determinants of trade, and the effects of trade policy, have been analyzed in some stylized models of this kind.[20] Even in the absence of rents there is some scope for trade policy since it can alter the range of product variety in the industry. But the formulations of demand in these models are so special that little empirical feel for the kind of policy that should be pursued emerges. This is another area where theory has run ahead of applied work, and the imbalance has restricted the usefulness of the research.

Political Economy

All of my discussion of trade policy thus far has assumed that the aim of the policy is to serve the general interest. This is the approach traditionally taken by economists. The result is a "normative" theory of trade policy, that is, of what the policy should be according to the specified or idealized criterion. An alternative, "positive" approach has recently gained in popularity among researchers.[21] This seeks to understand what trade policy is, or will be, in a society where individuals or groups, driven by their various special interests, operate in a political process that generates the policy.

Those who operate in the real world of trade policy do not need to be convinced of the truth and the significance of this viewpoint. Politicians offer promises designed to attract voters in important marginal states or constituencies. Lobbyists speed resources to persuade or influence legislators. Such political markets, rather than isolated computers maximizing some agreed general interest, determine what measures are actually adopted. Research that helps us understand this mechanism has been long overdue, and its recent growth is to be welcomed. Several important insights have emerged from it. Let me mention just a few basic ones that lead me to some thoughts on where this work should go next.

First, the political process is seen to operate in favor of concentrated groups and against dispersed ones. This is because each member of the former has far more at stake than each member of the latter and also because the more close-knit group is better able to avoid free-rider problems and marshal the resources that are necessary for a voting or lobbying campaign. Thus producers, or organized workers in one industry, are favored over consumers at large. Second, we see that established industries win at the expense of new emerging ones. Losses for larger numbers of workers and owners in established industries threatened with decline loom larger in political calculations than the prospect of future gains in areas where voters or lobbies are not yet very numerous or strong. Finally, we find that the policy measures that get adopted are indirect and opaque, for example, tariffs rather than subsidies and VERs rather than tariffs. This is because the groups that lose from such measures do not perceive the causal link so clearly and are therefore less effective in opposition. But such indirect and opaque policies are just the ones most harmful to the society's general interest.

Realistic though the picture may be, it is hardly an appealing one. The policy that emerges is very inefficient, costly to the large masses of consumers, and inimical to the healthy growth of new and dynamic industries. There is a distinct possibility that the various special-interest groups are caught in a prisoners' dilemma—each has an incentive to exploit the existing system in its own interest, but all might benefit from a move to a less exploitable, more efficient, system that generates a much greater total of output to be shared among them all. Can economists do anything to improve this state of affairs?

One possibility lies in a combination of the positive and the normative viewpoints. The existing political and legal structure of policy-making may be best approached from the positive angle. But the questions of possible reform of the structure, or the design of a very different one, are still amenable to normative analysis. Economists can therefore ask if a structure can be designed that is less subject to such capture by the concentrated and established groups and better serves the general interest, including that of future generations. Opportunities for such systemic reform do not appear frequently, but the recent calls for tax reform, industrial policies, reform of trade policy administration, and so on, may yet combine and swell to a point where such a large-scale change becomes thinkable. That will be the time to put a better structure in place, and economists can serve society well by being ready with ideas toward this end.

Even within the existing system economists can serve the disadvantaged groups—consumers, emerging industries, the future—by providing the persuasion and lobbying that these groups are unable to achieve for themselves. Over the years this role has been played with outstanding ability and style by Milton Friedman.[22] The impressive calculations of costs of protectionism, and other special-interest policies like the European Community's Common Agricultural Policy, are also very useful.[23] They should be continued; their cumulative weight cannot but have a desirable effect on the political process.

International Policy Interactions

The dominant mode of research on trade policy is the analysis of one government's decision, taking those of the others as fixed. In reality the policy choices of two or more governments interact in many ways. The most visible example of this is the joint decision-making process consisting of the rounds of negotiations under GATT. More subtly, any one country, when evaluating its policy choices, must be mindful of the reactions or retaliations that are likely from other countries. There are also instances of import restrictions that are imposed with the tacit agreement, and sometimes even approval, of the exporting countries. The MFA, and the VERs on Japanese automobiles, are examples of this phenomenon. Analysis of the process of such policy interactions, leading to an ability to explain and predict their outcomes, constitutes an important class of problems that deserves greater attention in future research.

The questions fall squarely in the domain of game theory. This theory has over the years contributed several useful insights on bargaining and negotiations. The problem of the prisoner's dilemma is well known, and possible solutions are beginning to be understood. Generally, Nash equilibria of noncooperative games show how the bargainers might end up in an inefficient outcome. The prospect of efficiency through collaboration is brought out in the theory of the core, and issues of sharing the gains are important in Nash's bargaining solution.[24] But these theories are often too simple and abstract to do justice to the rich complexities of actual negotiations. More useful, and much more insightful, are Schelling's ideas of "strategic moves" such as threats and promises and how they can be made credible to alter others' behavior to one's own advantage.[25] Recently Raiffa has brought together many of these theoretical approaches, the results of some bargaining experiments in a "laboratory" setting, and the observations from several case studies, to produce an eclectic methodology that offers interesting prospects for the study of trade negotiations.[26] I shall briefly mention a couple of prominent topics that seem worthy of more attention.

Prisoners' Dilemmas

Earlier we saw the possibility that two large countries or blocs, each restricting trade to drive up the prices of its exports and drive down the prices of its imports, could jointly end up with little price advantage and excessively restricted trade. Following Johnson's classic article on the subject, others have examined the issue in greater detail and asked how the two could extricate themselves from this dilemma.[27] Since each retains the incentive to restrict trade even after they have agreed not to, the question is how the promises they make to each other in such an agreement can be made credible. If their relationship is to last an indefinitely long time, then a reputation for integrity can have a useful role, and the use of strategies like "tit for tat" can serve to hold the temptations to cheat in check. But there are several dimensions to trade policy, and there is the risk that the cheating will simply shift to some less easily detected dimension, such as away from tariffs and into health or customs regulations. There is a belief that this has happened after the agreements to reduce tariffs in successive GATT rounds. There is room for empirical as well as theoretical research on the attempts to resolve such dilemmas.

Similar dilemmas also arise if two or more countries simultaneously try a neomercantilist policy of profit shifting. Although the possibility is recognized by the new mercantilists, its empirical significance has not been examined. I suspect that the dilemma is especially severe in such contexts (because import restrictions can make each country's market even more monopolistic) and difficult to avoid (since export subsidies come in many subtle disguises that increase the possibility of cheating on an agreement).

Threats

Many actions of trade policy are influenced by explicit or tacit threats—that is, expectation of what some other country or countries will do if we do not take this action. However, systematic economic analysis of these threats and their effects has hardly begun, and public discussion of policy is often confused about them.[28]

The most common error is the failure to distinguish between a response and a deterrent. Suppose the United States is dominant in commercial aircraft, and the Europeans are new entrants. Once they are in, it will generally be a poor policy for the United States to respond by subsidizing its firms to start a costly price war. But before the fact it may be perfectly sensible for the United States to threaten such a response, with the aim of making the Europeans fear the outcome, thereby deterring their entry and preserving the U.S.

profits. In practice, mercantilists, and proponents of the "level-field" argument, often propose an ex post response, although it is inappropriate in the general interest, whereas free-traders fail to recognize that there may be a genuine ex ante deterrent value to the threat.

The trick of course is how to make the threat credible when the other side knows that if the matter is put to the test, the action is not in the threatener's interest. Schelling discusses the matter in considerable detail and offers ideas such as (1) making a prior and irreversible commitment that makes fulfillment of the threat automatic, (2) acquiring a reputation for toughness, or even irrationality, and (3) arranging sufficiently severe penalties for failure to carry out the threat, thereby changing the ex post incentives. It would be interesting to examine what role these tactics have played or can play in trade negotiations. There is reason to suspect that the U.S. policy process is ill suited to making irreversible commitments or acquiring a consistent reputation, and research on its redesign would be useful.

There are other interesting points about threats: (1) The threat in principle can be totally unrelated to the action being deterred. Thus an action of trade policy might be deterred by a threat concerning defense in an alliance. This means that the outcome can depend sensitively on the choice of the agenda for negotiations. The parties' interests in this matter can differ widely, which can make it difficult even to start the process. (2) A threat can be probabilistic, that is, present a sufficiently large and credible risk that the threatened reaction will happen, instead of a certainty of it. Schelling calls this "brinkmanship" and examines its uses. In the context of U.S. trade negotiations, perhaps threats of what the Congress might do are of this kind. (3) There are threats to compel the other side to do something, as well as threats to deter it from doing something. The two kinds of threats work somewhat differently. Typically compellent threats must impose a deadline and often operate by administering some ongoing punishment that stops if compellence works. Deterrent threats can be passive: nothing need be done until and unless a transgression occurs. This distinction becomes important, for example, if one country is trying to get another to liberalize its trade regime.

It should be evident that all these issues have immediate relevance for bilateral as well as multilateral trade negotiations. More systematic theoretical and empirical research, as well as case studies of past negotiation processes, are badly needed.

Finally, consider what happens when we combine the positive or politico-economic view of each country's trade policy with the problem of international negotiation. In the game of bargaining at the world level, each country is no longer a single monolithic player but itself a coalition of many groups with some conflict of interests. The countries' internal political mechanisms now have a bearing on the way the intercountry game is played and on its outcome. Such considerations have been found to be of critical importance in many instances of political negotiations.[29] The same must be true of trade policy, but economists have hardly begun to confront these issues in their research.

A Summing Up

This was a somewhat unusual sightseeing tour of the city of trade-policy research. My task as the guide was not the usual one of pointing with pride to the beautiful medieval church and praising the stunning new cultural center. Instead, I had to concentrate on the slums and the follies of the brave new architects. This was dictated by my concern that future research should build on firmer foundations and have a better design. Comments of this kind were scattered throughout the journey; it will be useful to collect the most important of them into a short agenda.

1. *Validity of the profit-shifting argument*   This argument is the cornerstone of the emerging new mercantilism. I argued that the edifice does not rest on empirical bedrock and suggested that its validity is limited to a few particular industries, perhaps including civilian jet aircraft. I think it is very important to study this question by modeling and estimating the structure and conduct of a range of industries in international competition. I also argued that special care had to be exercised in modeling the process of R&D, to reveal the competition at an underlying stage with free entry.

Even in industries where profit shifting is shown to be important, trade policies can only be justified if no other superior policies are feasible. The study of such a hierarchy of policies, analogous to that available for the case of perfect competition, is an important task for theoretical research.

2. *Design of policy mechanisms*   Studies of the political economy of trade policy show that the mechanism favors the concentrated special-interest groups in established industries, and ignores the dispersed groups of consumers and new emerging industries. This is

very damaging to the general interest and can harm everyone in the longer run. It is of the utmost importance that normative research should focus on the design of a policymaking process that is less susceptible to exploitation by such special-interest groups. In the meantime economists can perform a useful service to the community by acting as forceful advocates of the general interest.

3. *Strategies in international negotiation* Some lessons from game theory have been fruitfully applied in political and military negotiations and in strategic thinking in general. Similar potential exists in the case of international trade policy. Research directed toward such issues can be of help in the formulation of policy for the United States (e.g., by avoiding the confusion between response and deterrence and making threats or promises more credible) and in rounds of multilateral negotiation (e.g., by designing schemes that avoid or overcome prisoners' dilemmas).

Urban renewal has been defined as the process of tearing down old slums and building new ones. If I might continue my simile of the guided tour, the prognosis for future research in this area would therefore appear to be dim. But the city does have its beautiful medieval churches. The idea that free trade promotes the general interest, and that departures from it are motivated by various special interests, is one such. In my judgment, this basic insight of Adam Smith and Ricardo still stands and continues to govern the overwhelming majority of the volume of world trade despite the demolition plans of the new mercantilists. In conclusion, I would like to make a personal plea to the architects of renewal in trade policy research. Don't be too tempted by radical new designs, and conserve some of the beauty of the old ones.

Notes

I thank Wilfred Ethier, Gene Grossman and Jean Baldwin Grossman for useful discussions and comments on an earlier draft. Further comments are welcome.

1. John Stuart Mill, *Autobiography* (London: Oxford University Press, 1949), p. 276.

2. Michael Innes, *The Weight of the Evidence* (London: Victor Gollancz), 1944.

3. An outstanding study of this process in action is Bruce Ackerman and William Hassler, *Clean Coal, Dirty Air* (New Haven: Yale University Press, 1981).

4. See the recent writings of Oliver Williamson, especially "Credible commitments: Using Hostages to Support Exchange," *American Economic Review* 73 (September 1983), pp. 519–540, for an elaboration of this point.

5. This part is based on Robert E. Baldwin, "The Case against Infant Industry Protection," *Journal of Political Economy* 68 (May–June 1969), pp. 295–305.

6. See Morton D. Davis, *Game Theory: A Nontechnical Introduction* (New York: Basic Books, 1983), pp. 108–119, and Robert Axelrod, *The Evolution of Cooperation* (New York: Basic Books, 1983).

7. Quoted in Paul A. Samuelson, *Economics*, 9th ed. (New York: McGraw-Hill, 1973), p. 694. But see F. W. Taussig, "Abraham Lincoln on the Tariff: A Myth," *Quarterly Journal of Economics* 28 (August 1914), pp. 814–820, and "Lincoln and the Tariff: A Sequel," *Quarterly Journal of Economics* 29 (February 1915), pp. 426–429.

8. See, for example, H. Katrak, "Multi-National Monopolies and Commercial Policy," *Oxford Economic Papers* (July 1977), pp. 283–291.

9. Many articles by James Brander and Barbara Spencer offer variations on this theme. See especially their "Tariff Protection and Imperfect Competition," in *Monopolistic Competition in International Trade*, H. Kierzkowski, ed. (Oxford: Oxford University Press, 1984).

10. See, for example, Avinash K. Dixit and Albert S. Kyle, "The Use of Protection and Subsidies for Entry Promotion and Deterrence," working paper, February 1984.

11. See, for example, Paul Krugman, "Import protection as export promotion," in Kierzkowski, ed. *Monopolistic Competition*, and Paul Krugman, "The Narrow Moving Band, the Dutch Disease, and the Economic Consequences of Mrs. Thatcher," working paper, June 1984.

12. From *World Motor Vehicles Data*, 1983.

13. See, for example, Gene Grossman and Carl Shapiro, "Research Joint Ventures: An Antitrust Analysis," Princeton University Woodrow Wilson School Discussion Paper in Economics No. 68, April 1984.

14. For discussion and criticism on this issue, see Gene Grossman and David Richardson, "Strategic U.S. Trade Policy: A Survey of Issues and Early Analysis," NBER Research Progress Report, 1984.

15. See David DeMeza, "Commercial Policy towards Multinational Monopolies—Reservations on Katrak," Oxford Economic Papers, 31 (November 1979), pp. 334–337.

16. See Dixit and Kyle, "Use of Protection and Subsidies."

17. For a definitive statement, see Jagdish Bhagwati, "The Generalized Theory of Distortions and Welfare," in *Trade, Balance of Payments and Growth* (Amsterdam: North-Holland, 1971).

18. See Kala Krishna, "Trade Restrictions as Facilitating Practices," Princeton University Woodrow Wilson School Discussion Paper in Economics No. 55,

February 1984, and Yoshiyasu Ono, "Profitability of Export Restrain," *Journal of International Economics* 16 (May 1984), pp. 335–343.

19. On the MFA, see Carl Hamilton, "Voluntary Export Restraint on Clothing from Asia: Price Effects, Rent Incomes and Trade Barrier Formation," Stockholm: IIES Seminar Paper No. 276, April 1984. On auto VERs, see "The Irony and Impact of Auto Quotas," *New York Times*, April 8, 1984.

20. For a detailed exposition of the determinants and effects of trade under monopolistic competition, see Elhanan Helpman and Paul Krugman, *Market Structure and Foreign Trade* (Cambridge, Mass.: MIT Press, 1985) chs. 6–9. Models of tariff policy include Anthony Venables, "Optimal Tariffs for Trade in Monopolitically Competitive Commodities," *Journal of International Economics* 12:2 (1982), pp. 225–241, and Kelvin Lancaster, "Protection and Product Differentiation," in Kierzkowski, ed., *Monopolistic Competition*.

21. See chapters 8–10 of *Import Competition and Response*, J. Bhagwati, ed. (Chicago: University of Chicago Press, 1982), and David C. Colander, ed., *Neoclassical Political Economy* (Cambridge, Mass.: Ballinger, 1984).

22. See the chapter on international trade in his *Capitalism and Freedom* (Chicago: University of Chicago Press, 1962) and various sections in *Free To Choose* (New York: Harcourt, Brace, Jovanovich, 1980).

23. Examples are: Stephen P. Magee, "The Welfare Effects of Restrictions on U.S. Trade," *Brookings Papers on Economic Activity* (1972:3), pp. 666–673, and C. N. Morris, "The Common Agricultural Policy," *Fiscal Studies* 1 (March 1980), pp. 17–35.

24. See Martin Shubik, *Game Theory in the Social Sciences* (Cambridge, Mass.: MIT Press, 1982), for an account of formal game theory.

25. Thomas Schelling, *The Strategy of Conflict* (Cambridge, Mass.: Harvard University Press, 1960), especially chs. 2, 5.

26. Howard Raiffa, *The Art and Science of Negotiation* (Cambridge, Mass.: Harvard University Press, 1982). For a more detailed research agenda in this area, see Avinash Dixit and Gene Grossman, "On the Analytics of Agreed Protection," report prepared for the World Bank, August 1984.

27. Harry Johnson, "Optimum tariffs and retaliation," *Review of Economic Studies* 21:2 (1953), pp. 142–153. For some recent work, see Wolfgang Mayer, "Theoretical Considerations on Negotiated Tariff Settlements," *Oxford Economic Papers*, 33 (February 1981), pp. 135–153 and Raymond Riezman, "Tariff Retaliation from a Strategic Viewpoint," *Southern Economic Journal* 48 (January 1982), pp. 583–593.

28. See Dixit and Kyle, "Use of Protection and Subsidies" for an analysis of the role of threats of this kind to deter entry of foreign firms.

29. See Graham Allison's *Essence of Decision: Explaining the Cuban Missile Crisis* (Boston: Little, Brown, 1971), and the case study of the Panama Canal negotiations in Raiffa, "Art and Science of Negotiation," ch. 12.

Index